Y0-CPD-232

# SIMON & SCHUSTER'S ILLUSTRATED YOUNG READERS' DICTIONARY

We are greatly indebted to K. W. Moody, former British Council English Language Officer, and Harry Lecomte, Headteacher of St Martin of Porres School, Haringey, London, for the advice and help they have given us during the compilation of this dictionary.

Wanderer edition edited by Jane Hyman, elementary reading specialist and school administrator in the Randolph (Massachusetts) School System.

First American edition, 1983

Published by Wanderer Books
A Simon & Schuster Division of
Gulf & Western Corporation
Simon & Schuster Building
1230 Avenue of the Americas
New York, New York 10020
This book was previously published in England
under the title THE KINGFISHER ILLUSTRATED DICTIONARY
10 9 8 7 6 5 4 3 2


ISBN 0-671-47144-9
Printed in Spain by Graficas Reunidas S.A., Madrid

SIMON & SCHUSTER'S

# ILLUSTRATED YOUNG READERS' DICTIONARY

WANDERER BOOKS
Published by Simon & Schuster, New York

## ABOUT YOUR DICTIONARY

A a B b C c D d E e F f G g H h I i J j K k L l M m N n O o P p Q q R r S s T t U u V v W w X x Y y Z z

What is a dictionary? It is a book like this one, which does two main jobs:

1 It explains the meanings of words. (It *defines* them, is another way of saying this.)
2 It shows you how to spell words.

### Alphabetical Order

A dictionary helps you to find the words you want. How does it do this? All dictionaries list the words they explain, or define, in *alphabetical order*. This means that the words are listed in the order of the letters of the alphabet. The order of the letters of the alphabet is shown at the side of these pages. To use a dictionary you need to know this order. It is very useful for looking up other things too. If you know the alphabetical order, you can use an encyclopedia, an index, or a telephone directory. It will also help you to find books in a library.

### Using the Alphabet to Find Words

Which comes first: *house* or *mouse*?
*tiger* or *axle*?
*watch* or *clock*?
*snake* or *lizard*?

But what do you do when you come to a more difficult problem? Which comes first, *flea* or *fork*? They both begin with "f" and therefore you will need to look at the second letter in each word. The second letter in *flea* is "l". The second letter in *fork* is "o". The letter "l" comes before "o", so *flea* comes before *fork* in the dictionary.

Now look at these words: *house* and *horse*. Which do you think would come first in a dictionary, and why?

And how about these words?

*fir* *first*
*see* *seed*
*so* *sow* *sowing*

Can you see why they come in that order in a dictionary?

You can see now why it is important to know the order of the alphabet. You would waste a lot of time if you had to go right through your dictionary to find a word, wouldn't you?

**Try it yourself**
Which comes first?
*first* or *fist*; *ghost* or *glue*; *bulb* or *bulrush*; *treat* or *tree*; *center* or *central*; *chess* or *chew*.

**Guide Words**

Maybe you want to find the meaning of the word *dinosaur*. First you would find the part of the dictionary where the "d" words are. If you do this, you will find that the "d" words start on page 44 and end on page 52. But you do not have to look at every page of "d" words to find *dinosaur*. You can look at the top outside corner of each page for the **guide words**. In this dictionary, the first guide word on the left-hand page tells you the first word on that page and the second guide word on the right-hand page tells you the last word on that page. You will find the word *dinosaur* on page 48. It is found between the guide words **DEVELOP** and **DIVE** because *dinosaur* comes between those two words in *alphabetical order*.

**Pronunciation**

You may not know how to say, or *pronounce*, some words. This dictionary has two ways of helping you to say them.

1 How do you pronounce *cello*? The dictionary tells you like this: **cello** (say *chello*)
2 How do you pronounce *choir*? The dictionary tells you like this: **choir** (rhymes with *fire*, say *kwire*)

**Helpful Sentences**

Some words are easier to understand if you see them in a sentence. Many words in this dictionary have a sentence to help you to understand their meaning. These sentences are printed in italics, like this: *Jane's aim was to learn French.*

A a B b C c D d E e F f G g H h I i J j K k L l M m N n O o P p Q q R r S s T t U u V v W w X x Y y Z z

## Which Word do I Need?

Some words are spelled the same, but have more than one meaning. Think of the word *spring*. How many meanings can you think of for that word? Look in the dictionary for *spring*. Did you think of all the meanings? You can see that the different meanings of *spring* are numbered 1 to 4.

What do you do when you do not quite understand a meaning? Look up the word *dinosaur* in the dictionary. Do you know what *extinct* means? Do you know what a *reptile* is? If you do not know, look up these words too. Then you should understand the meaning of *dinosaur* better.

## The Pictures

The color pictures in this book are very important. They have been chosen to show things that are often difficult to explain in words. For example, we say that a beaver is a "furry, flat-tailed animal that lives on land and in water". But the picture of the beaver really shows the fur, the flat tail, and other things too. And the caption to the picture tells you still more about the animal.

## The Spelling List

This dictionary is a bit different from other dictionaries. It ends with a Spelling List. This gives a list in alphabetical order of words that you may want to spell. There are no meanings given in the Spelling List. But most of these words are also in the main part of the dictionary Their meanings are given there.

Some words such as *banana*, *cucumber* and *guess* are not in the main part of your dictionary. You know what these words mean, and they do not have more than one meaning. But they are words which you could find difficult to spell. So they are in the Spelling List at the back of the book.

**A dictionary is a very useful tool. Learn to use it well.**

A a B b C c D d E e F f G g H h I i J j K k L l M m N n O o P p Q q R r S s T t U u V v W w X x Y y Z z

# Aa

**abacus** a frame with sliding balls, used for counting.
**abandon** 1 to stop doing something. *They had to abandon the game.*
2 to leave and not return. *They had to abandon the ship.*
**abbey** a church and other buildings where monks and nuns once lived; a great church.
**abbreviation** a short way of writing either a word or a group of words. *Tom is an abbreviation of Thomas.*
**aboard** on a ship, aircraft or train. *They went aboard the ship.*
**aborigines** (say *abo-rij-in-ees*) the first people who lived in a country, especially the first Australians.
**abroad** in another country.
**absent** not there.

There are over 200 kinds of oak tree, but all of them grow from **acorn** nuts.

**absorb** to take in water or some other liquid. *A sponge absorbs water.*
**accelerate** (say *ack-selerate*) to go faster.
**accept** (say *ack-sept*) to take something which is offered to you.
**accident** (say *ack-sident*) something that happens and is not expected, usually something bad.
**accurate** correct and exact.
**ache** (rhymes with *cake*) a pain that goes on for a long time, like a toothache.
**acid** (say *asid*) a substance which tastes sour, like vinegar. *Strong acids can burn you.*
**acorn** the fruit or nut of an oak tree.

Some **acids** are very strong. Others are harmless. The sharp taste of lemons comes from citric acid.

This **aircraft** was made by the American Glenn Curtiss. It won a speed trophy in 1909.

**acre** (say *aker*) a measure of land. *A football field has an area of about one and a half acres.*

**acrobat** a person who does balancing tricks, often in a circus.

**act** 1 to do something. *They will act very quickly.* 2 to play a part or pretend. *He acts the part of a pirate in our play.* 3 part of a stage play.

**active** busy, full of energy.

**actor** a person who acts in plays, in films or on the T.V.

**actress** a woman who acts in a play or film.

**add** to put things together to make more. *Colin added all the numbers together to find the total.*

**address** 1 the place where you live and to which your mail is sent. 2 a speech.

**adjective** a word that describes what something or somebody is like. *The black cat.* "Black" is an adjective.

**admire** to think very well of something or somebody.

**admission** being allowed into somewhere, and the money you pay to go in.

**adopt** to accept somebody else's child as a child of your own family. *The couple decided to adopt the boy.*

**advance** to move forward.

**adventure** an exciting happening.

**adverb** a word that tells us how, when or where something happens.

**advertise** to tell people about

The Sopwith Camel was one of the most famous fighter **aircraft** of World War

The HP42 Hannibal was one of the last of the famous biplane passenger **aircraft.**

something you want to sell. *People advertise in newspapers, on television, or by sticking up posters.*

**advertisement** a printed notice in a newspaper or a message about goods or services on radio or television.

**advice** something said to you to help you decide what to do. *We took our teacher's advice and borrowed a book about it from the library.*

**advise** to tell someone what you think they should do.

**affect** to make someone or something different in some way. *The hot weather affects her health.*

**afford** to have enough money to buy something. *He can afford that car.*

**after** 1 at a later time. *John will go to school after breakfast.* 2 behind. *The cat ran after the mouse.*

**afterward** later. *We watched television and afterwards went out to a play.*

**age** 1 the length of time a person has lived. 2 A length of time in history, such as the Stone Age and Bronze Age.

**agree** to say "yes" to. *If you agree, I will come too.*

**agriculture** farming.

**ahead** in front. *Father went ahead to get seats for us.*

**aid** 1 to help. 2 the help that is given.

**aim** 1 to point a weapon at something. 2 something you try to do. *Jane's aim was to learn French.*

**air** the mixture of gases we breathe.

**aircraft** any airplane or helicopter.

The British Harrier fighter **aircraft** can direct its jets downward so that it takes off vertically.

The **alligator** has a broader, flatter head than the crocodile.

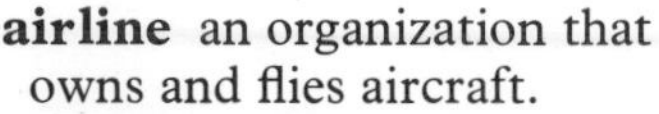

**airline** an organization that owns and flies aircraft.
**airplane** a flying machine driven by an engine or engines.
**airport** a place where aircraft land and take off.
**airtight** so tightly shut that air cannot get in or out.
**alarm** 1 a warning sound or signal. 2 to frighten.
**alike** 1 looking or acting the same. *People say my sister and I are very much alike.* 2 in the same way. *We were always treated alike.*
**alive** living.
**Allah** The name for God among Muslims.
**alligator** a reptile like a crocodile that lives in parts of the Americas and in China.
**allow** to let someone do something. *He allows us to play in his garden.*
**alloy** a mixture of metals.
**ally** (say *al-eye*) a friend, or a country that helps another.
**alone** by yourself; with no one else.
**aloud** in a voice that can be heard.
**alphabet** all the letters of a language arranged in order. *The English alphabet has 26 letters.*
**altar** the table in a church with a cross on it.
**alter** to change something. *You should alter the dress to make it fit.*
**altitude** height above sea level. *The aircraft flew at a very high altitude.*
**aluminum** a silvery metal which weighs less than most other metals. *Aluminum is used to make cooking pots and aircraft.*
**a.m.** the hours between mid-night and noon. *Nine a.m. is 9 o'clock in the morning.*
**ambassador** a person who represents one country in another country.
**ambulance** a vehicle for carrying people who are ill or injured.
**ambush** 1 to hide and wait for someone so that you can take them by surprise. 2 a hiding place for a surprise attack.
**ammunition** (say *am-mu-nishun*) things that are fired from guns.
**amount** the total sum; a quantity. *He needed a large amount of money to buy the car.*

This Renault **ambulance** was used during World War I.

**Amphibians** such as the frog at the top and the newt spend part of their lives in water and part as land animals. The tadpoles look very different from the adult frog.

**amphibian** an animal that lives both in water and on land. *A frog is an amphibian.*
**amplifier** electrical equipment used to make sounds louder.
**anchor** a heavy iron hook on a long chain. *An anchor is dropped into the water to stop a boat moving.*
**ancestor** one of the members of your family who lived long ago.
**ancient** (say *ayn-shent*) very old or very long ago.
**anesthetic** a drug used so that people do not feel pain during an operation.
**angel** a messenger from God.

A right **angle**

an acute **angle**

an obtuse **angle**

**angle** the space between two straight lines or surfaces that meet.
**animal** any living thing that is not a plant.
**ankle** the joint between the leg and the foot.
**anniversary** a day on which an event is remembered each year, like the anniversary of a wedding.
**annual** 1 happening every year. *Christmas is an annual event.* 2 a plant that lives for one year only.
**ant** a small insect that lives with many other ants.

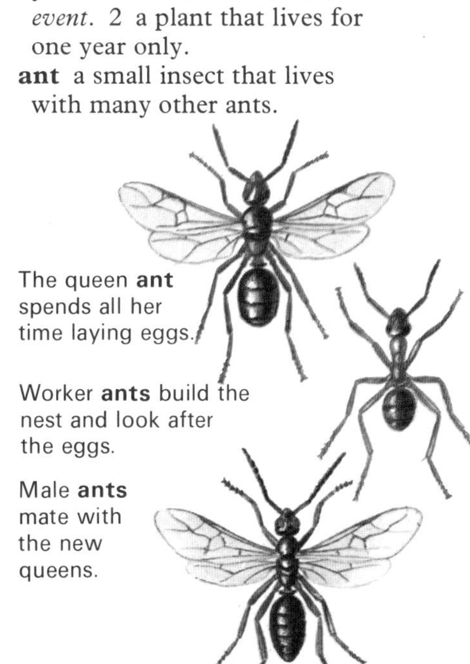

The queen **ant** spends all her time laying eggs.

Worker **ants** build the nest and look after the eggs.

Male **ants** mate with the new queens.

**antelope** an animal like a deer. *Antelopes have horns and can run very fast.*

**antenna** 1 one of a pair of feelers on an insect's or a lobster's head. 2 a wire or rod for sending out or receiving radio waves.

**antibiotic** a drug which helps to kill harmful bacteria. *Penicillin is an antibiotic.*

**antique** (say *anteek*) very old; a very old object. *Antiques are often valuable.*

**antler** the branched horn of a deer.

**apart** away from each other. *Our houses are 2 miles apart.*

**ape** a large monkey-like animal with no tail. *Gorillas and chimpanzees are apes.*

**apostle** one of the twelve men sent out by Jesus Christ to spread the ideas which he taught.

**apostrophe** (say *apostroffy*) a punctuation mark, like this '. It is used when letters are left out (*don't* means *do not*) or when "*s*" is added to a word to show ownership. *That is John's bicycle.*

**appear** 1 to come into sight. *A man appeared through the mist.* 2 to seem to be. *A microscope makes things appear larger.*

**appointment** a time agreed for a meeting.

**apricot** an orange-yellow fruit with a big, hard seed.

**apron** a piece of cloth or plastic worn over clothes to

**aquarium** a tank in which to keep fish or water plants.

**aqueduct** a bridge that carries water across a valley.

**arc** a curved line; part of a circle.

**arch** a part of a building curved like an arc, usually over a door or window.

**archer** a person who shoots with a bow and arrow.

**archery** the sport of shooting with a bow.

**architect** (say *ark-i-tect*) a person who designs and plans buildings.

**architecture** styles of buildings.

**area** 1 the size of a surface. Areas are measured in units like square yards and acres. *A football field is about 6000 square yards.* 2 a part of a country or the world. *They come from the Detroit area.*

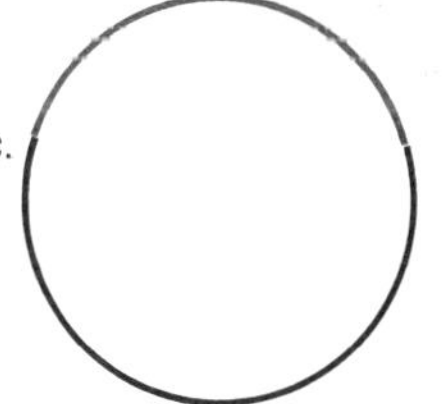

The part of the circle in red is an **arc**.

**argue** (say *arg-yoo*) to discuss the reasons for and against something. *They argue their case well.*

**arithmetic** sums; the science of numbers. *When we add numbers together we are doing arithmetic.*

**arm** 1 part of the body from the shoulder to the hand. 2 to give weapons to. *They will arm the soldiers with the latest weapons.*

When the Romans built their **aqueducts** to carry water, they used many simple machines. The treadmill wound up a rope that raised the huge stones into position.

**armor** a covering, usually made of metal, that protects the body in battle.

**army** a large number of soldiers.

**arrange** 1 to put in order. *She arranged all her toys on the shelf.* 2 to make plans. *Our teacher will arrange a visit to the zoo.*

**arrive** to reach a place. *The train arrived in the station.*

**arrow** a pointed stick that is shot from a bow.

**art** drawing, painting and modeling, and the things that are made that way.

**artery** one of the tubes that carries blood from the heart to all parts of the body.

**artificial** (say *art-i-fishel*) not natural, made by people and machines; not grown. *Natural rubber comes from the juice of a tree, but artificial rubber is made from coal.*

**artist** a person who draws, paints or carves.

**ash** the powder that is left after something has been burned.

**aspirin** a drug used to reduce pain.

**ass** a donkey.

Making and decorating **armor** was a skilled and costly craft.

**association** a group of people or organizations that work together.

**astronaut** a traveler in space.

**astronomy** the study of the Sun, planets, Moon and stars.

**athlete** someone who is good at sports or games that need strength or speed.

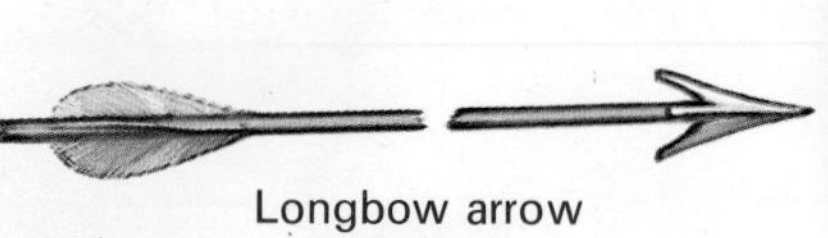

Longbow arrow

Bolt-heads for the crossbow

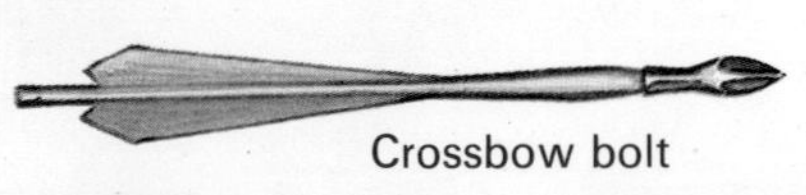

Crossbow bolt

Arrow-heads for the longbow

**atlas** a book of maps.
**atmosphere** the air around the earth.
**atom** the smallest particle of a chemical element.
**attach** to fasten or join one thing to another.
**attack** to try to hurt a person or capture a place. *The soldiers plan to attack the castle.*
**attempt** to try to do something. *Jack will attempt the climb tomorrow.*
**attend** 1 to be present. 2 to give thought to. *Please attend to what I am saying.*
**attic** a room in the roof of a house.
**attract** to pull towards.
**audience** people who watch a play or listen to music together.
**aunt** the sister of your mother or father.
**author** (say *awther*) a person who writes a book or a play.
**autobiography** the story of someone's life written by herself or himself.
**autograph** someone's name written in their own handwriting. *Georgia collected the autographs of famous authors.*
**automatic** working without being looked after, like an automatic washing machine.
**autumn** the season of the year between summer and winter.
**avalanche** a great mass of snow and rocks sliding down a mountain.
**avenue** 1 a road lined with trees. 2 broad street in a city.

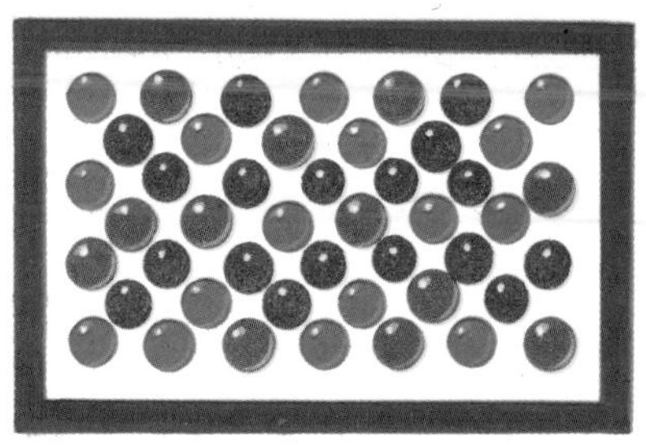

In a solid, **atoms** pack tightly.

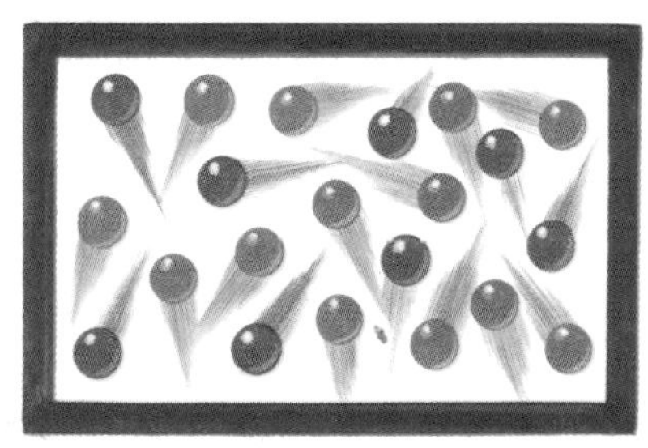

In a liquid, **atoms** move about.
In a gas, **atoms** move about a lot.

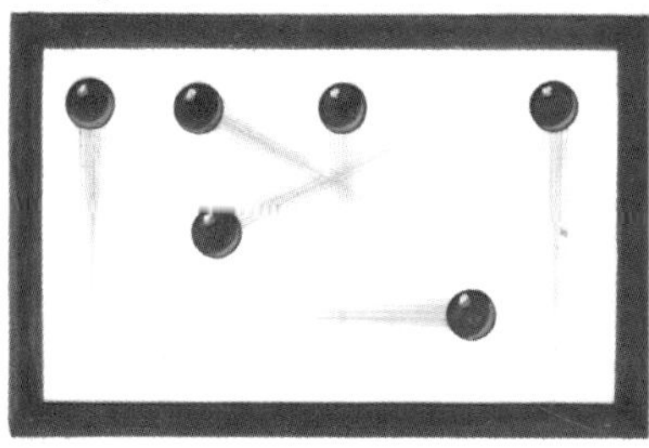

Everything is made of **atoms** – all solids, liquids and gases.

**average** 1 normal; usual. 2 a mathematical word. To find the average of 2, 4 and 6 you add them together and divide by 3. The answer is 4.
**awake** not sleeping.
**ax** a tool for chopping wood.
**axle** the rod on which a wheel turns.

# Bb

**baboon** a large kind of monkey.

**back** 1 the part of the body from the neck to the end of the spine. 2 the side opposite to the front. *I like to sit at the back of the class.* 3 to move backward. *Ask her to backup the car.*

**backbone** the bones that run down the back of a skeleton; the spine.

**background** the part of a scene or picture that is behind all the rest or in the distance.

**backward** towards the back, opposite of forward.

**bacon** smoked or salted meat from a pig.

**badge** something worn by a person, usually with a picture or message on it. *Badges often show that a person belongs to a school or club.*

**badger** dog-sized animal with a white mark on its forehead. It lives in holes (called *setts*) and comes out at night.

**bagpipes** a musical instrument with a wind-bag and pipes.

**bait** food used to attract fish or animals so that they can be caught.

**bake** to cook in the oven.

**baker** a person who makes cakes and bread and sells them.

**bakery** a place where bread is baked and may be sold.

**balance** 1 to keep steady. *Roger balanced the book on his head.* 2 an instrument for weighing.

**bald** (rhymes with *called*) without hair.

**Baboons** are fast runners because their front and hind legs are about the same length. They travel in bands called troops. Baboons are the largest members of the monkey family.

**ballad** a simple poem or song that tells a story.

**ballerina** a female ballet dancer.

**ballet** (say *bal-ay*) a stage show that usually tells a story with dance and music.

**balloon** a bag of thin material filled with air or gas.

**band** 1 a thin strip of material for fastening things together. 2 a group of people who do things together. 3 a group of musicians.

**bandage** a strip of material for covering a wound.

**bandit** a robber, often working in a group or band.

**banisters** rails up the sides of staircases.

**bank** 1 sloping ground. 2 land along the side of a river. 3 a place where people keep their money.

**banquet** (say *bang-kwet*) a feast.

**bar** 1 a long piece of hard material. 2 to stop someone going through. *The man tried to bar our way into the park.*

**barber** a person who cuts men's hair.

**bare** 1 not covered. 2 empty. *The room looked bare without its furniture.*

**barge** a flat-bottomed boat used on canals and rivers.

**bark** 1 outer covering of a tree. 2 the sharp cry of a dog.

**barn** a farm building for animals or for storing grain or hay.

**barometer** an instrument for measuring air pressure. *A barometer is used to forecast the weather.*

**barracks** a building where soldiers live.

**barrel** 1 a container with curved sides. 2 the tube of a gun.

**base** 1 the part of an object on which it stands. 2 a headquarters.

**basement** a floor of a building below the ground.

**bassoon** a large musical wind instrument that makes low notes.

The basic **ballet** positions were devised over 300 years ago. Each foot position has an arm position to go with it.

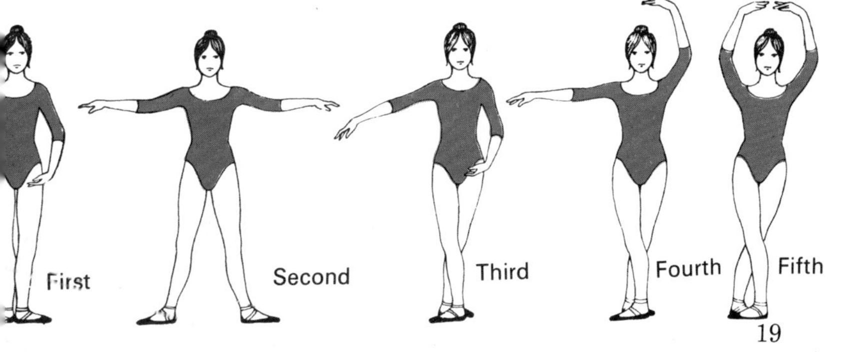

**bat** 1 a small mouse-like flying animal. 2 a piece of wood for hitting a ball. 3 to hit a ball with a bat.

**batch** 1 a number of cakes or loaves baked together. 2 a group of things that come together. *We must answer this batch of letters.*

**bathe** to swim or wash.

**baton** the stick with which a conductor beats time for an orchestra.

**batter** 1 to hit very hard. 2 a mixture of flour, eggs and milk cooked to make pancakes and other food.

**battery** a container for storing electricity.

**battle** 1 a fight between two armies. 2 to struggle. *The wind was so strong, we had to battle against it.*

**bay** part of the seashore that makes a wide curve inward.

**B.C.** time before Jesus Christ was born.

**beach** the shore between the high and low tide marks.

**bead** a small piece of wood, glass or other material with a hole through it. *Beads are used to thread on string to make necklaces and other jewelry.*

**beak** the hard outer part of a bird's mouth.

**beam** 1 a big heavy bar used as a support in a building or in a ship. 2 a ray of light, like *the beam of a torch.* 3 to smile widely.

**beard** hair that grows on the lower part of a man's face.

Birds' **beaks** have many shapes. They are used for catching moths, cracking nuts, eating seeds and insects, tearing up prey, or even tearing open pine cones.

**beast** an animal.
**beat** 1 to hit hard and often. *The cruel man beat the boy.* 2 to conquer or defeat. *John beat me at table tennis.*
**beaver** a furry, flat-tailed animal that lives on land and in water.
**became** past of **become**.
**become** to grow to be. *She has become a very pretty girl.*
**bed** 1 something to sleep on. 2 a place where flowers are planted.
**bee** an insect that makes honey. People keep bees in a *beehive*.
**beef** the meat of cattle.
**beetle** an insect with hard wing covers.
**beg** to ask someone for help, especially for money.
**beggar** someone who begs.
**behave** 1 to act in a particular way. *Sue behaved very badly at the party.* 2 To act well. *Do try to behave.*
**believe** to feel sure about the truth of something.
**bend** 1 a curve; not straight. 2 to curve over.
**bent** past of **bend**.
**berry** a small fruit with lots of seeds.

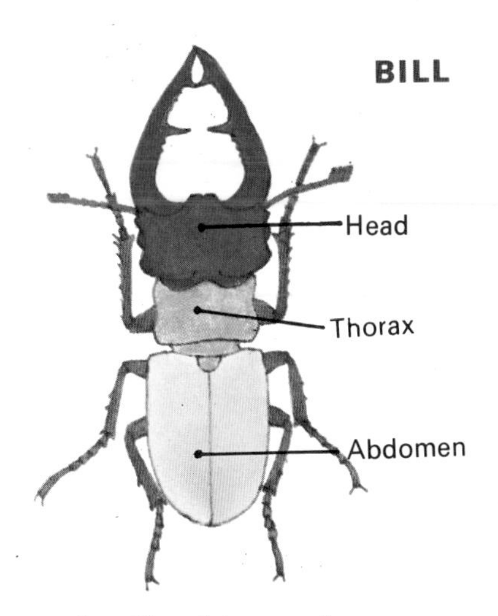


**Beetles**, like all insects, have bodies that are divided into three parts – a head, a thorax and an abdomen.

**berth** 1 a bunk or bed in a ship or train. 2 the place where a ship docks. *The ship was tied up at her berth.*
**besides** as well as.
**beware** be warned. *The sign said: "Beware of the dog".*
**beyond** on the far side of. *Julia's house is beyond the church.*
**bicycle** a two-wheeled vehicle.
**bill** 1 a paper showing how much you owe for something you have bought. 2 a bird's beak.

The **beaver** has large teeth for cutting down trees, a thick waterproof coat and a broad, scaly tail.

This French fighter aircraft of World War I was a **biplane**. The two sets of wings gave greater lift at the slow speeds of those days.

**billion** one thousand million (1,000,000,000).

**binary** made up of two parts or units.

**binoculars** field glasses; an instrument to make things far away look closer. *You look through a pair of binoculars with both eyes.*

**biography** the written story of a person's life.

**biology** the study of living things.

**biplane** an aircraft with two sets of wings.

**birth** coming into life.

**bison** a large animal of the cattle family, usually called a buffalo.

**bit** 1 a small piece. 2 a metal bar that goes in a horse's mouth; part of the bridle.

**bitch** a female dog, fox or wolf.

**bitter** sharp, unpleasant taste; not sweet.

**blackmail** the crime of demanding money from someone in return for keeping something secret. *The man said that if I gave him $5 he would keep quiet about the window I broke. This was blackmail.*

**blacksmith** a person who works with iron and makes shoes for horses.

**bladder** the part of the body where liquid wastes gather before they are passed out.

**blame** to say that it was the

fault of something or someone that something went wrong.
**blank** empty; with nothing written on it.
**blaze** a bright flame or fire.
**bleach** to make whiter.
**bleat** the cry of a sheep or goat.
**bless** to ask God to protect someone or something.
**blew** past of **blow**.
**blind** 1 not able to see. 2 window cover.
**blister** a swelling like a bubble on the skin, filled with a watery liquid.
**blizzard** a snowstorm with very strong winds.
**block** 1 a large lump of something. 2 a large building of apartments or offices. 3 to get in the way of. *A fallen tree can block a road.*
**blood** the red liquid that is pumped around our bodies by the heart.
**blossom** flower or mass of flowers, especially on fruit trees.

**blow** 1 a hard knock. 2 to make the air move. *The wind blows from the west.*
**blunder** a stupid mistake. *John made a blunder when he wrote 10 instead of 100.*
**blunt** not sharp.
**blush** to become red in the face because you are ashamed or shy.
**boar** (rhymes with *sore*) a male pig.
**board** 1 a long flat piece of wood; a plank. 2 a flat piece of wood or card used for a special purpose. *A chess board is used for the game of chess.* 3 to get onto a ship, train or airplane. *We must board the plane now.*
**boast** to talk about how good you think you are.
**boil** 1 to heat a liquid until it bubbles and steams. 2 a painful swelling on the body.
**bold** showing no fear
**bolt** 1 a metal fastening on a door or window. 2 a metal pin with a screw at one end that goes into a nut to fasten things. 3 to run away quickly.
**bomb** a container filled with explosives.
**bonfire** a big fire made in the open air.

The **bison** is usually called a buffalo. There used to be great herds of them in America. During the mating season, the males often fight.

The curved **boomerang** shown here, with an Aborigine shield, is used for sport, not hunting.

**boomerang** a throwing stick that comes back to the thrower. *Boomerangs were used by Australian aborigines.*

**boot** 1 a sort of shoe that also covers the ankle and sometimes the leg.

**border** 1 the part near the edge of something. 2 the land near the line dividing two countries.

**borrow** to get something from someone else which you use and then give back. The other person *lends* it to you.

**both** the two together. *She invited both of us to her party.*

**bounce** to spring up again like a ball that is dropped on the ground.

**boundary** a line separating one place from another. *That fence is the boundary between Mr. Brown's backyard and ours.*

**bow** (rhymes with *low*) 1 a piece of wood curved by a tight string. *A bow is used for shooting arrows.* 2 a knot with loops. 3 a stick with long hairs attached to it, which is used for playing musical instruments like violins.

**bow** (rhymes with *cow*) 1 the front end of a ship. 2 to bend at the waist to greet an important person.

**bowels** the part of the body where solid wastes gather.

**bowl** 1 a deep dish. 2 to roll a bowling ball.

**bracelet** a band worn round the arm or wrist.

**braille** (rhymes with *sail*) raised letters that a blind

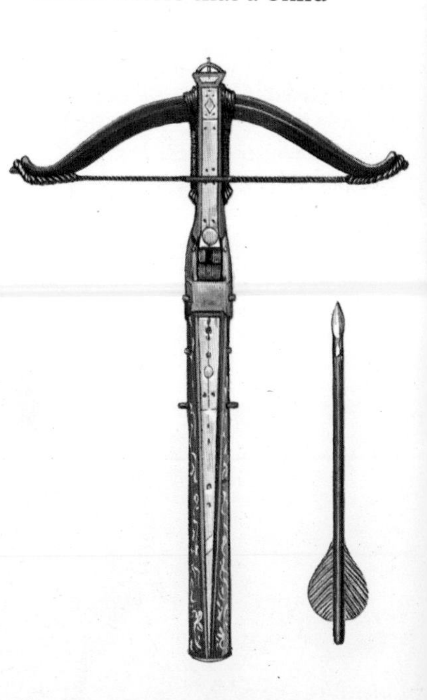
The **bow** of the crossbow was short and thick, and very hard to bend.

person can read by touching them.

**brain** the gray matter in the head which controls the work of the body, and with which you think.

**brake** something that is pressed against a wheel to stop it turning.

**branch** 1 one of the arm-like parts of a tree growing out of the trunk. 2 large stores and banks also have branches; separate buildings in different towns.

**brass** a bright, yellowish metal made by mixing copper and zinc.

**brave** 1 fearless. 2 an American Indian warrior.

**break down** 1 of a piece of machinery, to stop working. 2 to separate something into the parts it is made up of. *It's quite a big job, but if we break it down sensibly, we can do it.*

**breast** (rhymes with *rest*) the chest of a person or an animal.

**breathe** (say *breeth*) to take air into the lungs and let it out again.

**breed** 1 animals that produce others of exactly the same kind. *The Labrador is a breed of dog.* 2 to produce young ones.

**breeze** a gentle wind.

**bride** a woman who is about to be married or who has just been married.

**bridegroom** a man who is about to be married or who has just been married.

**bridesmaid** a girl who helps a bride at her wedding.

**bridle** the harness that goes on a horse's head, including the reins.

**bright** (rhymes with *bite*) 1 shiny, cheerful. 2 clever.

**brilliant** 1 very bright. *A brilliant star shone between the clouds.* 2 very clever.

**brim** the edge of a cup or container. *The bucket was full to the brim.*

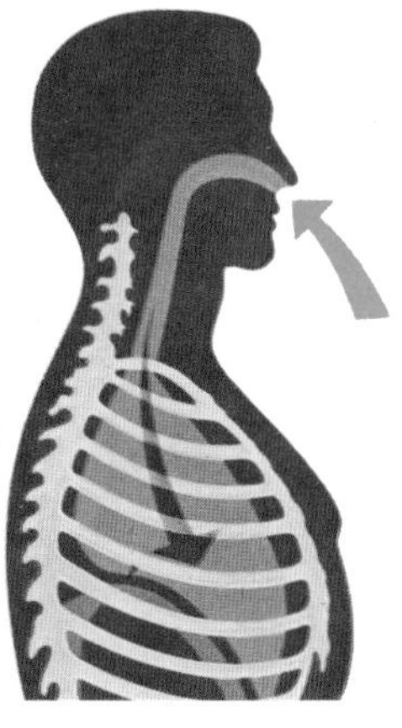

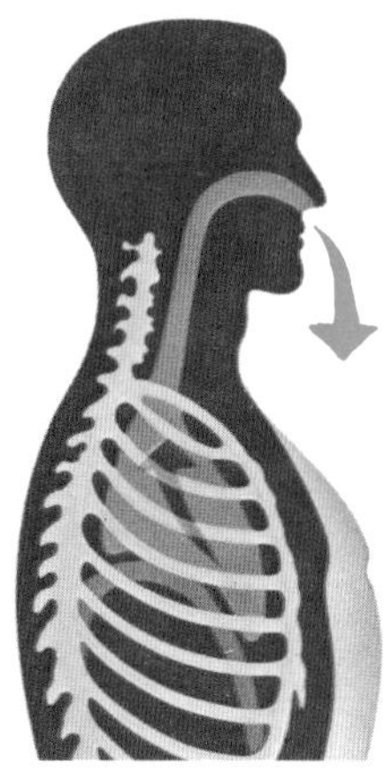

When we **breathe** our chest expands and air rushes in through our nose. When our chest muscles relax, the lungs are squeezed and air is pushed out.

**bring up** to care for a child as it grows.

**broad** wide, a long way across.

**broadcast** to send out in all directions, particularly by radio or television.

**bronze** a mixture of the metals copper and tin. *Bronze is reddish-brown in color.*

**Bronze Age** the time between the Stone Age and the Iron Age when people made weapons and tools of bronze.

**brooch** (rhymes with *coach*) a piece of jewelry that is pinned onto clothing.

**broom** a brush with a long handle.

**bruise** (say *brooze*) a blue-black mark on the skin caused by a knock.

**brush** 1 bristles or hair fixed to a handle, used for painting, sweeping or scrubbing. 2 to use a brush.

**bubble** a filmy ball of liquid filled with air.

**buck** 1 a male deer or rabbit. 2 (of a horse) to kick up the heels.

**buckle** a fastener, usually on a belt or strap.

**bud** a young flower or leaf before it opens.

**buffalo** 1 in Asia, a kind of wild ox. 2 in North America, a bison.

**bug** one of a group of insects with a mouth that can prick and suck.

**build** (rhymes with *milled*) to make something by putting

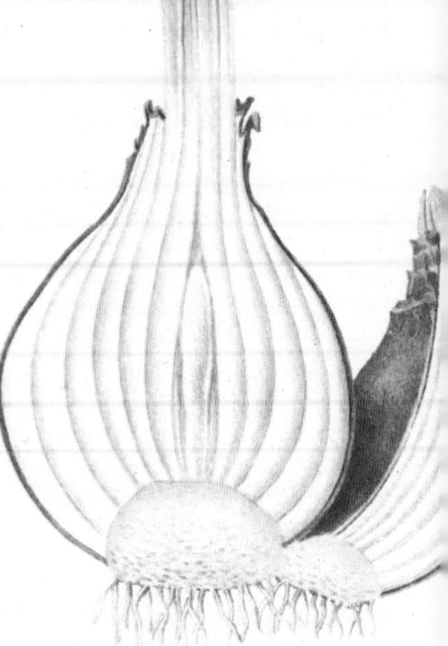

The **bulb** above has been sliced in half to show the fleshy layers round the central bud.

Terminal bud

Lateral buds

The main **bud** at the end of a stem is called the terminal bud. Side buds are called lateral buds.

different parts together. *This bird builds its nest from twigs and feathers.*

**building** a house or other structure that has been built.

**building site** the place where a building is being built.

**built** passed of **build**.

**bulb** 1 the roundish underground stem of some plants, like onions. 2 an electric lamp.

**bull** a male of the cattle family or a male elephant.

**bulldozer** a heavy machine for clearing land.

**bullet** a piece of shaped metal made to be shot from a gun.

**bully** a person who uses his or her strength to frighten other, weaker people.

**bulrush** a tall plant that grows near water.

**bumblebee** a large bee that hums noisily.

**bunch** a number of things of the same kind together, like a *bunch of grapes.*

**bundle** a number of things wrapped up together.

**bungalow** a house with all its rooms on the ground floor.

**bunk** a narrow bed fixed to the wall, often one above the other.

**buoy** (say *boy*) an anchored float marking a channel or a reef for ships.

**burglar** a person who breaks into a house to steal.

**buried** past of **bury**.

**burrow** a hole made in the ground by an animal as a home.

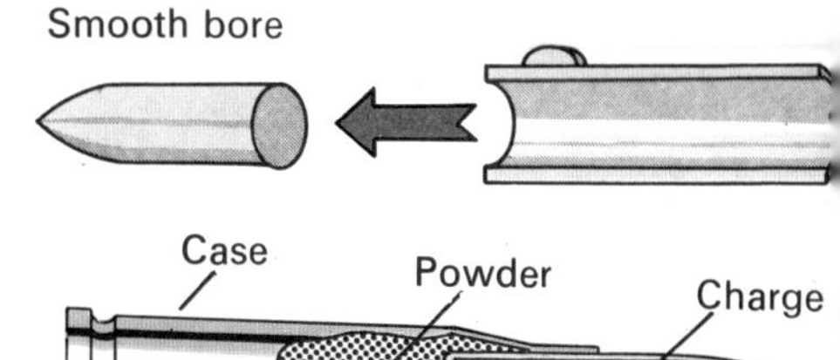


Grooves on the inside of a gun barrel (rifling) cause the **bullet** to spin. This gives it greater range and accuracy.

**burst** to break apart suddenly, or explode. *The balloon burst with a loud bang.*

**burst in** or **into** rush in. *Jane burst into the room.*

**bury** to put something in the ground; to hide away.

**bush** a shrub; a small thick tree.

**business** (say *biz-ness*) 1 a shop or organization. 2 a person's work or occupation. *My father's business is running a book shop.*

**busy** (say *bizzy*) having a lot to do.

**butcher** a person who kills or cuts up animals to sell their meat.

**butt** to hit with the head.

**butterfly** an insect with large, colorful wings. Unlike the moth, it flies during the daytime.

# Cc

The Polaroid **camera** above was invented in 1947. It develops and prints its own pictures in seconds.

**cabbage** a vegetable with thick green leaves growing very close together.
**cabin** 1 a room in a ship or aircraft. 2 a hut; a simple house.
**cactus** a prickly desert plant with a thick green stem.
**café** (say *caffay*) a place where meals are sold; a small restaurant.
**cage** a box with bars in which birds or animals are kept.
**calculate** to work out a sum.
**calculator** an electronic machine for doing sums.
**calendar** a list of the days, weeks and months of the year.

The barrel **cactus** swells up with water when it rains. During dry weather it loses water and shrinks in size.

**calf** (say *kaff*) (plural **calves**) 1 a young cow, seal, elephant or whale. 2 the fleshy back part of the leg below the knee.
**call off** to decide not to do something that has been arranged. *The game was called off because the field was flooded.*
**calm** (rhymes with *palm*) quiet, smooth.
**camel** an animal with a long neck and one hump or two on its back. *Camels can live in desert countries.*
**camera** an instrument for taking photographs.
**camouflage** to disguise guns, ships, aircraft, and so on with paint, tree branches, or nets so that they cannot easily be seen.
**camp** 1 a place where people stay in tents or huts. 2 to live in a tent.
**can** 1 to be able to. *Can you run faster than me?* 2 to be

Early **cannon** like this were clumsy and often blew up when fired.

allowed to. *Dad says I can stay up to watch television.* 3 a metal container.

**canal** a man-made waterway for barges or for taking water to fields.

**candle** a stick of wax with a string, or wick, through the middle, used to give light.

**candlestick** a holder for a candle.

**cannon** a big, heavy gun.

**canoe** (say *can-oo*) a light boat that is paddled through the water.

**canter** an easy gallop on horseback.

**canvas** a coarse cloth used for tents and sails. Artists also paint on it.

**canvass** to go to people and ask them to vote for your side. *We shall canvass for John Smith.*

**cape** 1 a coat with no sleeves, worn over the shoulders. 2 a piece of land that juts out into the sea.

**capital** 1 the city where the government of a country works. 2 uppercase letters written like this: A, M, R, Z.

**captain** 1 the officer in charge of a ship. 2 an army officer below a major and above a lieutenant.

**caption** the words near a picture which explain what it is.

**captive** a prisoner.

**capture** to take someone prisoner.

**caravan** 1 a home on wheels, pulled by a car or horse. 2 a group of people traveling together across a desert.

**cardboard** extra thick card or paper.

**cardigan** a woolen jacket that opens at the front.

**care for** to look after someone; to love someone.

**careless** not thinking about what one does.

**cargo** goods carried by ship or aircraft.

**carnival** a public occasion for making merry. *In New Orleans there is a famous carnival called Mardi Gras.*

**carnivore** an animal that lives on meat.

**carriage** 1 vehicle, usually with four wheels, pulled by horses. 2 a coach for passengers on a train.

**carry on** to continue doing something.

**cart** a two-wheeled vehicle pulled by a horse, ox or other animal.

**cartoon** a funny drawing, often of people in politics.

**cartridge** the case holding the explosive that fires a bullet.

**carve** 1 to shape a piece of wood or stone. 2 cut up meat to serve it at a meal.

**case** 1 a box for carrying things or storing them. 2 an example; an instance. *There was a case of whooping cough in the class.* 3 a trial in a law court. *The man and woman in the case were found guilty.*

**cash** money in paper notes and coins.

**cashier** the person who takes in and pays out money in a shop, hotel or other business.

**cassette** a container for holding magnetic tape used for recording.

**castle** a large building with thick walls, fortified against attack.

**cat** 1 a small, furry domestic animal. 2 any member of the cat family. *Lions, tigers and leopards are known as the big cats.*

**catalog** a list of things, such as the pictures in an exhibition or the books in a library.

**catamaran** a boat with two hulls joined together.

**catapult** 1 a Y-shaped stick with a piece of elastic fixed to it. *A catapult is used for throwing small stones.* 2 an ancient weapon for throwing large stones. 3 a device for launching aircraft from an aircraft carrier.

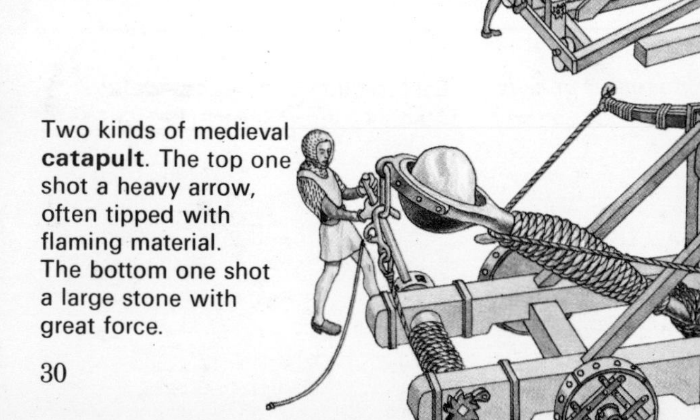

Two kinds of medieval **catapult**. The top one shot a heavy arrow, often tipped with flaming material. The bottom one shot a large stone with great force.

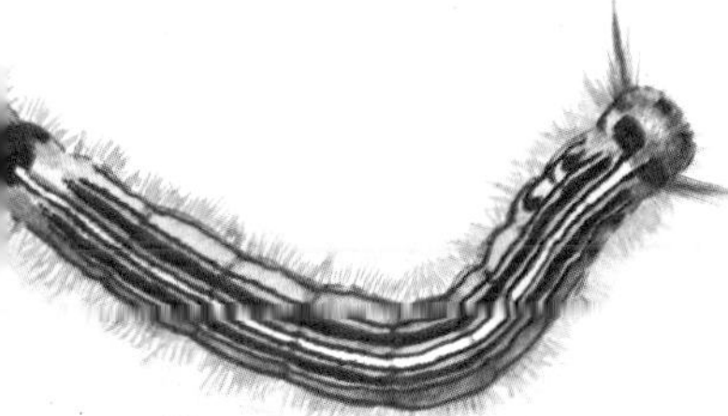

caterpillars spend their whole lives eating, so that they can grow and change into a butterfly or a moth.

**caterpillar** the larva stage in the growth of a butterfly or moth.
**cathedral** the main church of an area; the church of a bishop's region.
**cattle** all oxen or cows.
**cause** (rhymes with *saws*) to make something happen. *My dog was the cause of the accident.*
**cavalry** soldiers who fight on horseback.
**cave** a hole in the side of a hill or under the ground.
**caveman** a person who lived in a cave, especially during the Stone Age.
**cease** to stop.
**ceiling** (say *seeling*) the roof of a room.
**cell** 1 the smallest unit of living matter in animals and plants. *All living things are made up from a number of cells.* 2 a small room in a monastery, convent or prison.
**cellar** an underground room for storing things.
**cello** (say *chello*) a stringed instrument like a large violin. *A cello is held between the legs while it is being played.*
**cement** a gray powder that, when mixed with water, becomes very hard. *Cement is used in building.*
**cemetery** a place (not a churchyard) where people are buried.
**census** a counting of all the people in a country. *In the United States there is a census every ten years.*
**cent** an American coin. *There are 100 cents in a dollar.*
**centaur** an imaginary creature, half man and half horse.
**centennial** a hundredth anniversay.
**center** (rhymes with *enter*) the middle part of something.
**centigrade** a temperature scale on which water freezes at 0°C and boils at 100°C. *The centigrade scale was worked out by a Swedish scientist called Anders Celsius and is sometimes called the Celsius scale.*
**centimeter** a metric measure of length. *There are 100 centimeters in a meter.*

This line is 3 **centimeters** long.

Each section of a **centipede's** body has a pair of thin legs.

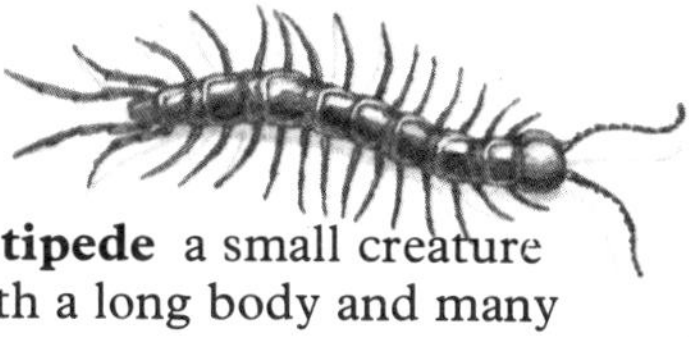

**centipede** a small creature with a long body and many legs.

**central** at or near the center. *Andy lives in central New York.*

**century** one hundred years. *We are now living in the twentieth century.*

**cereal** 1 grain crops such as maize, rice or wheat used for food. 2 breakfast food made from grain.

**ceremony** a dignified occasion. *The wedding ceremony took place in an old church.*

**certain** 1 sure. *I am certain they will come soon.* 2 some. *Certain people are color blind.*

**certificate** a piece of paper that is proof of something. *Nicola was given a certificate to show she had swum five lengths of the pool.*

**chain** a line of rings joined together. The rings in a chain are called "links".

**chalk** 1 a kind of soft, white rock. 2 white material used for writing on a blackboard.

**champion** the overall winner.

**championship** a competition to find the best person or team.

**chance** a possibility of something happening. *Leroy has a good chance of becoming champion, but Eric has no chance at all.*

**change** 1 to make something different. *The girls changed their clothes.* 2 the money given back when you give too much money for something you are buying. *I bought a loaf of bread and the storekeeper gave me change for my dollar.*

The most important **cereal** crops are, from left to right, barley, corn, rice rye, oats and wheat. Rye and wheat are mostly ground into flour. Oats and corn are often used to feed farm animals. Rice is eaten by more people than any other cereal. Barley is used to make beer.

Ancient Assyrian **chariots** usually carried a driver, an archer and two other soldiers to protect them. The Assyrians were among the first people to use chariots.

**channel** 1 a narrow strip of water joining two seas. 2 a narrow passage for water to run through.
**chapel** a small church, or part of a large church.
**chapter** one section of a book.
**character** 1 the things that make you the person you are. *Margaret's character was so kind that everyone liked her.* 2 one of the people in a book or play. *Little Red Riding Hood is a character in a story.*
**charge** 1 to rush forward and attack. 2 to ask a certain price for something. 3 **in charge of** responsible for. *Simon was left in charge of the store while the manager was out.*
**chariot** a vehicle used for fighting and racing long ago.
**charity** help and kindness given to poor people.
**charm** something that has magic power. *He carried a rabbit's foot charm.*
**charming** very attractive; delightful.
**chart** 1 a sea map for sailors, showing the sea depth, the position of buoys, rocks etc. 2 information shown by a diagram or graph.
**chase** to run after and try to catch.
**cheat** 1 to act dishonestly in order to help oneself. 2 someone who cheats.
**check** 1 to make sure that something is right. *Did you check that all the windows were closed?* 2 to stop, or hold back for a short time. *He was checked in the goal area, but still managed to shoot.* 3 a piece of paper which, when filled in and signed, tells a bank to pay money to someone.
**cheek** the fat part of your face

on either side of your mouth.
**cheer** 1 to make happy; comfort. 2 to shout joyfully.
**cheerful** looking and feeling happy.
**chef** (say *sheff*) a head cook who is in charge of a large kitchen.
**chemical** (say *kemical*) a substance used in chemistry.
**chemist** (say *kemist*) a person who is trained in chemistry.
**chemistry** a branch of science that is about what substances are made of and how they work together.
**chess** a game for two people played with 16 pieces each (**chessmen**) on a squared board.

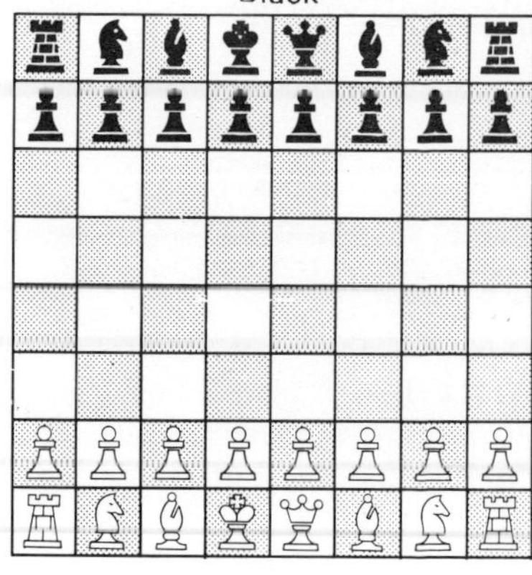


How the **chess** pieces are arranged at the start of the game.

**chest** 1 a large strong box with a lid. 2 the upper part of the front of one's body.
**chew** to crush food in your mouth with your teeth.
**chick** a baby bird.
**chicken** a young hen.
**chicken pox** a disease that causes red itchy spots on the skin.
**chief** 1 a ruler or leader. 2 most important; main. *Farming is the chief industry.*
**chimpanzee** an African ape.
**china** fine clay baked and glazed, made into plates, cups and so on.
**chip** 1 a small piece broken off something. 2 a tiny

**Chimpanzees** are just as happy in the trees as on the gound. They use their strong arms to swing from branch to branch.

The **chrysalis** stage of a butterfly is also called a pupa.

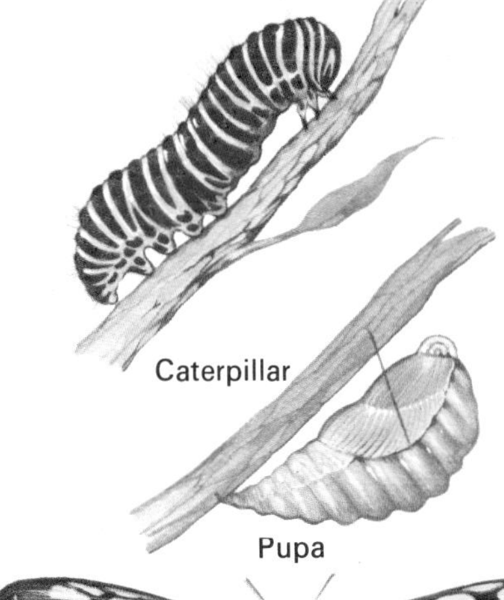


electronic device, usually made of silicon, that holds a circuit with thousands of transistors.

**chocolate** food or drink made from the ground and roasted beans of the cacao tree.

**choice** the act of choosing.

**choir** (rhymes with *fire*, say *kwire*) a group of people trained to sing together.

**choke** 1 not able to breathe because of something in your throat or lungs. 2 to block something up.

**chop** 1 to cut into pieces, often with an ax. 2 a thick slice of meat with a bit of bone in it.

**chorus** (say *korus*) part of a song that everyone sings after a solo part.

**christen** to give a name to and receive into the Christian Church; to baptize. *Our baby was christened Angela by the priest.*

**Christian** a believer in the religion of Jesus Christ.

**Christianity** the religion that was started by Jesus Christ.

**chrysalis** a stage in the development of an insect between caterpillar and adult. *The caterpillar turned into a chrysalis, and then it became a butterfly.*

**church** a building where Christians go to worship.

**cigar** tobacco rolled in a tobacco leaf for smoking.

**cigarette** a small roll of tobacco in thin paper for smoking.

**circle** a round flat shape; the line around this shape.

**circumference** the distance right around a circle.

**circus** a show, often held in a tent, with animal acts, clowns and acrobats.

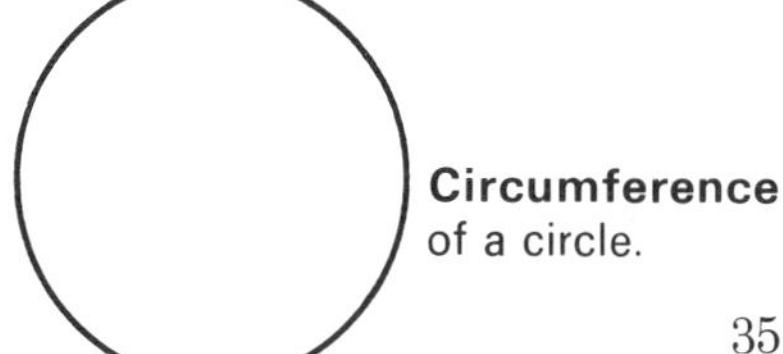

**Circumference** of a circle.

**citizen** 1 a person who lives in a town or city. 2 a person who has every right to live in a country. *She was an American citizen.*
**city** a large or important town.
**civilian** a person who is not in one of the fighting services.
**civilization** a group of people in an advanced stage of development.
**civilized** living in a well organized way.
**claim** 1 to say that something is yours. *You should claim your prize.* 2 to say that something is a fact. *He claims that he can lift great weights.*
**clarinet** a musical wind instrument with a single reed.
**class** a group of the same kind of people, like children who are taught together. *I go to the class at the ballet school.*
**claw** a pointed nail on an animal's foot.
**clay** a soft kind of earth that becomes hard when baked.
**clear** 1 easy to see through. *It was a clear day.* 2 easy to understand. *The meaning of the word was quite clear.* 3 free from obstacles. *Before you cross, make sure that the road is clear.*
**clerk** (rhymes with *jerk*) a person who works in an office writing things down.
**cliff** a very steep, high bank, especially by the sea.
**climate** the usual weather in a place.

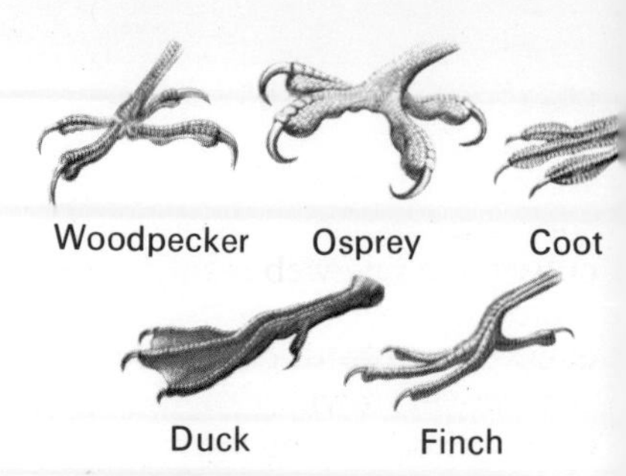


Birds' **claws** tell us about their way of life. The osprey's hooked claws, for example, are for grasping food.

**cloak** (rhymes with *poke*) a loose coat with no sleeves; a long cape.
**cloakroom** a place to leave your coat.
**clockwise** going around in the same direction as the hands of a clock.
**close** (rhymes with *toes*) 1 to shut. 2 to end. *The carnival will close with fireworks.*
**clown** a person who does funny things in a circus.
**club** 1 a heavy stick with which to hit things. 2 a group that people can join to do things together. *We have a chess club in our school.*
**clue** something that helps you to solve a puzzle.
**coach** 1 a four-wheeled carriage. 2 to teach someone, especially to teach a sport. 3 someone who helps others to prepare for examinations.
**coal** a black mineral that burns slowly and gives off heat.
**coarse** rough; not fine.

**coast** land along the edge of the sea.
**cobbler** a person who mends or makes shoes.
**cobweb** a fine web made by a spider.
**cock** a male bird, especially a farmyard fowl.
**cocoa** chocolate powder made from the seeds of the cacao tree.
**cocoon** covering made by a caterpillar to protect itself during the chrysalis stage.
**code** 1 a secret system of writing. 2 a set of rules. *Spies send messages in code.* 3 a signaling system. *Bob learned the Morse code.*
**coffee** a drink made from the roasted and ground beans of the coffee bush.
**coffin** a box in which a dead person is buried or cremated.
**cog** one of the teeth around the rim of a gear wheel.
**coil** to wind something in circles or spirals. *The old electric range had two coils of wire that gave off heat.*
**coin** a piece of metal money.
**collage** (say *co-ladge*) a picture made up of pieces of cloth, paper or other materials.
**collar** 1 part of a shirt or other clothing that goes around the neck. 2 a leather band around an animal's neck.
**collect** 1 to gather or bring together. *We collect coins.* 2 to gather from a number of people. *They went around to the houses to collect money for charity.*
**college** a place where people go to study after secondary school; part of a university.
**collide** to bump into something.
**colony** 1 a group of settlers in a new country who are still governed by their mother country; the country where the settlers live. *Hong Kong is still a British colony.* 2 a group of people or animals that live together. *He came upon a large colony of bees.*
**colt** a young male horse.
**column** a tall round pillar.
**combine** to join together.
**combine harvester** a large farm machine that cuts grain, threshes it and packs it together.
**come about** to happen. *It came about that we all met at the beach.*
**come across** to find something when you do not expect to. *I came across your letter when I was tidying my desk.*
**come to** total cost of several things. *When it is all added together it will come to $14.56.*

**Coffee** beans grow inside red berries.

**comedy** a funny play.
**comet** a body of (probably) ice and gas, which looks like a star but moves around our own Sun.
**comfort** to help someone who is unhappy. *Sandra comforted the little girl until her mother arrived.*
**comic** 1 funny. 2 a magazine with comic strip pictures.
**comma** a punctuation mark, like this , that is used to show a pause in writing.
**command** 1 to order someone to do something. 2 to be in charge of. *Grant took command of the whole army.*
**committee** a small group of people who are appointed by a larger group of people to discuss the larger group's affairs. *Our club's committee meets once a month.*
**common** usual, normal; often seen. *A thrush is a very common bird.*
**common sense** good, ordinary, sensible thinking.
**communicate** to pass on information or feelings to other people.
**communication** the passing of information from one person to another.
**community** all the people who live in a place.
**commuter** a person who travels daily to and from work.
**company** 1 an organization in business to make, buy or sell things. 2 visitors in your house. *We've got company for dinner on Sunday.*
**companion** a friend; someone who goes with you.
**compare** to look at things to see how alike or unlike they are. *Roger compared the two chairs and decided to buy the larger one.*
**compass** an instrument that shows direction. *The needle of a compass always turns toward north.*
**compasses** instruments for drawing circles or for measuring.
**compete** to take part in a contest. *All the girls will compete in the race.*
**competition** a contest in which a number of people take part to see who is the best.
**complain** to say that you are not pleased with something.
**complete** 1 whole; the full number. *When the party was complete it numbered 16 boys.* 2 to finish. *It will take three months to complete the new school.*

Some **conifer** trees. Left to right: Ginkgo, Monkey Puzzle, Cedar of Lebanon and Scots Pine.

**complicated** made up of many different parts; difficult to understand.

**compose** to write a story or make up a piece of music.

**composed** the way something is put together. *Our class is composed of 14 girls and 15 boys.*

**composer** a person who makes up music.

**compound** something made up of separate parts or elements. *Salt is a compound made up of the elements sodium and chlorine.*

**computer** an electronic calculating machine that stores information and works very quickly.

**concave** a surface that curves inward, like the inside of a saucer.

**concert** a musical entertainment.

**concrete** a hard building material made of cement, sand, gravel and water.

**condense** 1 to make something more solid; to shorten. *She condensed the story by cutting out some unnecessary sentences.* 2 to change from a gas into a liquid. *The steam condensed into water.*

**conductor** 1 a person who leads a group of singers or musicians. 2 a person who collects fares on a train.

**cone** 1 a solid body with a round bottom and a pointed top. 2 the fruit of a fir or pine tree. 3 a cone-shaped wafer for ice cream.

**congratulate** to tell someone you are glad that they have done well.

**conifer** an evergreen tree with cones for fruit. *Pine and fir trees are conifers.*

**conjurer** a person who performs tricks that look like magic.

**connect** to join things together. *This road connects our town to the main highway.*

**conquer** (say *conker*) to defeat an enemy.

**conservation** looking after things so they are not spoiled or destroyed.
**conserve** to keep something as it was without changing it.
**consider** to think about. *Did you consider buying a new belt?*
**consonant** any letter of the alphabet except a, e, i, o, u, which are **vowels**.
**conspire** to plot secretly for an evil purpose.
**constant** continuous; all the time.
**constellation** a group of stars which make a shape that you can recognize in the sky.
**construct** to build.
**consult** to try to get advice or help from someone or from a book. *When we do not know the meaning of a word we consult a dictionary.*
**contain** to hold something. *This box contains all my belongings.*
**container** a box, jar, pot or can in which things are put.
**contented** peaceful and satisfied.
**contents** 1 the things that are in something. *The contents of Rudolph's pockets were a penknife, a rubber band and two candies.* 2 a list of chapters at the beginning of a book.
**contest** a competition; a fight.
**continent** one of the seven main land masses of the world: North America, South America, Asia, Africa, Europe, Australia and Antarctica.
**continue** to go on being or doing. *We will continue collecting stamps.*
**contract** 1 to grow smaller. *A metal bar contracts as it is made colder.* 2 an agreement. *The butcher had a contract to deliver meat to the school.*
**control** 1 to be in charge of. 2 to operate machinery. 3 a lever, wheel or knob which is used to control machinery.
**convenient** suitable, handy. *Our new house is only two minutes from school. It is very convenient.*
**convent** a place where nuns live and work.
**conversation** talk.
**convex** a surface that curves outward, like an upturned saucer.
**convict** 1 a criminal who has been sent to prison. 2 to prove someone guilty of a crime.
**convoy** a group organized for protection in moving. *We spotted six trucks in a convoy on the highway.*

This lens is **convex** (thickest in in the middle). It makes the pin look larger.

The crocus **corm** sends up shoots from its thick bulb-like underground stem.

**cooperate** to work with others to do something. *If we cooperate we will finish the job sooner.*

**copper** a reddish-brown metal.

**copy** to make something look exactly like something else.

**coral** a hard pink or white material made in the sea from the bodies of tiny animals.

**core** the center of, the middle part. *Our dog likes to eat the core of my apple.*

**cork** 1 the light, tough bark of the cork-oak tree. 2 a bottle stopper made from cork.

**corkscrew** a tool for taking corks out of bottles.

**corm** a bulb-like swelling on the stem of a plant underground. *A crocus grows from a corm.*

**corn** 1 grain. The seeds of wheat, oats, rye and barley. 2 maize. *Indian corn is maize.*

**coronation** the ceremony when a king or queen is crowned.

**correct** 1 right; true; with no mistakes. *All my sums were correct today.* 2 to put right any mistakes. *Our teacher corrects our exercise books everyday.*

**corridor** a long passage in a building.

**cosmonaut** a Russian astronaut.

**cost** 1 the amount one has to pay for something. 2 to cause the loss of. *His attempt to save the boy cost him his life.*

**costume** clothes, especially the clothes worn by actors.

**cottage** a small house, often for vacation use.

**cotton** fiber from the seeds of the cotton plant. *Cotton is made into cloth.*

**couch** a long, soft seat.

**council** a group of people who meet to make decisions.

**counsel** 1 advice. *He gave Tom some wise counsel.* 2 an adviser in the law.

**counter** 1 a table or flat surface in a store. 2 a small piece used for moves in a board game.

**country** 1 the whole land where people live. *France is the country of the French.* 2 the land outside cities. *We like to walk in the country on weekends.*

**county** a part of a country with its own local government.

**couple** two; a pair.

**courage** bravery.
**course** the direction in which something goes. *We followed the course of the river to its mouth.*
**court** 1 the place where trials are held. 2 the place where a king or queen lives, and the people who live there. 3 an area marked out for certain games, as a tennis court or a squash court.
**cousin** the child of your aunt or uncle.
**cover** to put something over something else.
**covering** something that covers something. *Bark is the covering of a tree trunk.*
**cow** 1 a farm animal kept for its milk. 2 a female of the ox family or a female elephant, whale or seal.
**coward** a person who cannot hide fear.
**cowboy** a person who looks after cattle, especially on horseback.
**crab** an animal with a hard shell and ten legs, two of which have large claws. *Crabs live by or in the sea.*
**cradle** a bed for a small baby, usually on rockers.
**craft** 1 skilled work with the hands. 2 a boat; an aircraft.
**craftsman** a skilled person who works at a craft.
**crane** 1 a large water bird with long legs. 2 a machine that lifts and moves heavy things.
**crate** a large box made from thin pieces of wood. *The oranges were in a crate.*
**crater** 1 mouth of a volcano. 2 a hole in the ground made by the explosion of a bomb or shell.
**create** to make something; to bring something into existence. *Authors create characters for their stories.*
**creator** 1 the person who creates. 2 the God who created the universe.
**creature** any living thing.
**creep** 1 to move along close to the ground; to crawl. 2 to move stealthily.
**creeper** a plant that creeps along the ground or up a wall.
**crepe paper** (crepe rhymes

The Moon's surface is covered with **craters**. Some of them are 300 kilometers across.

with grape) a special sort of crinkly paper.
**crept** past of **creep.**
**crescent** a curved shape like the new moon.
**crew** the workers on a ship or aircraft.
**crib** a baby's bed.
**cricket** 1 a small insect like a grasshopper that leaps and makes a chirping noise. 2 an English outdoor summer game played with bats and a ball by teams of eleven players.
**crime** something done that is against the law.
**criminal** someone who is guilty of a crime.
**crimson** a deep red color.
**cripple** someone whose body is so badly hurt or formed that he cannot do things easily.
**crisp** 1 dry and hard, but easy to break. 2 clear, frosty weather.
**crocodile** a fierce, long reptile that lives in rivers.
**crooked** 1 not straight. 2 not honest or dishonest.
**crop** 1 the plants that are gathered each year from a farm. 2 to cut short.
**crossing** a place where people can go across the street. *It is safer to cross the road at the proper crossing.*
**crossroads** a place where two roads meet each other and cross.
**crow** 1 a large, black bird with a harsh cry. 2 to give a shrill cry like a cock. 3 to boast.

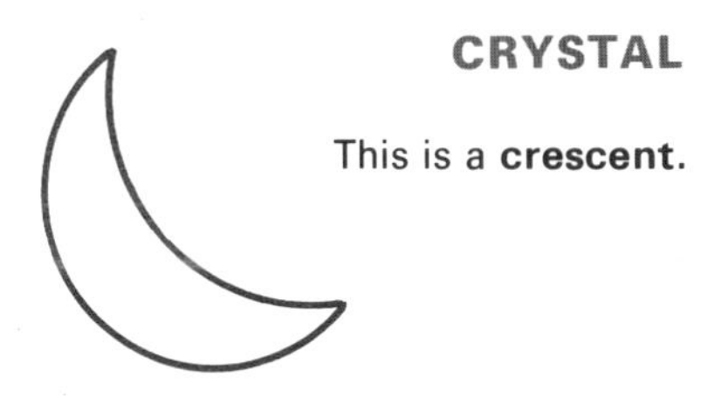

This is a **crescent**.

**crowd** a lot of people gathered together.
**crown** the headdress of a king or queen.
**cruel** liking to give pain to others.
**crumb** a small scrap of bread or other food.
**crumble** to fall or break into small pieces.
**crush** 1 to press on and break into pieces. *If you sit on the cookies you will crush them.* 2 to defeat. *Napoleon went on to crush all his enemies.*
**crust** a hard outer layer, like a crust of bread.
**crutch** something that helps a lame person to walk.
**crystal** 1 a hard glass-like mineral. 2 the shape which tiny pieces of many chemicals (such as salt) always take. 3 good quality, very clear glass.

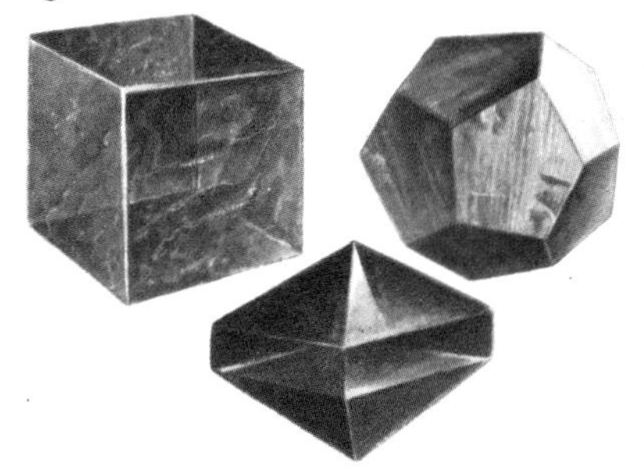

All the **crystals** that make up a substance are always the same.

**cub** a young bear, lion, fox, tiger, or some other animal.
**cube** a solid object with 6 equal sides. *A dice is a cube.*
**cuff** 1 the end of the sleeve. 2 to hit someone with the open hand.
**cultivate** to help plants to grow by preparing the soil well and looking after them.
**cunning** crafty; artful. *The fox is a cunning animal.*
**cure** 1 to make well. 2 to preserve some substances such as leather, tobacco and some meats by drying, smoking or salting them.
**curious** 1 odd; strange. *Jane was wearing a very curious hat.* 2 wanting to find out about something. *I am very curious as to why she is wearing that hat.*
**curly** something that is twisted into shape like a spiral or a coil, especially hair.
**currant** a small, seedless dried grape.
**currency** the money that is used in a country.
**current** 1 flowing water or air. 2 the flow of electricity.
**curry** a hot, spicy food, originally made in India and Pakistan.
**curve** a bend; a line that is not straight.
**custom** the usual way of doing something. *It is the custom in some countries to kiss people on both cheeks.*
**customer** a person who buys things from a store or business, sometimes regularly.
**cutlery** knives, forks and spoons.
**cygnet** (say *signet*) a young swan.
**cylinder** 1 a solid or hollow tubelike object. 2 the part of an engine in which the piston goes up and down.
**cymbals** (say *simbals*) a metal instrument. *Cymbals are two brass plates that are struck against each other to make a clashing sound. A cymbal can also be struck with a drumstick.*

# Dd

**dagger** a short, two-edged knife used as a weapon.
**daily** something that happens every day.
**dairy** a place where milk is kept and butter and cheese are made.
**dam** a thick wall built across a river so that a lake forms behind it.
**damage** 1 to do harm to something. *You will damage the gate if you swing on it.* 2 harm; injury. *Little damage was done.*
**danger** something that is likely to do harm to you. *The ice on the step is a danger to everyone.*

**dare** 1 to be brave enough to do something. *I wouldn't dare cross that road at night.* 2 to ask someone to show how brave they are. *I dare you to jump over the stream.*
**darn** to mend a hole in cloth by sewing threads across it.
**dart** 1 to move forward suddenly. 2 a small pointed arrow used in the game of darts.
**date** 1 the day, the month, the year, or all three together. *The date today is Friday, July 13th.* 2 the sweet, sticky fruit that grows on a date palm.
**dawn** sunrise.
**deaf** (say *def*) not able to hear.
**deal** 1 to tell about. *The book deals with butterflies and moths.* 2 to give out. *It is your turn to deal the cards.*

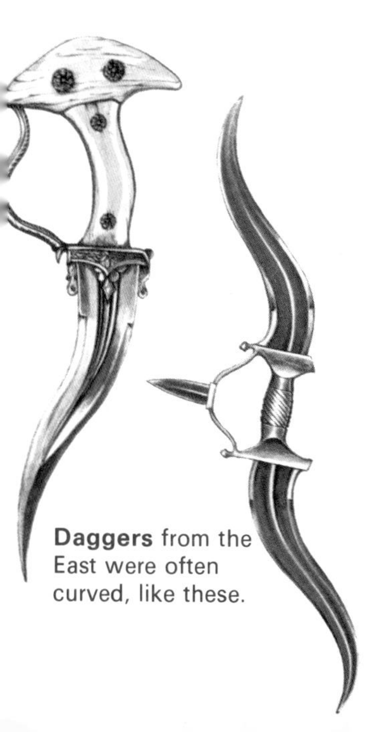

**Daggers** from the East were often curved, like these.

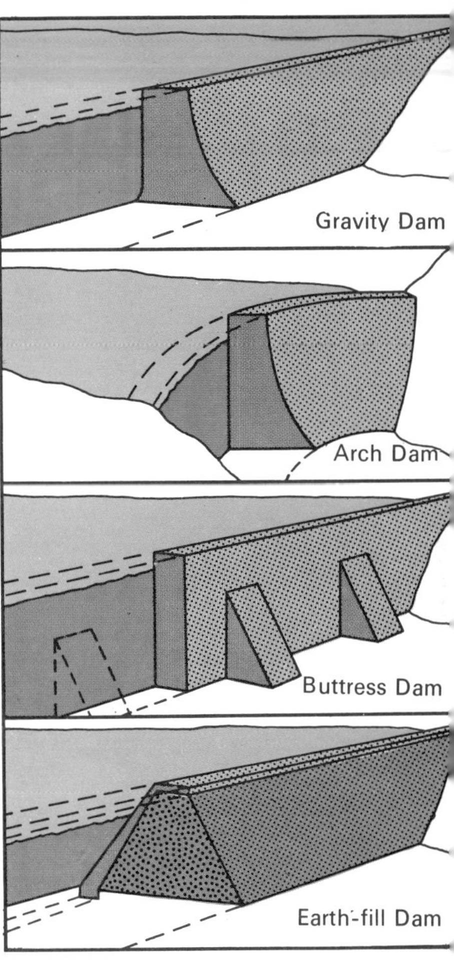


Four different kinds of **dam** are shown above.

**deal in** to buy and sell in. *The butcher deals in meat.*
**deal with** to do whatever has to be done. *You tidy this room and I'll deal with the kitchen.*
**debate** discuss or argue in public.

**debt** (rhymes with *yet*) something that you owe someone.
**decade** a ten year period.
**decay** to rot, to go bad.
**deceive** (say *de-seeve*) to make someone believe something that you know is not true; cheat.
**decide** to make up your mind about something.
**deciduous** deciduous trees such as maples and poplars lose all their leaves in winter.
**decimal** a way of writing fractions by using tens and tenths. Each place to the right of the decimal point stands for one tenth of the value of the place on its left, so; $2.1 = 2$ units + 1 tenth; $2.14 = 2$ units + 1 tenth + 4 hundredths; $3.276 = 3$ units + 2 tenths + 7 hundredths + 6 thousandths.
**deck** 1 the floor of a ship on which you walk. 2 dress up; decorate.
**declare** to make known publicly. *When we have all made an attempt, the teacher will declare the winner.*
**decorate** 1 to make more beautiful, to clean and paint. 2 to give someone a medal.
**decrease** to make or grow less.
**deed** something which is done, usually something good or bad or brave.
**deep** 1 going a long way down. *The river is very deep near the bridge.* 2 wide. *The shelf was not deep enough.* 3 dark. *The dress was a deep red.*

The female red **deer** is a graceful creature with sharp ears and a keen sense of smell.

**deer** a quick, graceful animal. *A male deer, or stag, has horns called antlers.*
**defeat** to beat someone at something.
**defend** to guard or make safe.
**defense** that which defends from attack. *A castle wall is a defense.*
**definite** certain, without doubt.
**degree** 1 a unit of measurement for temperature or angles. It is often written like this: 10° means 10 degrees. 2 a title given by a university to someone who has successfully completed a program of study.
**dehydrate** (say *dee-hi-drate*) to dry out the water from something. *Powdered milk is dehydrated.*
**delay** to make late or slow down.
**delicate** soft and not strong; dainty.
**delicious** (say *del-ish-us*) very pleasant to eat or smell.
**deliver** 1 to take things to a place where they are needed. *The boy delivers our newspaper*

*every morning*. 2 to give a speech. 3 to help at the birth of a baby. *The doctor arrived in time to deliver the baby.*

**delta** the triangle of land formed by rivers which have more than one mouth.

**demand** to ask for something that you think is due to you. *I shall demand payment of the money now.*

**democracy** 1 a country in which the government is chosen by all the adults. 2 this kind of government.

**den** the hidden home of an animal.

**denied** past of deny.

**dense** thick.

**deny** (say *den-eye*) to say that something is not true.

**depend on** to rely on someone for money or other things. *The child depends on us for all his needs.*

**depth** the distance from the top downward (how **deep** something is) or from the front to the back. *The depth of the shelf is just right.*

**descend** (say *de-send*) to go down.

The **delta** of the Nile River forms many smaller rivers.

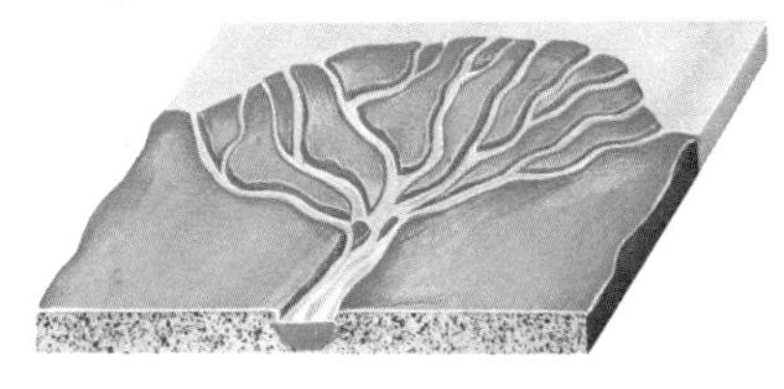

This map shows the world's **deserts**, about a third of the world's surface.

**describe** to say what something or somebody is like. *We can describe the man exactly.*

**desert** (say **dez**-*ert*) a large dry area of land where there is little water or rain.

**desert** (say *dez*-**ert**) to abandon; leave behind. *Why did you desert us when we most needed you?*

**deserve** to be worthy of something. *You deserve the prize because of all your hard work.*

**design** (rhymes with *line*) to make a plan or pattern for something.

**despair** to give up hope.

**dessert** (say *dez*-**ert**) the course served at the end of a meal; often it is sweet.

**detail** a small, sometimes unimportant piece of anything.

**detect** to discover.

**detective** a person who follows clues to find a criminal.

**detergent** a substance that removes dirt; a kind of soap.

**determined** with your mind firmly made up.

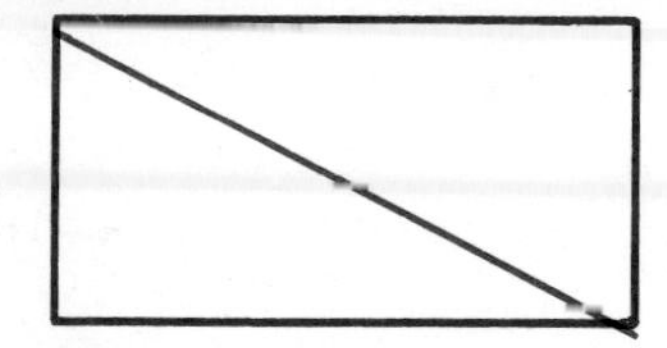

The red line is a **diagonal**.

**develop** to grow bigger and better. *A tadpole develops into a frog.*

**device** something made to do a particular thing.

**devil** an evil spirit, a demon.

**dew** the tiny drops of water that form on cool surfaces at night outside.

**diagonal** a straight line across an area from one corner to the opposite corner.

**diagram** a drawing that explains something. *The word "diagonal" is explained here with a diagram.*

**dial** 1 the face of a clock, watch or instrument. 2 the numbered part of a telephone.

**diameter** a line right across a circle passing through the center.

**diamond** 1 a very hard, brilliant precious stone. 2 a four-sided figure which is not a square.

The red lines show a **diameter** and a **diamond**.

**diary** a book in which you can write down what happens to you each day.

**dice** a small cube with one to six dots on its sides, used in games.

**dictionary** a book, like this one, that explains the meanings of words. *The words in a dictionary are listed in alphabetical order.*

**diesel** (say *deezle*) an engine that burns a certain kind of oil to supply power.

**diet** (say *di-et*) 1 the food you usually eat. 2 special meals that some people have to make them healthy, and others have to help them lose weight.

**digest** to change the food you have eaten in such a way that your body can use it to give you health and strength.

**dike** a bank or wall to keep back sea water and prevent flooding.

**dim** not bright.

**dinghy** a small, open boat.

**dinosaur** one of a group of reptiles that became extinct millions of years ago.

**dip** to put something into a liquid.

**direct** 1 to show or tell someone how to do something or go somewhere. 2 the quickest way from one point to another. *This train goes directly to Boston.*

**direction** the way from one place to another.

**disagree** 1 to quarrel, to have different ideas about something.

2 to have a bad effect. *I cannot eat onions; they disagree with me.*

**disappear** vanish; be seen no more.

**disappoint** to make someone sad by not doing what they had hoped for.

**disaster** a terrible accident. *Fifty people were killed in the disaster.*

**disciple** (say *dis-eye-pl*) a follower. *Jesus left twelve disciples to carry on his work.*

**discover** to find out something new.

**discuss** to talk about something with other people.

**disease** illness.

**disguise** to change what someone or something looks like. *His disguise was a mask and black cloak.*

**disinfect** to make something free from germs and disease.

**disk** a flat circle, like a stereo record.

**dismiss** 1 to send away. 2 to order someone to leave his job.

**disobedient** refusing to obey. *The girl did not do what her teacher told her. She was disobedient.*

**display** to show off something.

**dissolve** to mix something in a liquid so that it becomes part of the liquid. *Salt dissolves easily in water.*

**distance** the length between two points.

**distant** far away.

**district** part of a city or country.

**disturb** 1 to interrupt or annoy someone. 2 to move something from its usual position.

**ditch** a narrow channel for water.

**dive** to go into water head first.

A scene from over 100 million years ago. The fierce **dinosaur** Tyrannosaurus attacks a plant-eating Corythosaurus.

How a dry **dock** works. Water is let in from a harbor (1). Steel gates open and a ship sails into the dock (2). The gates close and water is pumped out of the dock (3). When the ship is repaired, water flows back in to refloat the vessel.

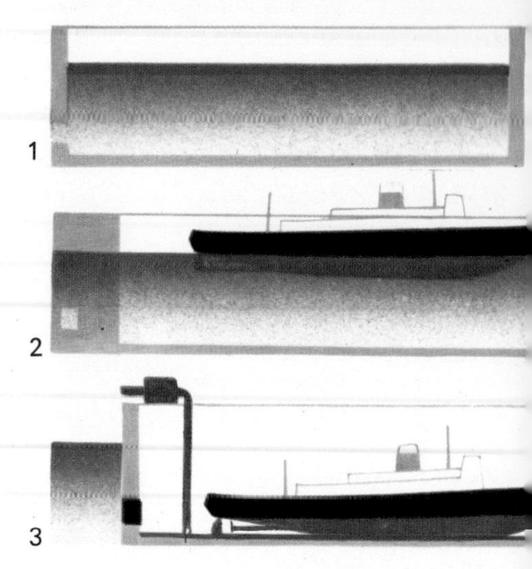


**diver** 1 someone who dives. 2 someone who goes deep into water for long periods by taking air with them, or who has air pumped down from the surface.
**divide** 1 to split into smaller parts. 2 to find out how many times one number goes into another number. *If you divide 8 by 2, the answer is 4.*
**dock** a place in a harbor where ships are loaded and unloaded.
**doe** a female deer or rabbit.
**dolphin** a small type of whale.
**dome** a rounded roof like an upside down bowl.
**domestic** to do with the home.
**domesticated** an animal that is used to living with people.
**donkey** an ass; an animal of the horse family with long ears.
**double** 1 twice the amount. 2 to fold over into two layers.
**doubt** (rhymes with *out*) to feel unsure about something. *I doubt whether you are right.*
**dough** (rhymes with *go*) a mixture of flour and water for making bread or pastry.
**down** 1 towards somewhere lower. *She went down the hill.* 2 very soft feathers.
**downward(s)** toward a lower level.
**dozen** twelve.
**draft** (rhymes with *raft*) 1 a flow of air, especially coming through a narrow gap in a door or window. 2 call up for military service. 3 the first plan or rough sketch of something.
**dragon** a fierce legendary creature that breathed fire.
**dragonfly** a brightly colored insect with long wings that lives near water.

**drain** 1 a pipe that takes waste water away. 2 to take water away through pipes and ditches. 3 to empty. *When he gives a toast, they will all drain their glasses.*
**drake** a male duck.
**draw** 1 to make a picture or diagram with pen, pencil or crayon, but not with paint. 2 the result of a game in which neither team or player wins. 3 pull. *They draw water from the well.*
**drawbridge** a bridge across a moat that could be pulled up when a castle was being attacked.
**dress** 1 a piece of clothing like a skirt and a shirt together worn by women and girls. 2 to put on clothes. 3 the way one dresses. *The national dress for women in India is the sari.*
**dresser** a piece of furniture like a chest of drawers.
**drift** to be carried slowly along by wind or water. *Without its engine, the ship will drift onto the rocks.*
**drill** 1 a pointed tool that is turned to bore holes. 2 exercises that are part of a soldier's training.
**drip** to fall in drops.
**dromedary** a fast camel with one hump.
**drop in** to visit someone without telling them you are coming.
**drought** (rhymes with *out*) a long period of dry weather.
**drown** to die in water.
**drug** 1 a medicine. 2 a substance that makes you sleepy or behave unusually.
**drum** a round, hollow musical instrument with a skin stretched over a frame. *A drum is beaten with a stick.*
**duck** 1 a webfooted water bird with a broad beak. 2 to bend down quickly to get out of the way of something.

Male **ducks** (drakes) have brighter feathers than female ducks.

Mallard Duck

Shoveler Duck

Pintail Duck

**duke** an important nobleman, next to a prince in rank. *A duke's wife is called a duchess.*

**dull** 1 not bright. 2 not sharp. 3 not interesting. *It is never dull when Mrs. Perfect teaches our class.*

**dumb** not able to speak.

**dune** a low hill of sand.

**dungeon** (say *dun-jun*) an underground prison.

**during** 1 throughout. *The old man slept during the whole speech.* 2 at some time in. *They arrived during the afternoon.*

**duty** something that you must do. *The policeman's duty is to arrest the burglar.*

**dwarf** a person, animal or plant that does not grow to full size.

**dwell** to live somewhere.

**dye** (rhymes with **lie**) to change the color of something by putting it in a special liquid, called a **dye**.

**dyke** see dike.

**dynamite** a powerful explosive used for blasting.

# Ee

**earn** 1 to get something by working for it. *He earns a good living.* 2 to deserve. *She earns every penny she gets.*

**earth** 1 the planet we live on. 2 the soil.

**earthquake** a sudden shaking movement of the surface of the Earth.

**easel** a frame to hold up a picture or a blackboard.

**east** the direction in which the sun rises. *East winds blow from the east.*

**ebb** the tide flowing back from land to sea.

**echo** (say *ecko*) a sound that is heard again when it bounces back or is reflected off something.

**eclipse** a time when the sun's light is cut off because the

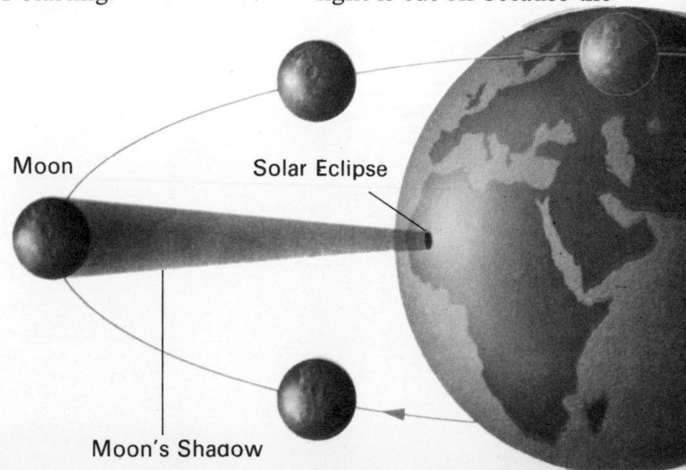

Moon passes between the Earth and the Sun (*an eclipse of the Sun*); a time when the Moon's light is cut off because the Earth passes between the Sun and the Moon (*an eclipse of the Moon*).

**ecology** the study of the habits of living things, the places where they live and how they depend on each other.

**edge** 1 the part along the side or end of something. *The path ran around the edge of the field.* 2 the cutting part of a knife.

**educate** to teach or train.

**effort** hard work.

**egg** 1 objects, that young birds, insects, fish and reptiles live inside before they are born. 2 an important kind of food.

**elastic** a material that stretches out and then goes back to the same size. *A rubber band is made out of elastic.*

**elbow** the joint between the upper and lower arm.

**elder** older. *My elder brother was born before I was.*

**eldest** the first born child in a family. *My eldest brother was born before my elder brother.*

**election** a time when people can choose by voting the men and women who will govern their town or country, society or club.

**electric** worked by electricity.

**electrician** a person who works with electricity or electrical equipment.

**electricity** energy that is used to make heat and light and is used to drive some machines. *Electricity moves along wires from generating stations to where it is needed.*

**electronics** the science that deals with things like television, radio and other pieces of apparatus that have devices such as transistors.

**element** a substance that cannot be divided into simpler substances. *There are only about a hundred elements in the universe. Everything is made up from them.*

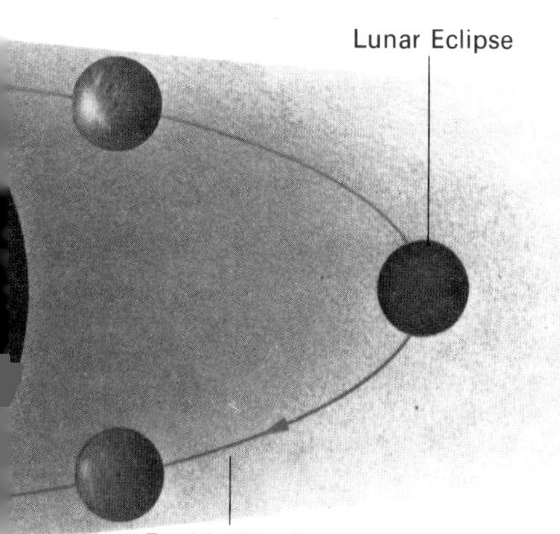


This diagram shows a solar **eclipse** as the Moon's shadow falls on the Earth, and a lunar eclipse as the Earth's shadow falls on the Moon.

# ELEPHANT

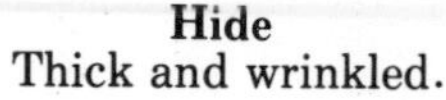


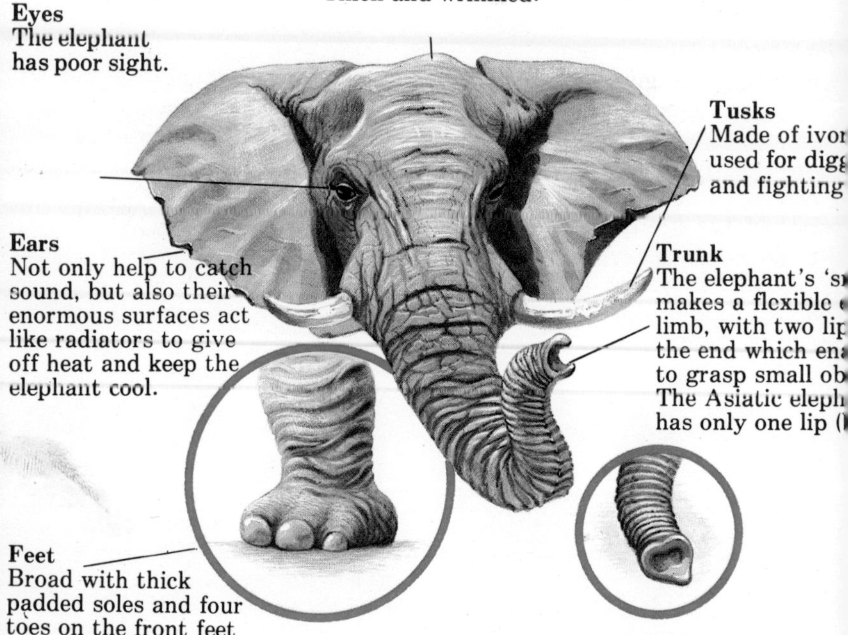


An African **elephant**.

**elephant** the largest four-footed animal. *An elephant has a long nose called a trunk and big, curved tusks made of ivory.*

**elf** (plural *elves*) in story books, a small fairy.

**embroidery** decoration on cloth made by sewing a pattern of colored stitches.

**embryo** an animal or bird in any early stage before it is born.

**emerald** a precious green stone.

**emergency** a sudden happening that needs quick action.

**emigrate** to go away from your own country to live.

**emperor** the male ruler of an empire. A female ruler is an **empress.**

**empire** a group of countries under one ruler. *The Roman Empire spread all around the Mediterranean Sea.*

**employ** 1 to pay people to work. 2 to use. *I employ a fine pen to fill in the details.*

**enamel** 1 a very hard, shiny paint. 2 a hard, shiny coating on metal pans, pottery or glass.

**enclose** to shut in on all sides.

**encourage** to make someone feel able to do something; to urge them on.

**encyclopedia** a book, or set of books, that give you information about many things. *An encyclopedia often lists things in alphabetical order.*

**energy** the strength or power to do work. *Machines have energy. The food we eat gives us energy.*

**engine** a machine that changes energy into power or movement. *The train was pulled by its great engine.*

**engineer** 1 a person who plans and builds bridges, roads, machines and big buildings. 2 a person who looks after or works with engines.

**enjoy** to get pleasure from. *I always enjoy going to the ocean.*

**enormous** very big.

**enter** go ino a place.

**entertain** 1 to amuse people with a show. 2 to have people as guests in your home.

**entire** whole; complete. *The magician entertained the entire school.*

**entrance** the place through which one enters or goes in.

**envelope** a paper covering for a letter.

**environment** surroundings; the place or kind of life surrounding an animal.

**envy** a feeling of wanting what someone else has; jealousy.

**equal** the same in size or number.

**equator** an imaginary line around the middle of the earth that is drawn on maps. *The equator is half way between the North and South Poles.*

**equinox** the time of year in spring and autumn when the day and night are of equal length. *The equinoxes happen about March 21 and September 23.*

**equipment** things needed to do something.

**erase** to rub out or wipe off.

**errand** a short journey to collect something; to take a message.

**error** mistake; something that is done incorrectly.

**escalator** a moving staircase.

**escape** 1 to get away from or to get free. *The lion escaped from its cage in the zoo.* 2 a leakage. *There was an escape of gas.*

**especially** more than normally. *I like raspberries, especially with cream.*

**estimate** to guess the size, weight or cost of something. *Can you estimate how tall that giraffe is?*

**estuary** the mouth of a large river.

**etcetera** (shortened as **etc.**) and so on, and other things. *Cats, cows, horses etc. are domestic animals.*

**eternal** having no beginning or end; lasting forever.

**eternity** time with no end.
**evaporate** to turn from a liquid into a vapor or gas, because of heat.
**evening** the time between afternoon and night.
**event** an important happening.
**eventually** in the end, at last.
**evergreen** a tree that has green leaves all the year round.
**evil** very bad, wicked.
**evolution** the process by which animals and plants develop and change over millions of years.
**ewe** (say *you*) a female sheep.
**exact** just right, perfectly correct.
**exaggerate** (say *eggs-aj-erate*) to make something sound bigger or smaller, or more or less important than it really is.
**exam, examination** 1 an important test to find out how much you know. 2 a close look at something.
**examine** to look at something very carefully.
**example** something which shows what something else is like or how it works. *This cake*

*is a good example of my cooking.*

**excavate** to uncover by digging.

**excellent** very good.

**exercise** 1 work that makes your body strong and healthy. 2 a piece of school work.

**exhaust** (say *eggs awst*) 1 to use up completely; to make very tired. 2 the part of an engine that lets out burned gases. 3 the burned gases.

**exhibit** 1 to show something in public. 2 the thing that is shown.

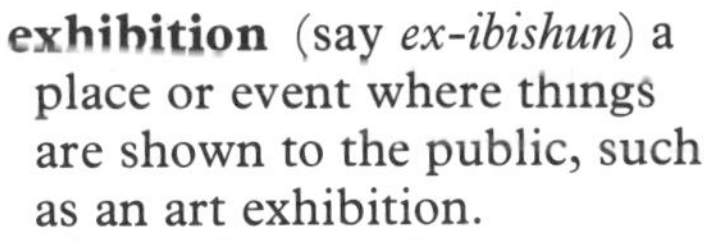

**exhibition** (say *ex-ibishun*) a place or event where things are shown to the public, such as an art exhibition.

**exist** to be or to live.

**exit** 1 to go out; to leave. 2 the place through which you go out. 3 a direction in a play which tells an actor to leave the stage.

**expect** to think that something will happen; to look forward to. *I expect they will be here soon.*

**expedition** a group of people making a journey for a special reason, such as climbing a mountain.

**expensive** costing a lot of money.

**experience** 1 something that happens to you, and from which you may learn. *Going to camp is a great experience.* 2 to feel; to meet with. *They will experience great heat in the center of Africa.*

**experiment** a test; a trial.

**expert** someone who knows a lot about something.

**explain** to show or make the the meaning clear.

**explode** to burst with a loud bang.

**explore** to look carefully around a place where you have not been before.

**explorer** a person who explores, especially places where people have not been before.

Voyages of some of the great **explorers**.

**explosion** (say *exploshun*) a loud noise when something explodes.
**explosive** anything such as dynamite used to make things explode or blow up.
**export** (say *ex*-**port**) to sell and send goods to another country.
**exports** (say **ex**-*ports*) the goods that are exported.
**extinct** a thing which was living is extinct when none of its kind is alive any more. *Dinosaurs have been extinct for millions of years.*
**extra** more than usual. *You will need extra clothes because it's so cold.*
**extraordinary** very unusual.
**extreme** very great or very far.
**eye-opener** something which suddenly surprises you or makes you suddenly understand.
**eyesight** your ability to see.

The light from an object we are looking at goes through the lens of the **eye** and throws an image onto the retina at the back of the eye.

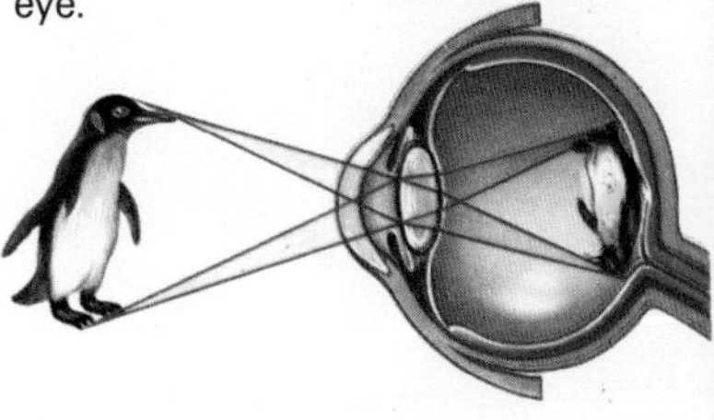

# Ff

**fable** a story that tries to teach us something. The characters are usually animals that talk.
**fabric** cloth.
**fact** something that really happened, so people know that it is true. *It is a fact that Abraham Lincoln was born in 1809.*
**factory** a building where people work together to make things.
**fade** 1 to lose color. *Our curtains have faded in the sun.* 2 to wither. *The flowers faded.* 3 to disappear slowly. *The ship faded from sight in the mist.*
**Fahrenheit** (say *Fa-ren-hite*) a thermometer scale in which the freezing point of water is 32° and the boiling point is 212°. It was invented by a German, Gabriel Daniel Fahrenheit (1686–1736).
**fail** to be unsuccessful.
**faint** 1 weak; not clear. *We could hear a faint sound when we listened carefully.* 2 to become dizzy, with everything going black, so you may fall down; become unconscious.
**fair** 1 acting in a just way, that is seen to be right. *Everyone should have a fair share of the cake.* 2 light colored. *Mary has fair hair and blue eyes.*

3 of weather, good. 4 a group of outdoor amusements, with sideshows.

**fairy** an imaginary small creature with magic powers.

**faith** 1 a strong belief; trust. *I have complete faith in her.* 2 religion.

**fake** something that looks real but is not.

**fall behind** to fail to keep up with. *He has no money, so he will fall behind with his rent.*

**false** not true; not real.

**familiar** well known.

**famine** a time when there is very little food in an area and people go hungry.

**fan** 1 a thing that moves the air and makes you cooler. 2 a person who greatly admires someone famous; a supporter.

Birds have two kinds of **feathers** Strong feathers cover the body and wings. Tiny hooks, or barbs, join the separate parts of the feather. Soft down feathers lie next to the skin.

**FEATHERS**

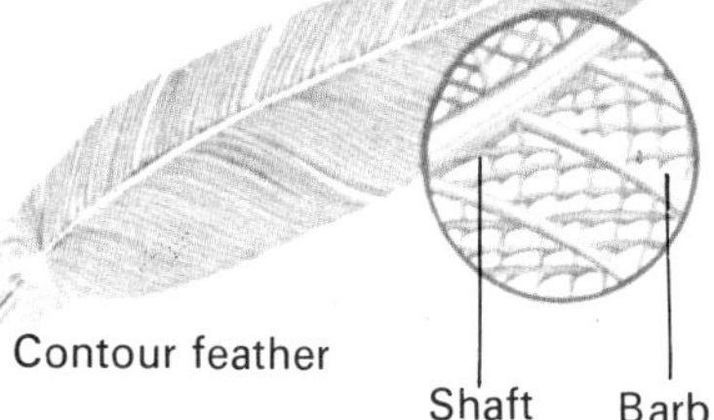


**fang** a long, sharp tooth.

**fare** the money you have to pay to go on a journey. *Children pay half fare on the trains.*

**farm** 1 land and buildings where crops are grown and animals reared. 2 to use land to grow crops or rear animals.

**farmer** a person who farms the land.

**fashion** a way of dressing or doing things that most people like to copy at a certain time. *There was a fashion for huge sweaters in our school last term.*

**fast** 1 very quick. 2 firmly fixed. *My boot was stuck fast in the mud.* 3 to eat no food for a period.

**farther** (*further*) more distant.

**farthest** (*furthest*) the most distant.

**fasten** to tie; to fix firmly.

**fault** (rhymes with *salt*) something that is not perfect; a mistake.

**favor** 1 an act of kindness or help. *Can you do me a favor by picking up my dress?* 2 to like one person or thing more than another.

**favorite** the best liked person or thing.

**fawn** a young deer.

**fear** 1 to feel frightened. 2 the feeling of being frightened.

**feast** 1 a very grand meal. 2 a religious festival.

**feather** one of the many light coverings that grow from a bird's skin.

**feature** 1 one of the parts of the face. *Your nose is one of your features.* 2 an important part of something.

**feeler** the antenna of an insect with which it touches, or feels, things.

**feeling** something that you know inside yourself, like knowing that you dislike someone. *A feeling of pain.*

**feet** more than one foot.

**felt** 1 past of feeling. 2 a kind of cloth made from bits of wool pressed together rather than woven.

**female** a woman; a girl; the opposite of male.

**fence** 1 a wooden or metal barrier. 2 to fight with special swords.

There are three **fencing** weapons: the foil (left), the épée (center), and saber (right). The target areas are shaded.

**fern** a plant with feathery leaves. *Ferns have no flowers. They reproduce from spores.*

**ferret** a small animal that can be trained to hunt rabbits and rats.

**ferry** a boat that carries people for short distances. *We crossed the river on the ferry.*

**fertile** able to produce a lot of good crops. *The Nile valley is very fertile.*

**fertilize** 1 to make fertile. 2 of plants and animals, to start to grow.

**festival** a time for dancing, music and feasting.

**fête** (rhymes with *late*) a kind of open air party where there are games and things to buy. *A fête is usually organized to collect money for charity.*

**fever** an illness in which you become very hot.

**fiber** 1 a very fine thread. 2 material made of fibers.

**fiction** a story that has been made up, that is not about real people or events.

**fierce** cruel and angry.

**figure** 1 a sign for a number, such as 5 or 9. 2 a diagram in a book. 3 the shape of the body. *Caroline has a very good figure.*

**file** 1 to put in order in a box or holder. 2 a metal tool with rough sides for smoothing surfaces.

**film** 1 a thin covering. 2 a roll of plastic that can be placed in a camera and used to take photographs. 3 moving pictures that may be shown in a movie.

**fin** part of a fish. *The fin helps the fish to swim and balance.*

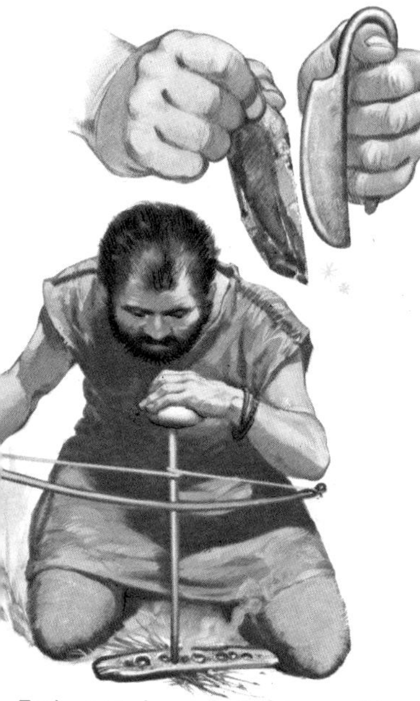

Early people probably learned to use **fire** by picking up branches from natural fires. Later they found that fire could be made by rubbing sticks together and by using the bowdrill (bottom). Fire could also be made by striking flints together.

**final** the last.
**finally** at last. *We finally reached land.*
**find out** to come to know something. *Can you find out where he has gone?*
**fine** 1 very thin or delicate. 2 of weather, good and clear. 3 money paid as a punishment.
**fingerprint** the mark left on something by the tip of your finger.
**fir** an evergreen tree with needlelike leaves and fruit called cones.
**fire** 1 the bright light and heat that comes when something is burned. 2 to shoot a gun.
**fire escape** a way out of a burning building.
**fireman** a person whose job it is to put out fires. *A fireman goes to a fire in a fire engine.*
**fireplace** the part of a room where a fire is or was built.
**firework** something that burns with noise or pretty colors, like a rocket or a sparkler.
**firm** solid, hard, steady.
**fisherman** a person who catches fish.
**fist** the tightly closed hand.
**fit** 1 in good health. 2 to be the right size. *Are you sure that shoe fits you?*
**fix** 1 to mend something. 2 to decide. *We will fix a date for the match.* 3 a difficult position. *We are in a fix.*
**flag** a piece of cloth with a pattern on it to show the

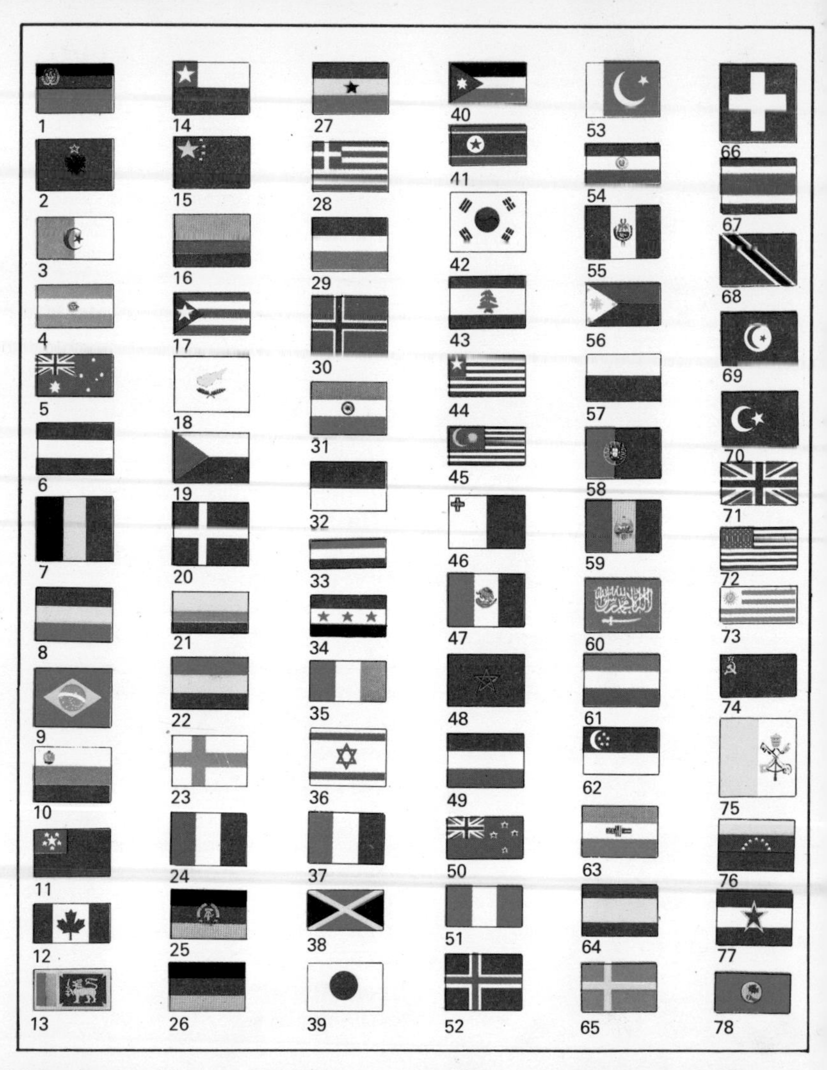


*1. Afghanistan 2. Albania*
*3. Algeria 4. Argentina*
*5. Australia 6. Austria*
*7. Belgium 8. Bolivia*
*9. Brazil 10. Bulgaria*
*11. Burma 12. Canada*
*13. Sri Lanka 14. Chile*
*15. China 16. Colombia*
*17. Cuba 18. Cyprus*
*19. Czechoslovakia*
*20. Denmark 21. Ecuador*
*22. Ethiopia 23. Finland*
*24. France 25. E. Germany*
*26. W. Germany 27. Ghana*
*28. Greece 29. Hungary*
*30. Iceland 31. India*
*32. Indonesia 33. Iran*
*34. Iraq 35. Ireland*
*36. Israel 37. Italy*
*38. Jamaica 39. Japan*
*40. Jordan 41. N. Korea*
*42. S. Korea 43. Lebanon*
*44. Liberia 45. Malaysia*
*46. Malta 47. Mexico*
*48. Morocco 49. Netherlands*
*50. New Zealand 51. Nigeria*
*52. Norway 53. Pakistan*
*54. Paraguay 55. Peru*
*56. Philippines 57. Poland*
*58. Portugal 59. Romania*
*60. Saudi Arabia*
*61. Sierra Leone 62. Singapor*
*63. South Africa 64. Spain*
*65. Sweden 66. Switzerland*
*67. Thailand 68. Trinidad & T*
*69. Tunisia 70. Turkey*
*71. United Kingdom 72. USA*
*73. Uruguay 74. USSR*
*75. Vatican City 76. Venezuel*
*77. Yugoslavia 78. Zaire*

Left: Some national **flags.**

country or organization to which it belongs.

**flake** a small, light piece of something, like snow.

**flame** the burning gas from a fire.

**flap** 1 a piece of material that hangs down over an opening. 2 to make something move up and down. *The wind flapped the clothes on the line.*

**flash** a sudden burst of light.

**flat** 1 level and smooth. 2 a separate home in a building, or block of apartments.

**flatter** to please someone by praising them more than they deserve.

**flavor** the taste and smell of food.

**flea** a small insect that jumps. *Fleas feed on blood by biting animals.*

**fledgling** a young bird that is just able to fly.

**flee** to run away from.

**fleece** a sheep's wooly covering.

**fleet** a number of ships under one leader.

**flesh** the soft part of the body covering the bones.

**flight** (rhymes with *bite*) 1 the act of flying. 2 a journey in an aircraft. 3 running away from danger.

**flipper** an arm-like part used by seals and other water animals to swim.

**float** 1 to be held up in air or in water. 2 a piece of cork or wood on a fishing line or net.

**flock** a large group of animals, particularly sheep or birds.

**flood** (say *flud*) a lot of water that spreads over the land.

**floor** 1 the part of the room on which you walk. 2 one level or story of a building. *Nick lives on the second floor.*

**flour** a powder made from grain and used in cooking. *Bread is made from flour.*

**flow** to move along as water does in a river

**flower** the colored part of a plant that produces seeds.

**flu** short for influenza.

**fluid** any liquid or gas that can flow easily.

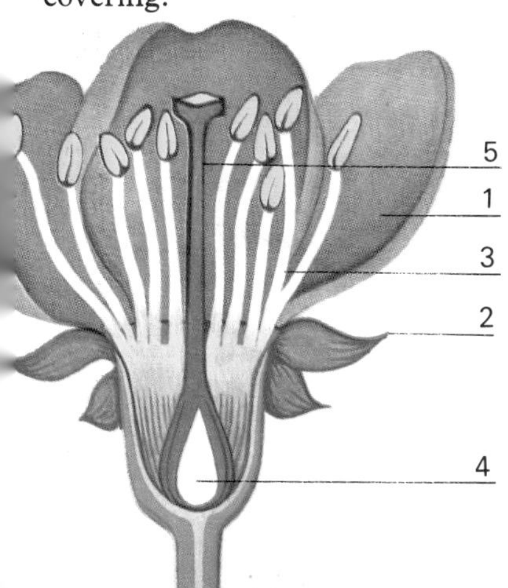


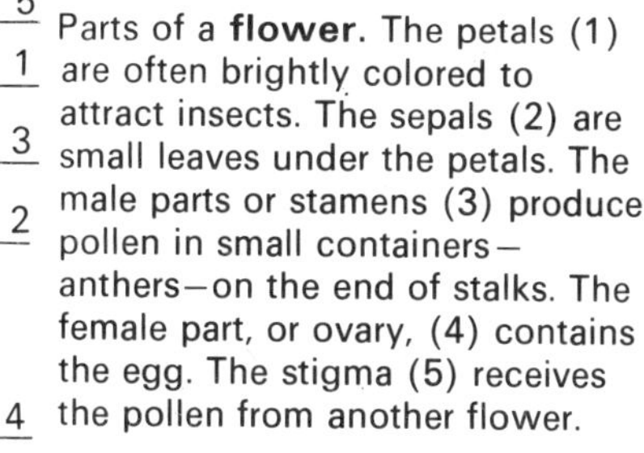

Parts of a **flower**. The petals (1) are often brightly colored to attract insects. The sepals (2) are small leaves under the petals. The male parts or stamens (3) produce pollen in small containers—anthers—on the end of stalks. The female part, or ovary, (4) contains the egg. The stigma (5) receives the pollen from another flower.

**flute** a wind instrument with holes in the side.
**foal** a young horse.
**foam** a white mass of small bubbles; froth.
**foe** an enemy.
**fog** a thick mist that it is difficult to see through.
**fold** 1 to bend part of a thing back over itself. 2 part of material that is folded; a crease.
**foliage** the leaves on plants.
**folk** (rhymes with *smoke*) people.
**foolish** without much sense; silly.
**footprint** the mark left by a foot on the ground.
**force** 1 to make someone do something they do not want to do. 2 power; strength. 3 a group of people who work together such as the police force.
**ford** a shallow place where a river can be crossed by walking across it.
**forecast** 1 to say what is likely to happen before it does. 2 what is forecast. *Every morning we listen to the weather forecast on the radio.*
**forehead** the part of the face above the eyebrows.
**foreign** (say *for-rin*) from or of another country.
**foreigner** a person from another country.
**forest** a large area of land covered thickly with trees.
**forgave** past of **forgive.**
**forgery** writing or a picture that is made to look as if someone else has done it.
**forgive** to stop being angry with someone for something they have done to you; to pardon.
**fork** 1 a tool with two or more points for lifting food to the mouth. 2 a large pronged tool for digging earth. 3 a place where something divides. *Go on until you reach the fork in the road, and then keep to the left.*
**form** 1 the shape something has. 2 a printed paper with spaces where the answers to questions have to be filled in. *I filled out the forms to take the driver's test.* 3 to make into or turn into. *Water forms ice when it freezes.*
**fort** a strong building that can be defended.
**fortify** to make a place strong so that it is difficult to attack.
**fortunate** lucky, having or bringing good luck.
**fortune** 1 luck. 2 a lot of money. *James inherited a fortune from his uncle.*
**fossil** the remains of a prehistoric animal or plant that have been turned to stone.
**foster mother** a woman who takes a child into her own home when the real parents cannot look after it.
**foundations** the strong base of a building, usually below ground.

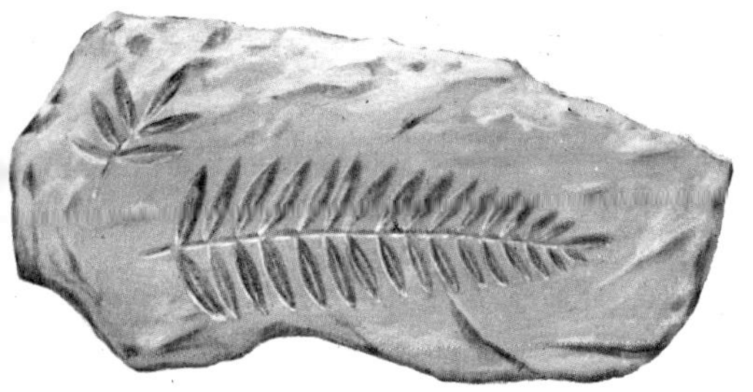

Some **fossil** remains of plants show every detail.

**foundry** a place where metals or glass are melted and molded.
**fowl** any bird, particularly those that are kept for their eggs or meat.
**fox** a wild animal of the dog family. *A fox has soft red-brown fur and a bushy tail.*
**fraction** (say *frack-shun*) 1 a number that is less than a whole number. *½ (one half) and ¼ (one quarter) are fractions.* 2 a small part of something. *We only got a fraction of what we expected.*
**fracture** 1 to break; to crack. 2 a break or crack.
**fragment** a small piece.
**fragrant** sweet smelling.
**frame** 1 a number of pieces that fit together to give something its shape. *The frame of our tent is made up of two upright poles with a pole going across between them.* 2 the border around the edge of a picture.
**frank** open and honest.
**free** 1 costing no money. 2 able to do what you want.
**freedom** the state of being free, and able to do what you want.
**freeze** to turn from a liquid to a solid because of cold. *Water freezes into ice.*
**freezer** a box or compartment kept very cold. *Food can be kept in a freezer for a long time.*
**freight** (rhymes with *late*) cargo, goods that are carried from one place to another.
**freighter** (rhymes with *later*) a ship or aircraft that carries freight.
**frequent** happening often.
**friction** 1 rubbing of two things together. 2 the resistance something meets with when it rubs against something else.

The fronts of space capsules have to be made of special material to withstand the great heat of **friction** with the air.

**fridge** short for **refrigerator.**
**friendship** the close feeling between friends.
**frighten** to make afraid.
**frog** a small amphibian that jumps.
**frontier** part of a country touching another country.
**frost** the powdery ice that covers things when it is very cold.
**frown** to pull the eyebrows together when you are cross or thinking hard.
**froze** past of **freeze.**
**fruit** (rhymes with *boot*) that part of a plant that has seeds in it and which is often eaten.
**fuel** anything that is burned to make heat or give energy, such as coal, oil, gas, or wood.
**funeral** the ceremony when someone who dies is buried.
**function** (say *funk-shun*) 1 the special work of a person or thing. *A hammer's function is to knock in nails.* 2 to do something. *This tool functions well.*
**fungus** a plant with no leaves, flowers or green coloring. *A fungus such as a mushroom lives on other plants or rotten matter.*
**funnel** 1 a tube with a wide top and a narrow bottom. *A funnel is used to pour liquid into a container with a narrow opening.* 2 a tube to let out the smoke from a steamship or steam engine; a smokestack.
**fur** soft, thick hairy covering on some animals.
**furniture** chairs, tables, beds, desks and other similar things.
**furrow** a straight, narrow rut made in the ground by a plow.
**future** the time yet to come.

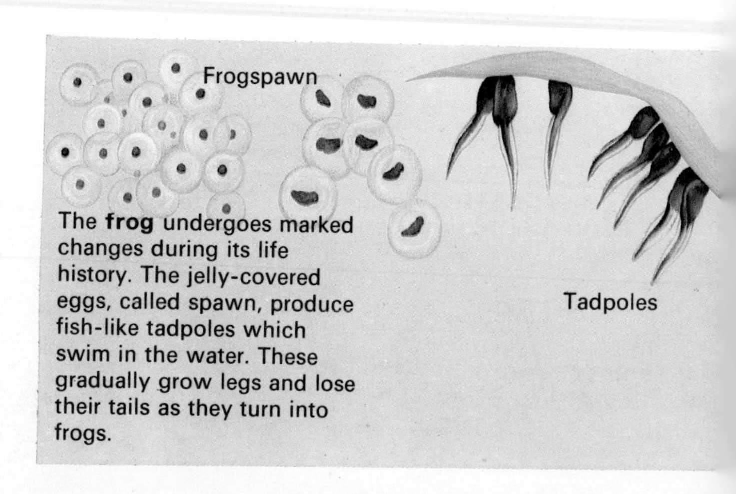

The **frog** undergoes marked changes during its life history. The jelly-covered eggs, called spawn, produce fish-like tadpoles which swim in the water. These gradually grow legs and lose their tails as they turn into frogs.

# Gg

**gadget** a small thing made to do a particular job. *A can opener is a gadget.*

**gag** something tied around someone's mouth to stop them speaking.

**gain** (rhymes with *lane*) to win or reach. *Eric is sure to gain five pounds if he eats too much.*

**galaxy** a very large group of stars in outer space. *The Milky Way is a galaxy.*

**gale** a very strong wind.

**galleon** a large ancient Spanish sailing ship with a high stern.

Two views of our **galaxy** (side and top) showing how the stars are arranged in a flat spiral. The red arrows show the position of our Sun.

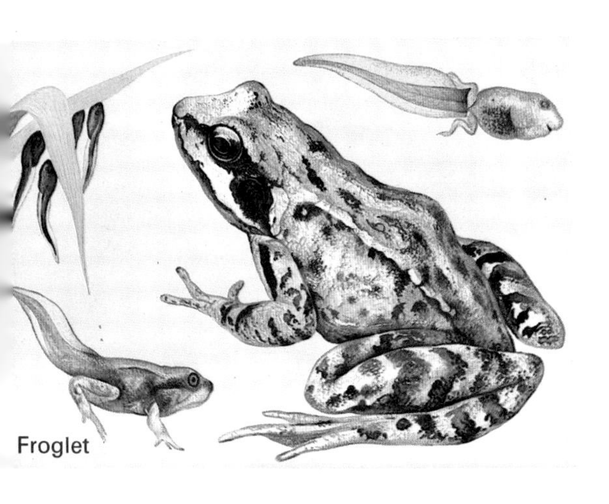

Froglet

**gallery** 1 a building where pictures or other works of art are shown. 2 the highest part of a theater or church where people sit.
**gallon** a liquid measure. *There are 4 quarts in a gallon.*
**gallop** the fastest pace of a horse.
**game** 1 a form of indoor or outdoor play, usually with rules. 2 wild animals that are hunted for food or for sport.
**gander** a male goose.
**gang** a group of people working together.
**gangster** a member of a gang of criminals.
**gap** 1 an opening; a space. 2 a space of time. *There was a long gap in the conversation.*
**garage** a place where cars are kept or repaired.
**garbage** waste; trash.
**garden** a piece of ground where flowers, fruit or vegetables are grown.
**gargle** to clean your throat by bubbling liquid around it.
**garment** a piece of clothing.
**gas** 1 any substance like air. *They fill balloons with helium gas because it is lighter than air.* 2 the gas used for heating. *We cook with gas in our house.*

The small **gear** wheel above has 8 teeth. It will turn twice as fast as the big wheel with 16 teeth.

**gasoline** fuel for car engines (abbreviated as **gas**).
**gasp** 1 to struggle to breathe. 2 to breathe in short, quick breaths.
**gather** to bring or come together. *Marian gathered a bunch of roses.*
**gauge** (rhymes with *rage*) 1 an instrument for measuring. 2 the distance between a pair of railroad lines.
**gay** cheerful and full of fun.
**gaze** to look at something for a long time.
**gear** a set of toothed wheels working together in a machine.

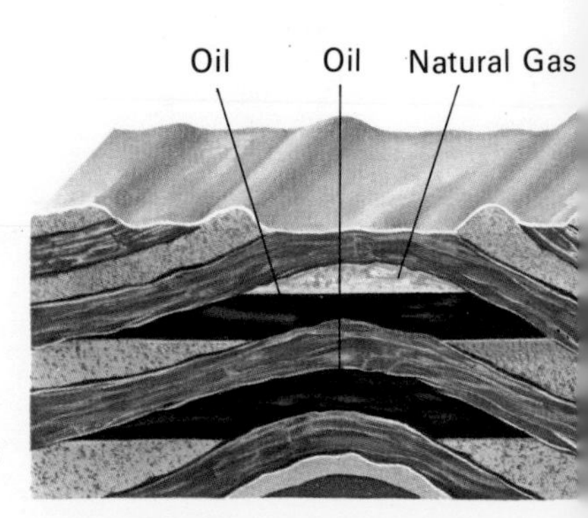


Natural **gas** is often found near oil, trapped between layers of rock beneath the Earth's surface.

**geese** more than one goose.
**gem** (say *jem*) a jewel or precious stone.
**general** 1 to do with most people or things. *There is a general feeling that dogs should be kept on leashes in the street.* 2 a very senior officer in the army.
**generate** to make, especially electricity.
**generation** all the people of about the same age. *I get along well with people of my mother's generation.*
**generator** a machine that produces electricity.
**generous** ready to give freely and happily.
**genius** (say *jean-ius*) a particularly clever person.
**gentle** kind and friendly, never violent.
**genuine** real and true.
**geography** the study of the Earth and what happens on it.
**geology** the study of the Earth's history as shown in the rocks.
**geometry** the mathematical study of lines, surfaces, angles and solids.
**germ** a microbe, especially one that makes people ill.
**germinate** to start to grow, especially of plants.
**gesture** to move the hand or head to show someone something. *She gestured towards the gate and they all ran out.*
**get away with** to avoid the result of something you have done or not done. *I did my work badly, but I will get away with it.*
**ghost** the spirit of a dead person that some people believe walks at night.
**giant** a huge animal or plant.
**gift** a present, something that is given to someone.
**gigantic** (say *ji-gantic*) very, very large.
**giggle** to laugh in a silly way.
**gill** the part on each side of a fish through which it breathes.
**Gipsy (Gypsy)** a member of a dark-haired group of wandering people.
**giraffe** an African animal with very long legs and neck.

The **giraffe** can reach the topmost branches to strip off leaves with its long tongue.

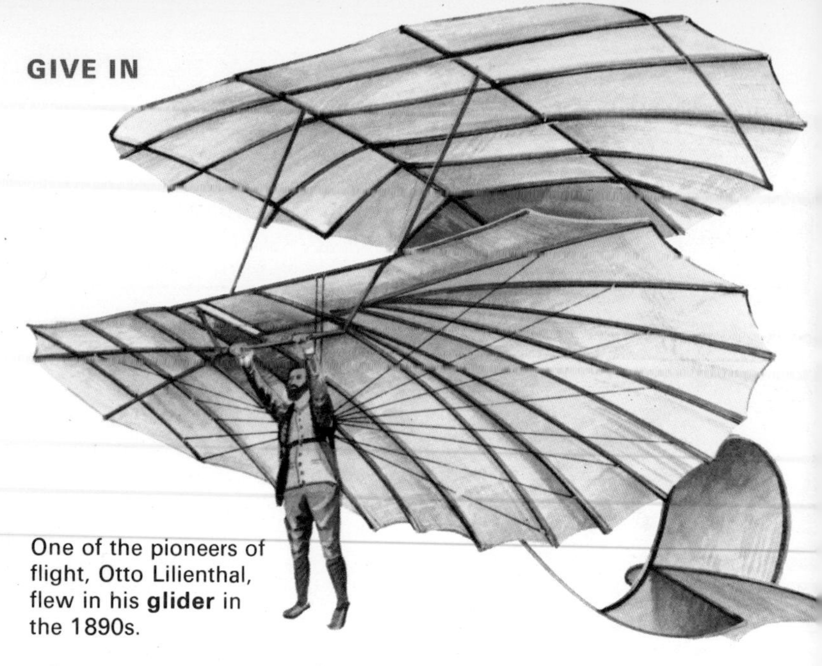

One of the pioneers of flight, Otto Lilienthal, flew in his **glider** in the 1890s.

**give in** to agree to something unwillingly. *Bill kept asking for another ice cream, and at last his father gave in.*

**give up** to stop doing something. *My father will give up smoking on New Year's Day.*

**glacier** a mass of ice and snow moving very slowly down a valley.

**glasses** spectacles; lenses in frames to help someone see better.

**glaze** a mixture coated on pottery to give it a shiny surface.

**glide** to move very smoothly.

**glider** an aircraft that flies without an engine.

**glitter** to shine brightly and reflect light. *The Christmas tree decorations glitter in the candlelight.*

**globe** a thing shaped like a ball, expecially a map of the world shaped like a ball.

**glossary** a list, like a dictionary, of special words used in a book.

**glue** sticky substance used for joining (gluing) things together.

**gnaw** (rhymes with *paw*) to chew at. *Our dog loves to gnaw a bone.*

**gnome** (say *nome*) a small goblin that lives under the ground.

**goal** (rhymes with *hole*) 1 the posts between which a ball must be sent in some games. 2 points scored by doing this. 3 something you are trying to achieve or some place you are trying to reach.

**goat** an animal with horns. *Some goats are wild, others are domesticated.*

The mask of Tutankhamen was made of solid **gold**. He was a pharaoh of Egypt in the 1350s BC.

**goblin** a legendary ugly, and usually evil, spirit or fairy.
**god** a being that is worshipped because people believe that it has control over their lives.
**goggles** large glasses that protect the eyes from water, wind or at work.
**gold** a precious, shiny yellow metal.
**goods** 1 things that are bought and sold. 2 things that are carried on trains or trucks. *They took the goods off the truck and put them on the train.*
**goose** a large water-bird.
**gorilla** the largest of the apes.
**gosling** a young goose.
**gossip** to talk about other people and what they are doing.
**govern** to rule; to control people or a country.
**government** the people who are chosen to rule or govern a country.
**gown** 1 a woman's dress. 2 a long flowing garment.
**grab** to seize quickly and roughly.
**graceful** moving beautifully.
**gradual** happening slowly. *The change was so gradual we hardly noticed it.*
**graft** to cut part of one thing and join it to another so that it grows.
**grain** 1 the small, hard seeds of all plants like wheat, rice and corn. 2 the natural pattern of wood.
**gram (or gramme)** a small unit of measuring weight. *There are 1000 grams in a kilogram.*
**grammar** the rules for using words and putting them together.
**granary** a building where grain is stored.
**grand** important, splendid.
**grandstand** rows of seats at a sports ground, usually covered.
**grape** a green or purple berry that grows in bunches on a vine. *Grapes are used to make wine.*
**graph** (rhymes with *laugh*) a diagram used to show how numbers and amounts compare.

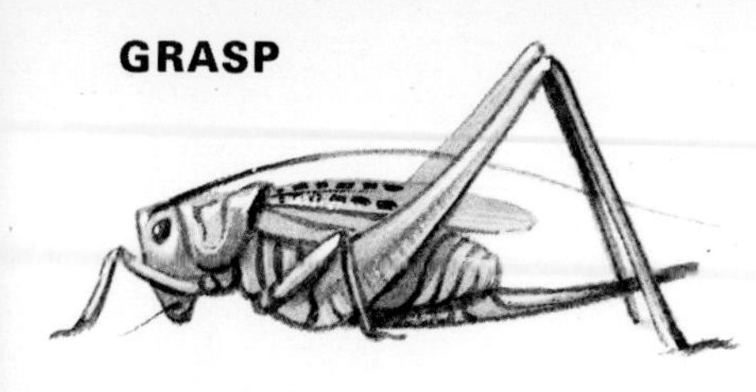

Male **grasshoppers** chirp by rubbing their back legs on their wings.

**grasp** to hold tightly.
**grasshopper** an insect that chirps and has long, strong back legs. *A grasshopper can jump ten times its own length.*
**grateful** feeling of thanks for something. *She was very grateful to the nurses who looked after her in the hospital.*
**grave** 1 a hole in the ground in which a dead body is buried. 2 serious, solemn.
**gravel** small stones used in the making of roads and paths.
**graveyard** a place where people are buried, near a church.
**gravity** the force that pulls things towards the center of the Earth. *Gravity makes things fall.*
**gravy** a hot sauce made with meat juices.
**gray** a color between black and white.
**graze** 1 to eat growing grass. 2 to scrape lightly.
**grease** any thick oily substance.
**greedy** wanting more food or money than you need.
**green** 1 a color like grass or leaves. 2 an open, grassy area.
**greenhouse** a building with a glass roof and glass walls in which plants are grown.
**greet** to welcome. *She always greets me with a kiss.*
**grew** past of **grow**.
**grief** (rhymes with *reef*) great sadness.
**grin** a wide smile.
**grind** to crush to a powder. *They grind wheat into flour at that mill.*
**grip** to hold firmly.
**groan** to make a deep sound because you are in pain or very sad.
**grocer** a person who sells foods like tea, sugar, cereals and jam.
**groom** 1 to brush and clean a horse. 2 a person who looks after a horse for someone else. 3 a bridegroom.
**groove** a long, narrow cut in a surface.

Greenhouses are warm inside because heat rays from the Sun warm up everything inside. The heat is then trapped in the greenhouse.

**ground** 1 the surface of the Earth. 2 the soil. 3 past of **grind**.

**group** (say *groop*) a number of people, or things gathered together or belonging together.

**growl** a low, angry noise, as made by a dog.

**grown up** any person who is not a child.

**grow up** to stop being a child.

**grub** the larva stage of an insect.

**grumble** to complain in a cross way.

**grunt** to make a low noise like a pig.

**guarantee** a promise to do something, especially to mend or replace something which goes wrong after it has been bought.

**guard** 1 to protect someone or something. *The police will guard the exhibition of jewels.* 2 a person who guards things.

**guerrilla** a fighter who does not belong to a country's army.

**guest** a person who is visiting another person's house or who stays in a hotel.

**guide** 1 to show someone the way. 2 a person who guides other people.

**guilty** having done something wrong. *The dog looked very guilty when we found the meat had gone.*

**guitar** a musical instrument with six strings. *The strings of a guitar are plucked with the fingers.*

**gulf** a large area of the sea almost surrounded by land.

**gull** a kind of large sea bird, or seagull.

**gum** 1 the pink flesh in which the teeth are set. 2 chewing gum.

**gunpowder** an explosive made by mixing special amounts of charcoal, sulfur and saltpeter.

**guts** the intestines.

**gutter** a small channel for carrying off rainwater.

**guy** (rhymes with *lie*) 1 a man or boy. 2 a rope or wire attached to something to hold it steady.

**gym** or **gymnasium** a room for sports and training.

**gymkhana** a competition for horses and ponies and their riders.

**gymnast** a person who does exercises to make the body strong or as a sport.

An old print showing men mixing saltpeter, charcoal and sulfur to make gunpowder.

# Hh

**habit** something that a person or animal does so often they do not think about it.
**hail** 1 frozen rain. 2 to greet someone by calling out to them.
**hairdresser** someone who cuts and looks after other people's hair.
**hall** 1 the entrance room of a house. 2 a large room for meetings, plays and other activities.
**Halloween** October 31st, the eve of All Saints' Day.
**halo** a circle of light around something.
**halt** to stop.
**halve** to divide into two equal parts.
**ham** salted or smoked meat from a pig's thigh.
**hamburger** a round patty of chopped beef inside a bun.
**hammer** a tool for driving in nails or breaking things.
**hamster** a small, roundish rodent, often kept as a pet.
**hand** 1 the part of the arm beyond the wrist with five fingers (one of which is the thumb). 2 a measure of the height of horses or ponies equal to 4 inches. 3 give something with the hand.

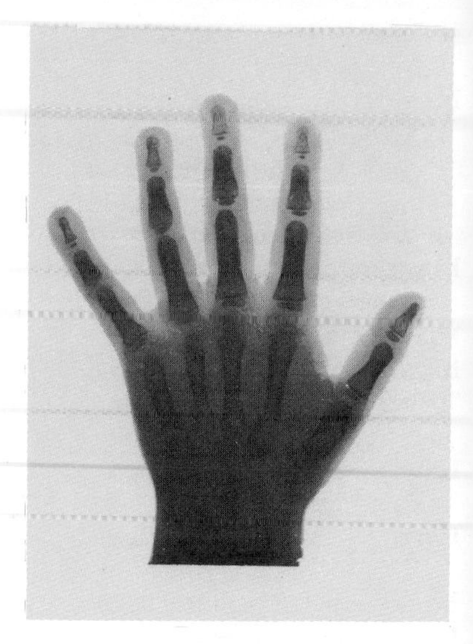

An X-ray photograph of a 4 year-old child's **hand**, showing the bones.

*Please hand me a glass of milk.*
**hand over** to give something to someone else, often when you do not want to. *The thief made us hand over our money.*
**handcuffs** a pair of bracelets for locking a prisoner's hands together.
**handicap** anything that makes it more difficult to do things.
**handle** 1 part of an object by which it is held. 2 to feel something with the hands.
**handsome** good looking, usually applied to men.
**hang** to hold from above so that the lower part is free. *Ripe red cherries hang from that tree.*

**hangar** a large building where aircraft are kept.

**happen** 1 to take place. *The sales happen every year in January.* 2 to be by chance. *My friend and I happen to share the same birthday.*

**happening** something that happens; an event.

**harbor** a shelter for ships.

**hardly** only just. *She had hardly reached home when the telephone rang.*

**hardy** strong, able to face difficulties.

**hare** an animal like a large rabbit.

**harm** to hurt, to cause damage.

**harness** all the leather straps and other equipment by which a horse is controlled.

**harp** a large musical instrument played by plucking the strings with the fingers of both hands.

**harpoon** a spear on a rope for catching whales and large fish. *A harpoon is thrown or fired and can then be pulled back.*

**harvest** 1 the time for cutting and bringing in grain and other crops. 2 the crops brought in at harvest time.

The sparrowhawk is a **hawk** that chases other birds.

The **hare** has longer ears and legs than a rabbit.

**haste** hurry, quickness of movement.

**hatch** to come out of an egg.

**haul** (rhymes with *ball*) to pull a heavy load.

**haunt** of a ghost, to visit a place often.

**hawk** 1 a bird of prey. 2 someone who supports a warlike policy.

**hay** dried grass for feeding animals.

**haystack** a large pile of hay.

**hazel** 1 a small nut tree. 2 the brownish green color of some people's eyes.

**headache** (rhymes with *bake*) a pain in the head.

**headlight** one of the main lights at the front of a vehicle.

**headline** a few words in larger print at the top of a story in a newspaper.

**headquarters** the main office of an organization; an army base.

The nuts grow in clusters on **hazel** trees.

**heal** to make better, particularly of a wound.
**health** (say *helth*) how well or ill your body or mind are.
**healthy** well and strong.
**heap** a pile of things.
**heart** the part of the body that pumps blood around the body.
**heat** 1 hotness. *We had to rest in the heat of the day.* 2 to make hot.
**heaven** (say *heven*) the home of God.
**hectare** a metric measure of area. *A football field is about ⅔ of a hectare.*
**hedge** a row of bushes making a fence around a field or garden.
**hedgehog** a small animal that is covered with prickles. It defends itself by rolling into a ball.
**heel** the back part of the foot.
**heifer** (rhymes with *deafer*) a young cow that has not had a calf.
**height** (rhymes with *bite*) the measurement from the bottom to the top of something.
**heir** (say *air*) the person who will inherit somebody's property or position. *Prince Charles is heir to the British throne.*
**helicopter** an aircraft with wings that turn above it. *A helicopter can go straight up and down, go backward or forward, or hover in one place.*

This 14th century **helmet** protected the head and face.

**hell** the home of the devil.
**helmet** a strong covering that protects the head. *The motorcyclist wore a crash helmet.*
**helpless** not able to look after yourself. *A baby bird is helpless if it falls out of the nest.*
**hem** the edge of cloth or clothing that is turned over and sewn.
**hemisphere** 1 half a sphere. 2 half of the Earth. *America is in the western hemisphere.*

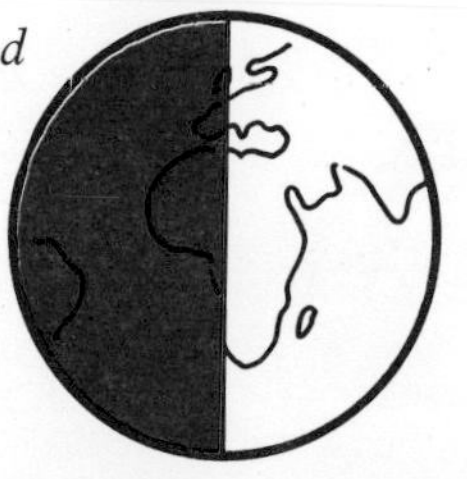

The red areas show the western and northern **hemispheres**.

**hen** any female bird, but especially a farmyard chicken.
**herb** plants with leaves that are used for flavoring food or for scent.
**herd** a group of animals grazing or moving together.
**hermit** a person who chooses to live alone, usually for religious reasons.
**hero** 1 a man admired for his bravery. 2 the most important male character in a play, film or story.
**heroine** 1 a woman admired for her bravery. 2 the most important female character in a play, film or story.
**heron** a long-legged water bird.
**hesitate** to stop briefly.
**hexagon** a six-sided figure.
**hibernate** to spend the winter asleep. *Many animals hibernate when cold weather comes.*
**hide** 1 to put something where others cannot find it. 2 to go into a place where you cannot be seen. 3 the skin of a large animal.
**hieroglyphics** picture writing. *The ancient Egyptians used hieroglyphics to write.*
**highway** a main road.
**highwayman** a robber on horseback.
**hijack** to seize control of a vehicle or aircraft during a journey.
**hinge** a joint on which a door or gate swings when it is opened or shut.

Some of the common **herbs** used in cooking.

**hint** to suggest something without really saying it. *Carol hinted that she would like a new dress for her birthday.*
**hip** the joint where the leg joins the trunk of the body.
**hippopotamus** a large African animal that lives in and near lakes and rivers.
**hire** to rent; to pay for the use of something. *We hired a car for a week when we were on vacation.*

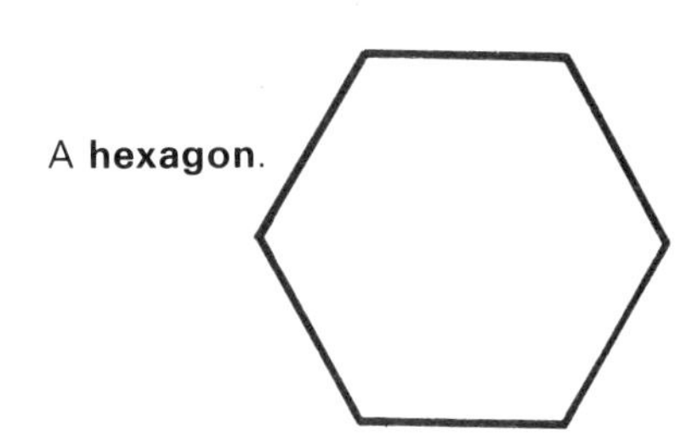

A **hexagon**.

**historic** famous in history. *The Battle of Gettysburg was an historic event.*

**history** the study of what has happened in the past.

**hive** (or **beehive**) a place for bees to live in.

**hoarse** of the voice, rough or croaking.

**hobby** something a person likes doing when they are not working. *Nick's hobby is collecting stamps.*

**hockey** a game in which a ball is hit with a bent stick.

**hoe** a tool for loosening the earth and digging out weeds.

**hold** 1 to keep firmly in the hand. 2 part of the hull of a ship where cargo is stored. 3 to contain. *This can holds 5 quarts.*

**hollow** 1 not solid; empty inside. *The squirrels lived in a hollow tree.* 2 a hollow place or small valley.

**homesick** sad at being away from your home.

**homework** school work that is done at home.

**honest** (say *on-est*) truthful, not likely to cheat.

**honey** the sweet substance made by bees from the nectar of flowers.

**honeycomb** the wax container made by bees in which to store their honey.

**honeymoon** a vacation for a newly married couple.

**hood** a covering for the head and neck.

**hoof** the hard part of the foot of a horse, and of some other animals.

**hook** a bent piece of metal, such as a fishhook.

**hop** to jump along on one leg, or (of a bird) with both feet together.

**hopeful** having hope.

**hopeless** without hope.

**horizon** the line where the land and the sky seem to meet.

**horizontal** flat; level with the horizon.

**horn** 1 one of the long,

Inside the hive of the honeybee are cells made of wax—the **honeycomb**.

The **hovercraft** rides on a cushion of air that is forced down under the vessel.

pointed growths on the head of some animals. 2 a brass musical instrument that is blown.

**horsepower** a unit for measuring the power of engines.

**hose** a long flexible tube through which water and other liquids can pass.

**hospital** a building where sick people are looked after.

**host** (rhymes with *toast*) a person who has guests in his house.

**hostage** a person who is held prisoner and threatened until certain demands are agreed to.

**hostess** 1 a woman who has guests in her house. 2 a woman who looks after travelers.

**hotel** a building where travelers pay to stay and have meals.

**houseboat** a boat on which people live.

**household** all the people who live together in a house. *Our household consists of my mother, my brother and me.*

**housekeeper** a person who looks after a house for its owner.

**housewife** a person who looks after a home.

**housework** the work of cleaning and caring for a home.

**hovel** a small, very poor house or cottage.

**hover** to stay in the air in one place. *A dragonfly hovers over the water.*

**hovercraft** a vehicle that moves over water or land. *A hovercraft is held up by the pressure of air pumped underneath it.*

**howl** a long, sad cry.

**hull** the body of a ship.

**human** behaving or looking like people.

**humor** sayings, drawings or stories that make you laugh. *Dominic has a very good sense of humor.*

**hump** a round lump like that on a camel's back.

**hunger** the feeling of needing food.

**hunt** 1 to go after, and often kill, animals for sport or food. 2 to look for something.

**hunter** a person who hunts animals.

**hurricane** a violent storm.

**hutch** a cage or box for rabbits or other small animals.

**hydroelectric** producing electricity from the power of water.

**hydrofoil** a boat with fins that skims over the surface of the water. *When the hydrofoil moves the fins raise the boat above the water.*

**hydrogen** a gas that is lighter than air.

**hymn** (rhymes with *rim*) a religious song praising God.

**hyphen** a mark like this "-" showing where a word has been divided at the end of a line, or where two words have been joined to make one as **self-defense.**

**hypnosis** a condition like deep sleep in which someone's actions can be controlled by another person.

**hypodermic syringe** an instrument for injecting drugs under the skin; a hollow needle.

**hysterical** in a state of wild excitment.

# Ii

As the **hydrofoil** moves forward, underwater wings lift it clear of the water.

**ice** frozen water.

**iceberg** a mass of ice floating in the sea.

**icicle** a pointed piece of ice. *An icicle is made from dripping water that freezes.*

**icing** sweet covering for cakes.

**idea** a thought, a plan in the mind.

**ideal** perfect, just what you want. *We thought that the plans for the holiday were ideal.*

**identical** exactly the same.

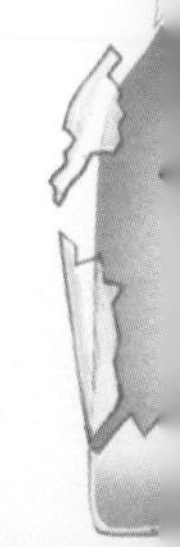

If a sealed bottle of water is frozen it will burst. This shows that when water becomes **ice,** it expands.

**idiot** a person who is so weak-minded that others have to look after him or her.
**igloo** an Eskimo hut made of blocks of snow.
**ignorant** knowing very little; uneducated.
**ignore** to take no notice of something or somebody. *The man ignored us and walked straight past.*
**illegal** against the law.
**illustrate** to explain with pictures.
**illustration** picture in a book or magazine.
**imaginary** not real; existing only in a person's mind. *David has made up an imaginary friend called Little David.*
**imagine** to make a picture in the mind.
**imitate** to copy another person.
**immediately** now; without losing time. *I must run down to the shops immediately or they will close.*
**immigrate** to come to live in a country.
**immigrant** a person who comes to live in a country that is not his own.
**immunize** to make safe from an illness.
**imp** in stories, a little devil.
**impatient** not patient; not wanting to wait for others.
**implement** a tool or instrument.
**import** to bring goods into your country.
**impossible** not possible; something that cannot be done.
**improve** to make something better.
**incense** a substance that gives off a sweet smell when it is burned.
**income** money received for work and from other sources during a period. *My income each month is only $300.*
**increase** to make greater in size or amount. *There has been a large increase in the number of pupils at our school.*
**incredible** something that cannot be believed.
**incubate** to hatch eggs by keeping them warm.
**indeed** really; in truth. *It was a very big dog indeed.*
**independent** free; not controlled by others.
**index** a list at the end of a book, giving all the subjects in the book in alphabetical order and the pages on which they appear.
**Indian** 1 a person from India. 2 one of the original people of America.
**indigestion** difficulty in digesting food.
**individual** of or for one person only. *We each had an individual parcel of food.*
**industry** 1 work done in factories. 2 a trade or business. *Steel is an important industry.*
**industrial** to do with manufacturing.

**infant** a baby or a young child.

**infection** an illness that can be spread by harmful germs.

**infinity** a time or space without end; too big to be imagined.

**inflate** to blow full of air or other gas.

**influenza** an illness with fever and a cold, abbreviated as **flu.**

**information** knowledge about something; news.

**inhabit** to live in a place.

**inhabitant** a person who lives in or inhabits a place or country. *The American Indians were the first inhabitants of this continent.*

**inherit** to receive money or property from someone who has died.

**initial** (say *in-ish-al*) 1 at the beginning. 2 the first letter in a name. *Simon Powell's initials are S.P.*

**injection** medicine given with a hypodermic syringe.

**injure** to hurt or damage.

**inland** away from the sea. *Chicago is an inland city.*

**inn** a public house where food and drink are sold and people can stay.

**innocent** 1 not guilty. 2 doing no harm.

**inquire** to ask about something or someone.

**inquisitive** wanting to find out about things.

**insect** one of a group of animals with six legs and no backbone. *All insects' bodies are divided into three parts. Bees, flies and ants are insects.*

**Insects** of different kinds are found all over the world. They range from tiny fleas to beetles as big as your hand.

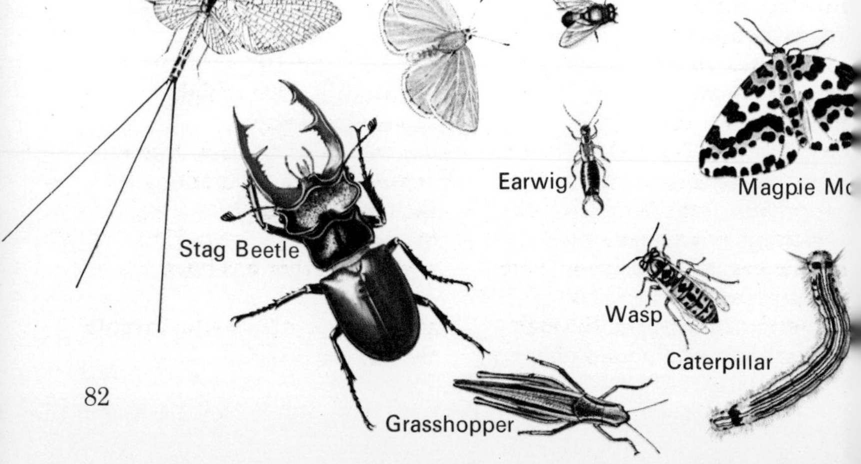

Mayfly
Bee
Common Blue Butterfly
Green Bottle Fly
Earwig
Magpie Mo
Stag Beetle
Wasp
Caterpillar
Grasshopper

**insecticide** a mixture used to kill insects.
**inspect** to examine carefully.
**instant** a moment; a very short time.
**instantly** at once.
**instinct** something that makes animals do things that they have not learned to do; in-born behavior. *Birds build their nests by instinct.*
**instrument** 1 a delicate tool or implement for a special purpose. 2 something used for making musical sounds. *A musical instrument.*
**insult** (say *in*-**sult**) to be rude to someone.
**insult** (say **in**-*sult*) a rude remark. *It was an insult to call Bill a stupid, lazy fellow.*
**intelligent** clever and able to understand easily.
**interested** wanting to know and learn about. *Robert is very interested in ships and borrowed three books about them.*
**interfere** 1 to meddle in other people's affairs. 2 to get in the way of something.
**international** affecting two or more nations. *The United Nations is an international organization.*
**interpret** 1 to show the meaning of. *He interpreted the signs as meaning that it would rain.* 2 to translate from one language to another.
**interrupt** to disturb someone who is doing something.
**intestines** the tubes through which our food passes after it has been through the stomach.

The potter wasp lays eggs in pots of soil. The wasp puts a caterpillar in each pot. When the young wasps hatch, they eat the caterpillars. All this is done by **instinct.**

**introduce** 1 to make people known to each other. *Edward introduced me to his mother.* 2 to bring forward for the first time.
**introduction** the first part of a book which tells you what the book is about.
**invade** to go into another country or place to fight against the people.
**invalid** an ill or weak person.
**invent** to make something for the first time.
**invention** (say *inven-shun*) something that has been invented.
**inventor** someone who invents things.

Spiders, butterflies and earthworms do not have a backbone. They are all **invertebrates**.

**invertebrate** an animal with no backbone, such as an insect, a worm or snail.

**invisible** unseen; cannot be seen. *The hem was sewn so neatly that it was invisible.*

**invitation** spoken or written words that ask you, or invite you to come.

**invite** to ask someone to come somewhere. *Susan's aunt may invite her to go to India next year.*

**iris** 1 a flower with pointed leaves. 2 the colored part of the eye.

**iron** 1 a heavy, common metal. 2 a tool for pressing clothes. 3 to press clothes.

**irrigate** to take water to dry land to help crops to grow.

**Islam** the religion taught by the prophet Mohammed.

**island** a piece of land surrounded by water.

**isolate** to set apart from others. *We had to isolate John when he had measles.*

**isthmus** a strip of land joining two larger pieces of land.

**italics** words that are printed at a slope *like this.*

**item** a single unit on a list. *How many items of furniture should there be?*

**ivory** the white bone material from which elephants' tusks are made.

An ancient Egyptian using a shaduf to **irrigate** his garden. The shaduf is a beam balanced on a pillar. It has a bucket at one end and a weight at the other.

**jack** a tool for raising heavy weights off the ground.
**jail** see prison.
**jam** 1 to push things together tightly. 2 food made by boiling fruit and sugar together.
**jaw** the bones of the mouth. *Your teeth are set in your jaw.*
**jealous** (say *jel-us*) being unhappy because you want what others have.
**jellyfish** a stinging sea animal that looks like a lump of jelly.
**jersey** a knitted top.
**jet** 1 a fast stream of liquid or gas. 2 an aircraft with an engine that sucks in air and pushes it out at the back, so pushing the aircraft forward.
**jewel** a precious stone.
**jeweler** a person who makes or sells jewelry.
**jewelry** ornaments with jewels or other decorations.
**jockey** a person who rides horses in races.
**jog** to run at a slow, steady pace.
**join** to put together.
**join up** to join the army, navy or air force.
**joint** a point where two parts join. *The knee is the joint between the upper and lower bones of the leg.*
**journalist** a person who writes about the news in magazines and newspapers.
**journey** 1 a distance traveled. 2 to travel
**joy** great happiness.
**judge** 1 to decide what is right or best out of a number of people or things. 2 a person who judges, particularly in a law court or competition.
**juggler** an entertainer who tosses things in the air, catches and throws them up again.
**juice** (rhymes with *loose*) the liquid part of fruit or other food.
**jungle** thick forest in hot countries.
**junior** younger or less high in rank.
**junk** 1 rubbish. 2 a Chinese sailing boat.
**jury** people who are chosen to decide whether an accused person is guilty or not guilty in a law court.
**juvenile** a young person.

This is the ball and socket **joint** of the hip. It allows movement in any direction.

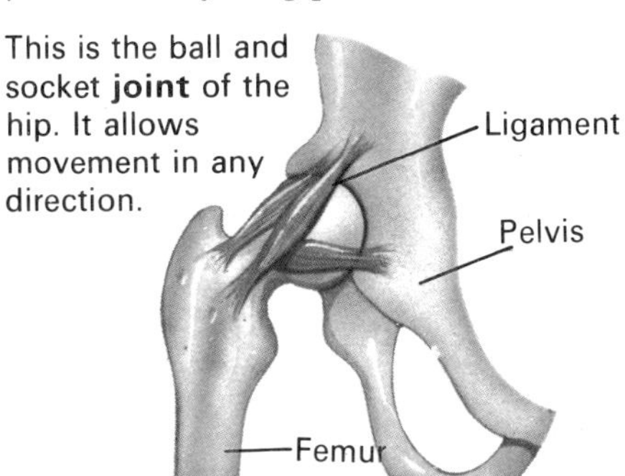

# Kk

**kaleidoscope** a tube with mirrors and pieces of colored glass in it. *You look through one end of a kaleidoscope and the mirrors reflect the glass in patterns.*

**kangaroo** an Australian animal. *A kangaroo has strong back legs and a pouch in which it carries its baby, or joey.*

**kayak** (say *ki-ack*) an Eskimo canoe made of sealskin.

**keel** the heavy strip of metal or wood running along the bottom of a ship.

**keen** eager; enthusiatic.

**keep** 1 to have something and not give it to anyone else. 2 to look after something for somebody. *Keep the book until I see you again.* 3 a strong tower in a castle.

**keep on** to continue doing something. *Stan keeps on talking, even when the teacher tells him not to.*

**keep up with** not to lag behind. *He managed to keep up with the others in the race.*

**kennel** a shelter for a dog.

**kept** past of **keep.**

When they are born, baby **kangaroos** are tiny and quite helpless. For six months they never leave their mother's pouch.

**kernel** the soft inner part of a nut that we can eat.

**kerosene** see paraffin.

**ketchup** a sauce made mostly from tomatoes and spices.

**key** (rhymes with *me*) 1 a metal device to undo a lock or wind a clock. 2 part of a machine or instrument pressed with the fingers. *The piano keys were made of ivory.*

**kid** 1 a young goat. 2 a child.

**kidnap** to steal someone, often to get money as a ransom.

**kidney** one of a pair of bean-shaped organs of the body that remove waste matter from the blood.

**kiln** an oven or furnace for baking bricks or pottery to dry them and make them hard.

**kilogram** a measure of weight, often shortened to kg. *There are 1000 grams in one kilogram.*

**kilometer** a measure of length, often shortened to km. *There are 1000 meters in a kilometer.*

**kilt** a skirt often made of tartan cloth. *Kilts are worn by men and women in Scotland and some other countries.*

**kimono** a loose gown with wide sleeves worn in Japan.

**kingdom** a country ruled by a king or a queen.

**kite** a frame of wood covered with light material. *A kite can be made to fly on a long string.*

**kiwi** (say *kee-we*) a New Zealand bird that cannot fly.

**knead** (say *need*) to work dough, or clay, with the hands.

**kneel** (say *neel*) to go down on your knees.

**knight** (say *nite*) 1 in the middle ages, a mounted nobleman who served his king. 2 now a man with the title "Sir".

**knob** (say *nob*) a round handle.

**knowledge** (say *noll-edge*) understanding; information in the mind. *Vanessa has a great deal of knowledge about geography.*

**knuckle** (say *nuckle*) the bone at the finger joint.

**koala** a small Australian animal that climbs trees. *A koala looks like a bear, but is not.*

**Koran** the holy book of Muslims.

**kosher** food that has been prepared according to Jewish law.

The **kiwi** hides in a burrow during the day and hunts at night. It lays a huge egg for its size.

The **koala** is a marsupial. Its only food is eucalyptus leaves.

# Ll

**label** a piece of paper or card with writing on it attached to something. *The label may say what the thing is or where it is going.*

**labor** work, particularly

**laboratory** a place used for scientific experiments.

**lace** a delicate fabric made with patterns of threads.

**lacrosse** a team game played with a racket with a net in it. A ball is caught and thrown with this.

**ladder** two lengths of wood or other material fastened with cross bars (called rungs). *A ladder is used for climbing up and down walls.*

**ladle** a large deep spoon used for serving soup.

**lagoon** a shallow salt water lake separated from the sea by a sand bank.

**lair** a wild animal's den.

**lake** a large area of inland water.

**lamb** 1 a young sheep. 2 the meat of a young sheep.

**lame** not able to walk properly.

**land** 1 all those parts of the Earth's surface which are not sea. 2 the area owned by someone. *Farmer Green's land goes as far as the river.* 3 to come to land from the sea or the air. *Our plane should land early.*

**landmark** something that can be seen from a distance and which helps you find the way. *A church steeple is often used as a landmark.*

**landscape** what you see when you look across a large area of land.

**language** the words that we use to talk or write to each other. *Many different languages are spoken in Africa.*

**lantern** a case with glass sides for holding a light so that it does not blow out.

**lap** 1 the upper legs when sitting. 2 to drink with the tongue like an animal.

**larder** a room where food is stored; a pantry.

**larva** (plural *larvae*) an insect in the first stage when it comes from its egg.

**laser** a device for sending out very strong light waves.

**lass** a girl.

**lasso** a long rope with a loop used by cowboys to catch cattle and horses.

**lather** a foam that is formed when soap is moved around in water.

**latitude** a distance measured in degrees north or south of the Equator.

**laughter** the sound you make when you laugh.

**launch** (say *lonch*) 1 a type of boat. 2 to put a boat into water or a rocket into space.

**laundromat** a shop with washing machines where people pay to do their washing.

**laundry** 1 a place where clothes are washed. 2 the clothes that have to be washed.

**lava** hot liquid matter that flows from an active volcano.

**lavatory** a toilet; a room with a toilet in it.

**law** a set of rules usually made by a government, that people have to obey.

**lawn** 1 an area of short cut grass. 2 a fine material used for nightgowns, blouses and other clothes.

**lay** 1 past of **lie.** *We lay down on the lawn.* 2 of a bird, to lay (produce) eggs.

**lay off** to stop employing a worker for a time.

**layer** something that is spread over the surface of something else. *A thick layer of clay had washed over the bank.*

**lazy** not wanting to do much work; idle.

North Pole
45° North
45° South
South Pole

The dotted lines show 45° north and 45° south **latitude**.

**lead** (rhymes with *bed*) a soft, heavy gray metal.

**lead** (rhymes with *reed*) 1 to go in front to guide others. 2 the first place. *Chris had a lead of about a yard in the race.*

**leader** a person who leads.

**leaf** (plural *leaves*) 1 one of the flat, green parts of a plant growing from the stem of a branch. 2 a sheet of something.

**league** (say *leeg*) 1 a group of sports clubs that play matches against each other. 2 an alliance; nations that agree to help each other.

**leak** a hole through which liquid or gas can escape.

**lean** 1 to be or to put in a sloping position. *The ladder leans against the house.* 2 thin, having little fat.

**leap** to jump high or far.

**leaped (leapt)** past of **leap.**

**least** the smallest in size or quantity.

**leather** (say *lether*) material made from animal skins. *Shoes are made of leather.*

**leaves** more than one leaf.

**led** past of **lead.**

**ledge** a narrow shelf on a wall or cliff.

**legal** (say *leegal*) 1 to do with the law. 2 correct by the law. *Is it legal to ride a bicycle on the sidewalk?*

**legend** an old, old story.

**legendary** told about in old stories.

**leisure** rest, time free from work.

**lend** to give something to someone for a time, expecting to get it back. The other person **borrows** it.

**length** from one end to the other in distance or time.

**lens** a piece of glass with a curved surface, used in cameras, glasses, telescopes and microscopes.

**Lent** the 40 days before Easter Sunday.

**lent** past of **lend.**

**leopard** (say *lepard*) large African and Asian animal with black spots on a yellowish coat.

**leotard** (say *lee-o-tard*) a one-piece garment worn for gymnastics and other sports.

**leprechaun** (say *lepri-con*) an Irish fairy.

**less** a smaller amount.

**let** to allow someone to do something. *Bob let us see his scar.*

**let down** to fail to do something that somebody expected you to do. *The workmen promised to mend our roof, but they let us down, and the rain came in.*

**level** 1 flat; even. *The surface of the table is perfectly level.* 2 height. *The height of mountains is measured from sea level.*

**lever** a tool used to lift something heavy or force it open.

**liable** 1 likely. *You are liable to be cold if you go out without a coat.* 2 responsible by law.

**liar** someone who does not tell the truth.

**liberty** freedom.

**librarian** a person who looks after the books in a library.

**library** a room or building for books.

**lice** more than one louse.

**license** 1 a permit to do something. *He has a license to drive a car.* 2 to give a license.

**lichen** (say *liken or litchen*) a small dry looking plant that grows on rocks or trees.

**lick** to touch something with the tongue.

**lie** 1 to say something that is not true. 2 to put yourself down flat. *If you lie on the*

Most **leopards** have blotchy spots called rosettes. They are very fierce, strong and agile hunters. They catch and eat antelopes, goats, dogs and sometimes people.

*floor, you can see the crack.*
3 to be in a certain place. *The small islands lie just off the coast.*
**life** 1 all living things. *When did life begin on earth?* 2 the time between birth and death. 3 liveliness; energy. *The young children were too full of life.*
**lifeboat** a boat for rescuing people at sea.
**lift** to raise up.
**lighthouse** a tower with a light in it that warns ships away from dangerous rocks.
**lightning** a flash of light in the the sky during a thunderstorm. *Lightning is caused by electricity passing between clouds and the ground, or from cloud to cloud.*
**likely** expected to happen. *It is likely to rain today.*
**limb** a leg or an arm.
**limerick** a funny five line poem with this form:
There was a young man of Nepal
Who went to a fancy dress ball;
He thought he would risk it
And go as a biscuit,
But a dog ate him up in the hall.
**limit** 1 a line or point that you cannot or should not go beyond. *The speed limit in the town is 30 miles an hour.*
2 to restrict something. *You should limit her to three candies before lunch.*
**limp** 1 not stiff. *The skirt became very limp after she washed it.* 2 to walk unevenly.

In **lighthouses,** a powerful light is shone through many lenses joined together.

**line** 1 a long, thin mark.
2 a piece of rope or string.
3 a row of people or things. *We stand in line for dinner.*
4 a transport system. *There goes a Green Line bus.* 5 to put a lining into something.
**linen** cloth made from the fibers of the flax plant.
**liner** a big passenger ship.
**lining** a layer of material inside something. *Her coat has a red silk lining.*
**link** 1 one loop of a chain.
2 to join things together.
**lion** a large member of the cat family. *The male lion has a mane.*
**lioness** a female lion.
**lipstick** makeup for the lips.
**liquid** a substance like water that flows. *A liquid is not a gas or a solid.*

**lisp** to speak using a "th" sound for "s". *"Thith ith my thithter," she lisped.*

**list** a number of names of things written down one above the other. *Did you put bread on the shopping list?*

**liter** (rhymes with *heater*) a measure of liquids; 1000 cubic centimeters.

**litter** 1 rubbish thrown away in a public place. 2 all the newly born babies of an animal. *Our cat had a litter of four kittens.*

**live** (rhymes with *hive*) living. *There are no live animals in the museum.*

**liver** an organ of the body which does many jobs, including getting rid of things the body does not want and making things it needs.

**livestock** farm animals.

**living** alive.

**lizard** a small four-legged reptile with a tail.

**load** (rhymes with *code*) 1 something that has to be carried. *She took a load of washing to the laundromat.* 2 to put something onto something. *They loaded the car with luggage.*

**loan** something that has been lent to you, usually money.

**lobster** a shellfish with a hard shell and ten legs, two of which carry large claws.

**local** belonging to a fairly small area. *This newspaper gives local news about our town.*

**lock** 1 to fasten something. 2 a fastening for a door or a box that needs a key to open it. 3 a piece of hair. 4 a section of a canal or river where the water levels can be changed by opening and shutting large gates.

**locker** a cupboard that can be locked.

**locket** a small case worn on a chain around the neck. *A locket may contain a picture.*

**locomotive** a machine on wheels which pulls trains. *A locomotive's power may come from steam, diesel oil or electricity.*

In 1829, George Stephenson built a **locomotive** called the *Rocket*. It was very fast for those days, reaching speeds of 36 miles an hour.

**lodge** 1 a small house at the gates of a large house. 2 to stay in someone's house and pay to stay there. 3 a beaver's home.

**loft** a room at the top of a house often used for storing things; an attic.

**log** a length of a tree that has been cut down.

**lonely** 1 without friends. 2 away from other people. *They had a lonely house in the woods.*

**longitude** a distance measured in degrees east or west from a line on the map joining Greenwich, England and the North and South Poles.

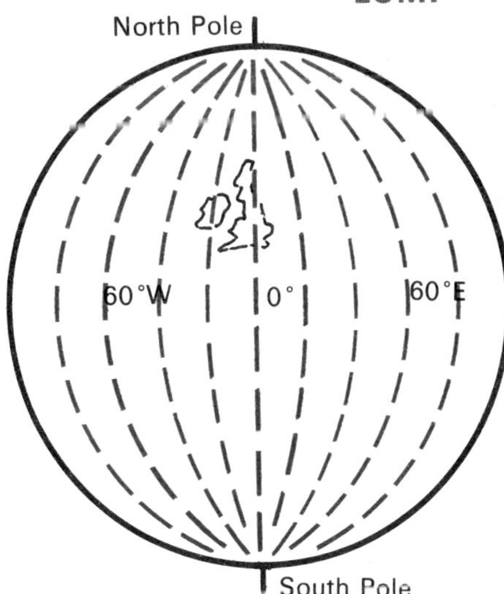


The dotted lines are lines of **longitude**.

**look after** to take care of. *Can you look after our cat while we are away?*

**look forward to** to think with pleasure about something that is going to happen.

**look out** 1 watch to see whether anyone is coming, or whether something will happen. 2 a sentry.

**look up** to find a word or item in a dictionary, encyclopedia or other book.

**look up to** to admire someone. *I always looked up to my brother because he was so good at football.*

**looking glass** a mirror.

**loom** a machine for weaving cloth.

**loop** a circle or part circle of wire, string or other material.

**lord** a nobleman.

**loudspeaker** part of a radio or record player that makes electric waves into sound.

**lounge** 1 to sit or stand in a lazy way. 2 a living room.

**louse** (plural *lice*) a small insect that lives on animals' or humans' bodies.

**lower** 1 not as high as. 2 to make something less high.

**loyal** true to others. *We trust him as a loyal friend.*

**lubricate** to use oil or grease to make a machine work smoothly.

**luggage** the cases, bags and other containers that are taken on a journey.

**lullaby** a song that is sung to send a baby to sleep.

**lumber** rough timber.

**lump** a bump, a swelling.

**lunar** of or about the Moon. *There will be a lunar eclipse this week.*

**lung** one of the two parts inside your body with which you breathe.

**lurk** to wait unseen. *Strange creatures lurk in these woods.*

**luxury** an expensive thing that is not really needed. *Most people think that a fur coat is a luxury.*

# Mm

**macaroni** long tubes of flour paste to be cooked and eaten. *Macaroni and spaghetti are Italian dishes.*

**machine** a tool that has movable parts working together to do something. *Joe put some money into the machine and out popped a ticket.*

**machine gun** a gun that can fire many bullets very quickly without being reloaded.

**machinery** 1 machines. 2 the moving parts of machines.

**mackintosh** a waterproof coat.

**magazine** 1 a book of text and advertisements that comes out periodically. 2 part of a gun that holds the bullets.

**magician** (say *maj-ishun*) a person who does magic tricks.

**magnet** a piece of iron or steel that can pull other pieces of iron or steel towards it.

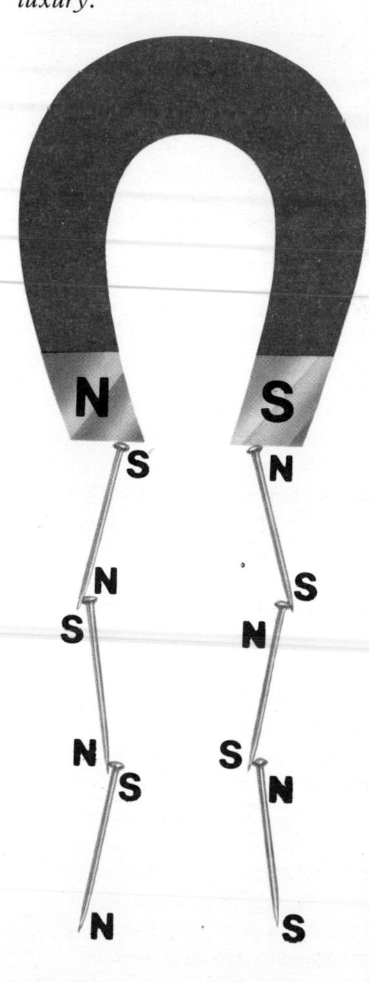


If you hang pins on a horseshoe **magnet**, each pin becomes a little magnet with North and South poles.

Woolly **mammoths** lived during the Ice Ages. They roamed the plains of Europe and North America.

**magnetic** acting like a magnet.
**magnify** to make something appear bigger. *If you look through a drop of water, it will magnify things.*
**magnifying glass** a lens that magnifies things.
**maid** 1 a girl. 2 a female servant.
**mail** letters and parcels sent by post.
**main** the most important; largest. *The main road runs near our house.*
**majority** the greater part of a number. *The majority of the class voted to go swimming.*
**make up** the cosmetics (lipstick and powders) people put on their faces.
**make up for** to do something good after you have done something bad. *I was nasty to my sister, but I made up for it by helping her this afternoon.*
**male** 1 a boy or man. 2 the opposite of female.
**mammal** any of the animals that feed their young with milk from their bodies.
**mammoth** a large animal like an elephant, but now extinct.
**man** a grown up male human; sometimes also used to mean all people, men and women.
**manage** 1 to take charge of something. *My father manages a supermarket.* 2 to succeed in doing something even though it is not easy. *I can just manage to keep up with James when we run together.*
**manager** a person whose job is to take charge of other people at work.

**mane** the long hair on the neck of a horse or lion.

**manger** a box for horses or cattle to eat from in a stable.

**mankind** all people everywhere.

**man-made** artificial; made by humans. *A canal is a man-made river.*

**manner** the way a thing is done or happens.

**manor** in the Middle Ages, a lord's house and the land he owned.

**mansion** (say *man-shun*) a large, grand house.

**manufacture** to make things in a factory.

**map** a drawing of the Earth's surface or part of it, often showing things like rivers, mountains, countries and cities.

**marble** 1 a hard stone that can be carved and polished. 2 a small glass or china ball used in games.

**march** 1 to walk like a soldier. 2 a piece of music to which people can march.

**mare** a female horse or donkey.

**margarine** a fat used instead of butter. *Margarine is made from vegetable and animal oils.*

**margin** the blank space around the edge of a page of printing or writing; border.

**marine** (say *mareen*) to do with the sea. *A whale is a marine animal.*

**marionette** a puppet moved by strings.

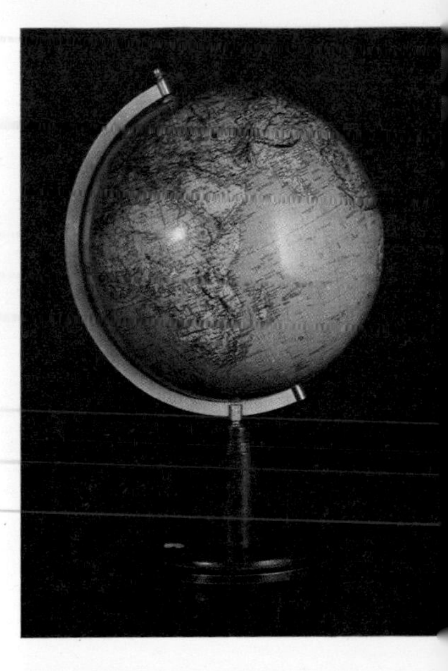

The globe is the only true **map** of the world. But globes are awkward to carry around, and they do not show much detail.

**mark** 1 a spot or pattern on something. *There is a dirty mark on your shirt.* 2 to correct work and write things on it. *The teacher will mark our papers.*

**marmalade** a jam made from oranges or lemons.

**marriage** (say *maridge*) a wedding.

**marry** to become husband and wife.

**marsh** low-lying, wet land.

**marsupial** one of a group of mammals in which the females carry their young in a pouch on their bodies. *A kangaroo is a marsupial.*

**mascot** a person, animal or thing thought to bring good luck. *Dad says they had a goat as a mascot when he was in the army.*
**mask** a covering for the face; a disguise.
**mass** 1 a large amount. 2 the amount of material in something.
**massive** huge and solid.
**mast** the pole that holds a ship's sails.
**master** a man who has other people working for him; the captain of a merchant ship.
**mat** a floor or table covering.
**mate** 1 a companion, or, with animals, one of a pair. 2 of animals, to produce young. 3 an officer of a ship under the captain.
**material** any substance from which something is or can be made. *Bricks, wood and cement are all building materials.*
**mathematics** (abbreviated as **math**) the science of numbers and shapes.
**matter** 1 the stuff of which things are made. 2 to be important. *We think it matters that you are late.*
**mauve** (rhymes with *rove*) a pale purple color.
**maximum** the greatest possible. *The maximum speed limit is 55 miles per hour.*
**mayonnaise** a cold sauce made with oil, vinegar and eggs.
**mayor** (rhymes with *hair*) the head of a town or city.
**maze** a network of winding paths from which it is difficult to find a way out.
**mean** 1 to stand for; to show. *A red flag means danger.* 2 to plan to do something. *We always mean to be good, but often we aren't.* 3 miserly; unwilling to share with others.
**meaning** what something means. *The English meaning of the French words "le chat" is "the cat".*
**meant** past of **mean.**
**meanwhile** (or **meantime**) during the same time. *We were in the garden. Meanwhile our mother hid the presents in the house.*
**measles** an infectious disease which causes red spots on the body and a fever.
**measure** 1 to find the size or amount of a thing. 2 something with which size, weight, length etc. can be found. *A foot is a measure of length.*
**mechanic** (say *meckanic*) a person who works with machines.
**mechanical** 1 to do with machines. 2 worked by machinery.
**medal** a flat piece of metal, often like a coin, with words or a picture on it, given as a prize or for bravery.
**medicine** (say *med-isin*) something taken to make you better when you are ill.

**medium** (say *mee dium*) middle size. *The robber was of medium height with fair hair.*
**meeting** a coming together of two or more people.
**melt** to turn from a solid to a liquid by heating it *My ice cream melted in the sun.*
**member** a person who belongs to a group or team of people. *Winston is a member of the football team.*
**memory** 1 the ability to remember things. 2 what is remembered. *I have a very clear memory of being in the hospital.*
**men** more than one man.
**menu** a list of food you can have at a meal in a restaurant.
**merchant** a person who makes a living by buying and selling things.
**mercury** a heavy, silver colored liquid metal; quicksilver. *Mercury is used in thermometers.*
**mermaid** a legendary creature with a woman's body and a fish's tail.
**merry** happy and cheerful.
**merry-go-round** a machine with toy animals and vehicles that you ride on as it goes around.
**mess** 1 untidiness and dirt. 2 a place where soldiers and sailors eat their meals.
**message** a piece of information sent to somebody.
**messenger** a person who carries a message.
**metal** any sort of material like iron, steel, tin or copper.
**meteor** (say *meet-eor*) a small solid body that rushes from outer space into the Earth's atmosphere; a shooting star *Meteors burn up brightly.*
**meteorite** a meteor that reaches the Earth without burning up.
**meter** 1 an instrument for use in our house. 2 a measure of length. *There are 100*

This early **microscope** belonged to Robert Hooke. In 1665 he wrote a book about all the strange things he could see through it.

*centimeters in a meter.*
**method** a way of doing something.
**metric** the system of measuring based on the meter, the kilogram and the liter.
**microbe** a tiny creature that can only be seen through a microscope.
**microphone** an instrument that picks up sound waves and turns them into electric waves for broadcasting or recording.
**microscope** an instrument for making very small things big enough to see.
**midget** a very small person.
**midnight** twelve o'clock at night.
**mighty** very strong.
**migrate** to move from one place to another to live, as birds do in the fall.
**mild** 1 soft, gentle. 2 of weather, warm.
**mile** a measure of distance; 5280 feet.
**military** to do with soldiers and war.
**mill** 1 a building where grain is ground into flour. 2 a factory with machinery in it.
**million** one thousand thousand (1,000,000).
**millionaire** a very, very rich person who owns a million dollars.
**milligram** a very small measure of weight; one thousandth of a gram.
**millimeter** a small measure of length, shortened to *mm.* (10 mm = 1 centimeter).
**mime** to act without using words.
**mimic** to imitate someone.
**minaret** a tall tower by a mosque from the top of which Muslims are called to pray.
**mince** 1 to cut into tiny pieces. 2 meat that is chopped up finely.
**mincemeat** a mixture of dried fruits and fat that is cooked in pies and tarts, especially at Christmas.
**mind** 1 that part of a person which thinks, has ideas, and remembers; the brain. 2 to look after. *Our dog minds the house when we are out.* 3 to object to something. *I don't mind being left alone.*
**mine** 1 belonging to me. 2 a deep hole in the ground from which coal or other minerals are taken. 3 to take minerals from the ground.
**miner** a person who works at a mine.
**mineral** a natural material that comes from the ground. *Coal, salt and diamonds are all minerals.*
**minimum** the least possible amount. *The minimum price of a seat was $5.*
**minister** a clergyman; a parson.
**minor** not very important.
**mint** 1 a green, leafy herb used for flavoring food. 2 a place where coins are made.
**minus** the mathematical sign "–" meaning take away or less than; (6–4 = 2).

**minute** (say *min-it*) a short period of time. *There are 60 minutes in one hour.*
**minute** (say *my-nute*) very tiny.
**miracle** a remarkable event that cannot be explained.
**mirror** a shiny surface that reflects things; a looking-glass.
**mischief** naughtiness.
**miser** a person who loves money for itself; a mean person.
**miserable** very unhappy.
**miss** 1 to fail to hit, catch or see something that you want to. *If Sally does not hurry she will miss the train.* 2 to be sad because someone is not with you. *When mother was in the hospital we all missed her very much.*
**Miss** the title that goes before the name of an unmarried woman. *Miss Moody is the head teacher of our school.*
**missile** an object or weapon that is thrown or sent through the air, often by a rocket.
**mission** (say *mishun*) people sent to do some special work; an errand.
**missionary** a person who goes to another country to tell people about his or her religion.
**mist** a thin fog; water vapor in the air.
**mister** (written as **Mr.**) the title that goes before a man's surname. *Our teacher is called Mr. Todd.*
**mitten** a type of glove with places for four fingers together and the thumb separately.
**mixer** a machine for mixing things.
**mixture** anything made by mixing things together.
**moat** a deep ditch around a castle.
**model** 1 a copy of something, usually smaller. *The architect showed us the model he had made of the new building.* 2 to make a model. 3 someone who sits while an artist or photographer paints or photographs them. 4 someone whose job is to wear and show new clothes.
**modern** of present or recent times. *My mother likes living in a modern house, but my father would like to move to an older one.*
**moist** slightly wet.
**mold** (rhymes with *sold*) 1 a hollow container. *When a hot substance is poured into a mold it cools into the shape of the container.* 2 a small fungus that grows on damp decaying things.
**mole** 1 a small furry animal that lives in a tunnel underground. 2 a small dark mark on the skin.
**mollusk** one of a group of animals with soft bodies. *Most mollusks, like snails, limpets and oysters, have hard shells.*
**molt** (rhymes with *colt*) to

change old feathers or an old skin for new ones. *Snakes molt and have new skin under the old one.*

**monarch** (rhymes with *bark*) a king or queen.

**monastery** a place where monks live and work.

**mongrel** a dog that is a mixture of different types of dogs.

**monk** (rhymes with *bunk*) a member of a religious group of men who live together in a monastery.

**monkey** (say *munky*) a furry animal that belongs to the same group as apes and people.

The magpie **moth**. When butterflies rest, they hold their wings upright. Moths spread theirs flat.

This **mosaic** from the ruins of the Roman town of Pompeii warns visitors to "beware of the dog".

**monorail** a railway with only one rail.

**monster** 1 very large. 2 a large and frightening creature.

**month** one of the twelve parts into which the year is divided.

**mood** the way you feel.

**moonlight** the light from the moon.

**moor** 1 an open area often covered with heather. 2 to tie up a boat.

**moped** (say *mo-ped*) a motorized small bicycle.

**Morse code** a system of sending messages with a series of dots and dashes for letters.

**mortar** a mixture of cement, lime, sand and water. *Mortar is used to hold bricks together.*

**mosaic** a picture made from little bits of colored stone or glass.

**Moslem** (see **Muslim**)

**mosque** (say *mosk*) a building in which Muslims worship Allah.

**mosquito** (say *moskeeto*) a small flying insect that sucks blood. *Some mosquitoes carry a disease called malaria.*

**moss** small green or yellow plants that grow on damp surfaces.

**motel** a roadside hotel for people who arrive by car.

**moth** a winged insect that usually flies at night.

**motor** an engine that uses electricity, gas or oil to produce movement. *This pump is driven by an electric motor.*

**mottled** marked with spots of different colors.

**mountain** a very high hill.

**mountaineer** a person who climbs mountains.

**mourning** great sadness after someone dies.

**mouse** (plural *mice*) a small rodent.

**mouth** 1 the opening in the face into which you put food and through which your voice comes. 2 that part of a river where it flows into the sea.

**mouth-organ** a small musical instrument played by blowing and sucking.

**movement** activity; the act of moving.

**mow** (rhymes with *toe*) to cut grass or corn.

**Mr.** (say, and see, **Mister**)

**Mrs.** (say *missis*) the title that goes before the surname of a married woman.

**Ms** a title used before the surname of a woman. It does not show whether or not she is married.

**muddle** an untidy mess.

**mule** a horse-like animal that is the foal of a male ass and a female horse or pony (a mare).

**multiply** to make something a number of times bigger. *When you multiply by 3, the answer is 3 times bigger.*

**mummy** the preserved body of a human or animal.

**mumps** an illness that makes the neck and sides of the face swell.

**mural** a picture painted on a wall.

**muscle** (say *mussel*) one of the fleshy parts in your body that make you move. *You make movements by tightening the right muscles.*

**museum** (say *mu-see-um*) a building where old things are kept and shown to the public.

**mushroom** a kind of fungus that is often safe to eat.

**music** the sounds made by someone who sings or plays a musical instrument.

**musician** (say *mu-zish-un*) a person who makes music.

**Muslim** a follower of the Islamic religion.

**mystery** something that is difficult to explain or understand.

**myth** an old story about imaginary people.

**Music** is made by four kinds of instruments – stringed, woodwind, brass and percussion.

# Nn

**nail** 1 the hard layer over the outer tip of a finger or toe. 2 a thin piece of metal with a point at one end and a flat head at the other, used to fasten things together.

**naked** bare, without any clothes on.

**nap** a short sleep.

**napkin** a cloth for wiping fingers and lips and for protecting clothes at meals.

**narrow** not wide, small in width.

**nation** (say *nay-shun*) a country and the people who live in it.

**national** (say *nash-unal*) belonging to one country. *The national flag of the United States is the Stars and Stripes.*

**nationality** being a member of a nation. *He has American nationality.*

**native** a person who was born in a country. *Lincoln was a native of America.*

**natural** made by nature, not by people or machines.

**nature** the whole universe and all its life. *Nature includes everything that is not made by people or machines.*

**navigate** to find the way for a ship or aircraft.

**navy** a country's warships and all the people who sail in them.

**neat** tidy, having everything in the right place.

**necessary** that which has to be done. *It is necessary to have a license to drive a car.*

**necklace** (say *neck-less*) a string of beads or other ornaments worn around the neck.

**nectar** a sweet liquid in flowers that is collected by bees.

**needle** 1 a pointed instrument used for sewing or knitting. 2 a pointer in a meter or a compass.

**neglect** 1 to give little care to. *If you neglect your garden it will become full of weeds.* 2 not to do something you should do. *Never neglect your duty.*

**neighbor** (say *nay-ber*) someone who lives near you.

**neighborhood** the area around the place where you live.

**neither** not one or the other.

**neon** a colorless gas used in light tubes.

**nephew** the son of your brother or sister.

**nerve** a fiber that carries feelings and messages between the body and the brain.

**nervous** easily frightened.

**nestling** a bird too young to leave the nest.

**net** 1 a material made of loosely woven string, thread or wire, so there are many holes between the threads. 2 something that is made from this sort of material. *Toby caught a fish in his fishing net.*

Some birds' **nests.** The golden oriole makes a hanging nest (top); the tailor bird weaves a nest between leaves; the tit's mossy nest is almost enclosed; the American robin's nest is a cup of mud and twigs.

**nickname** a name given instead of your proper name. *We call Mr. Baker by his nickname, Floury.*
**niece** (rhymes with *fleece*) the daughter of your sister or brother.
**nightmare** a frightening dream.
**nip** to pinch like a crab.
**nit** the egg of a louse, found in the hair.
**noble** (or **nobleman**) a man of high rank, like a duke.
**nod** to bow the head slightly.
**noisy** making a lot of noise.
**nomad** a member of a group of people who wander from place to place.
**nonsense** foolish talk or behavior.
**noon** twelve o'clock midday.
**noose** a loop of rope. *The noose becomes tighter when one end of the rope is pulled.*
**normal** usual, as expected. *The normal buses will run on the holiday.*
**north** one of the compass points. *When you face the sunrise, north is on your left.*
**nostril** either of the openings in the nose through which you breathe and smell.
**note** 1 to write down a few words to remind yourself or someone else about something. 2 a short letter. 3 a single musical sound. *Catherine played one note on the piano.*
**notice** (say *no-tiss*) 1 something written down or shown to people to tell them something. *Our teacher put up a notice about the swim meet.* 2 to see something. *I noticed that she had a new coat.*
**noun** the name of a person, place or thing. *John, Paris and cat are all nouns.*
**novel** a long story that is made up by the writer.
**now** at this very moment in time.
**nowadays** at the present time.
**nowhere** not anywhere.
**nuclear** to do with atomic energy. *When the nucleus of an atom is split it produces nuclear energy.*
**nucleus** a center part of something.
**nude** naked, bare, having no clothes.
**nuisance** something or somebody that causes trouble.
**numb** (rhymes with *gum*) not able to feel.
**number** 1 a word or figure showing how many. *5, 37 and six are all numbers.* 2 a quantity or amount. *There were a large number of books left on the shelf.*
**nun** a woman who has taken vows to live a religious life.
**nurse** a person who is trained to look after people who are ill, very young or very old.
**nut** 1 the fruit of certain plants with a hard shell. 2 a piece of metal with a hole in the center that screws onto a bolt to fasten it.
**nylon** an artificial, or man-made, fiber.

# Oo

**oak** a large tree on which acorns grow.
**oar** (rhymes with *sore*) a pole with a flat end for making a row boat move through water.
**oasis** (say *o-ay-sis*) a fertile place in the desert.
**oat** grain from a cereal. *Ground oats are called oatmeal and are used to make porridge.*
**obedient** doing what you are told. *Our dog was very naughty as a puppy, but now he is quite obedient.*
**obey** (say *o-bay*) to do what you are told.
**object** (say **ob**-*ject*) anything that can be touched.
**object** (say *ob*-**ject**) to say that you do not agree with something, *She objected to the way the people were chosen.*
**oblong** a rectangle; a flat figure with two parallel pairs of straight sides, two longer than the others.
**oboe** a musical instrument made of wood and played by blowing.
**observe** to watch carefully.
**obstinate** not easily made to agree to do something. *A donkey can be very obstinate if it does not want to work.*
**obvious** easily seen or understood.
**occupation** what you do or are doing; your job.
**occupy** to live in or be in. *Sam will occupy the second floor of the building.*
**ocean** (say *o-shun*) one of the seven great bodies of sea water that surround the continents.
**octagon** a flat figure with eight equal sides.
**octopus** a sea animal with a soft body and eight arms. *An octopus is a mollusk.*
**odd** 1 peculiar, strange. 2 a number that cannot be divided exactly by two. *3, 27 and 101 are odd numbers*
**offer** 1 to say that you will do something for somebody. *I thanked him for his offer to help me clean the room.* 2 to hold out something to somebody. *Sean offered me a bag of candies.*



Two views of the world as seen from space. The **oceans** cover three-quarters of the Earth.

**office** a place where people work whose business needs writing and recording.

**officer** a senior person in the army, air force or navy.

**offspring** the child or children of a family, young animals.

**ogre** (say *oger*) a cruel giant in stories that eats people.

**oil** kinds of liquid that do not mix with water and usually burn easily. *Oils are used for power (gasoline); for making surfaces slide easily against each other (engine oil); and for cooking (corn and olive oil).*

**ointment** a medicine made in a paste or cream.

**old-fashioned** out of date, not worn or used nowadays.

**opening** a place that is not closed, like a gap in a fence.

**opera** a play in which the words are sung.

**operate** 1 to work. *Do you know how to operate the machine?* 2 to carry out a surgical operation.

**operation** (say *opper-ashun*) 1 a treatment by a doctor in which the patient's body is cut. 2 a carefully planned action.

**opinion** what someone thinks; an idea with which not everyone agrees.

**opportunity** a good chance to do something. *While the children were out, their mother took the opportunity to clean their rooms.*

**opposite** 1 entirely different. *Fat is the opposite of thin.* 2 on the other side. *The house on the opposite side of the road is painted blue.*

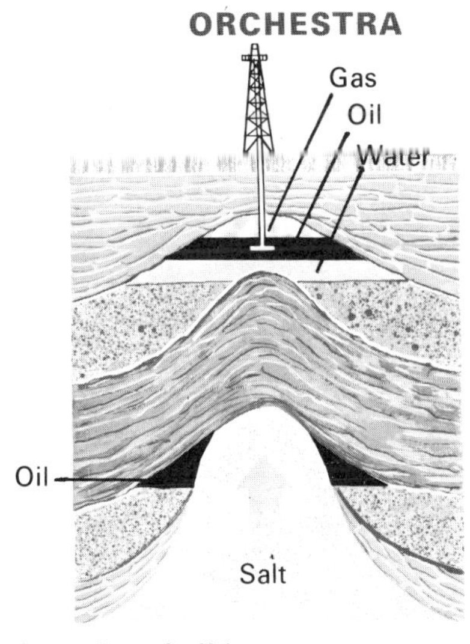


The formation of **oil** began millions of years ago when dead plants fell to the bottom of the seas. Layers of rock pressed down on top and the plants were turned into crude oil.

**optician** (say *optishun*) a person who tests eyes and sells glasses.

**orange** 1 a round, juicy fruit with a thick skin. 2 a color like an orange.

**orbit** the path followed by any body in space around another body. *The Earth has an orbit around the Sun, and the Moon has a smaller orbit around the Earth.*

**orchard** a piece of ground where fruit trees are grown.

**orchestra** (say *ork-estra*) a group of people who play musical instruments together. *There are always stringed instruments in an orchestra.*

**order** 1 command somebody to do something. *The officer gave the order to advance.* 2 a list of things that you want. *She gave the order to the grocer.* 3 **in order** in a tidy way. *Please put all your books in order.*

**ore** rock or earth from which metals can be taken.

**organ** 1 any part of an animal's body that has a particular job to do. *The heart is the organ that pumps blood around the body.* 2 a musical instrument with a keyboard and pipes.

**organization** an organized group of people.

**organize** to make arrangements for something to happen.

**original** the earliest or first; new, not copied.

**ornament** something which is used as a decoration.

**orphan** a person whose parents are dead.

**ostrich** a very large bird that lives in southern Africa. *Ostriches have long legs and cannot fly.*

**otherwise** 1 in another way. 2 if not, or else. *You'd better hurry, otherwise we'll go without you.*

**ounce** a small measure of weight. *There are 16 ounces (oz.) in one pound (lb.). An ounce equals 28.35 grams.*

**outboard motor** a motor for driving a small boat. *It is hung over the stern (back) of the craft.*

**outgrew** past of **outgrow.**

**outgrow** to become too large for something. *Robert will soon outgrow his gray pants.*

**outing** a day's holiday away from home or school.

**outlaw** a person who has broken the law; a bandit.

**outline** 1 the outside shape of something. 2 a drawing that shows only the shape of something. 3 the main facts about something.

**outskirts** the edges of a town.

**oval** an egg-shaped figure.

**oven** the enclosed part of a stove where food is baked or roasted.

**overcoat** a thick coat.

**overflow** to flood, to spill out. *I left my bath running and it overflowed all over the floor.*

**overhang** to hang out over something.

**overhaul** 1 to examine thoroughly and repair if

**Ostriches** run very fast on two long toes that help to lengthen the big bird's leg and give a long, swift stride.

necessary. 2 to overtake.
**overhead** raised up high, above your head.
**overhear** to hear something when the speaker does not know you can hear.
**overlap** to cover one thing partly with another.
**overtake** to pass another moving thing, particularly a vehicle.
**overtime** 1 time spent working after the usual hours. 2 extra wages paid for such work.
**owe** (rhymes with *low*) to need to pay money to someone. *I borrowed money from Bob. I still owe him a dollar.*
**owl** a bird of prey that flies in the dark.
**own** 1 to possess or have. *Father owns that field.* 2 belonging to one person only. *It is father's own field.*
**owner** someone who owns something. *My father is the owner of that field.*
**ox** a male animal of the cattle family.
**oxen** more than one ox.
**oxygen** one of the gases in the air. *All animals and plants must have oxygen to live.*

# Pp

**pack** 1 to put things into a bag or other container ready for a journey. 2 a holder for carrying things on a journey. 3 a group of animals that hunt together.
**package** a parcel or bundle of things packed together.
**packet** a small parcel.
**pad** 1 to walk along softly. 2 a kind of small cushion used to protect something from rubbing. 3 sheets of paper joined together at one edge.
**paddle** a short oar for making a canoe move through water.
**painting** a picture that has been painted.
**pair** two of the same kind. *Look at the pair of doves sitting on my windowsill.*
**palace** the home of a ruler, such as a king or queen.
**pale** having not much color.
**palm** (say *pam*) 1 the inner surface of the hand. 2 a tree with no branches but a lot of large leaves near the top. *There are date palms and coconut palms in hot countries.*
**pancake** a flat cake made from batter cooked in a frying pan.

**panda** a bear-like animal from Asia.

**pane** a single sheet of glass in a window.

**pant** to breathe in and out quickly.

**pantomime** a kind of play with music and dancing; the story is told mainly by body and face movements.

**pants** 1 underclothes for the lower part of the body. 2 trousers are also called pants.

**papier-maché** (say *pap-uh-mash-ay*) pulped paper used for modeling.

**papyrus** (say *pap-eye-rus*) a kind of paper made from the papyrus reed in ancient Egypt.

**parable** a story that teaches a simple lesson.

**parachute** an umbrella-like apparatus used for floating down from an aircraft.

**parade** 1 a procession. 2 soldiers gathered for inspection.

**paraffin** an oil used for burning in jet engines, heaters and lamps (also called **kerosene**).

The African gray **parrot** can imitate almost any sound.

**paragraph** several sentences grouped together because they deal with one main idea.

**parallel** lines that are the same distance from each other along their full length. *The tracks of a railroad are parallel.*

**paralyzed** unable to move or feel.

**parasite** an animal or plant that lives on other living things. *Mistletoe is a plant parasite. A flea is an animal parasite.*

**pardon** to forgive someone.

**parent** a mother or father.

**parliament** the group of people who are elected to make the laws in some countries.

**parrot** a brightly-colored tropical bird with a hooked beak. *Some parrots can be taught to say words.*

**particle** a very small part of something.

**particular** one rather then another. *This particular book is very interesting.*

**particularly** one more than any other. *I particularly like this book.*

**partner** a person who does something with someone else. *Alice is my partner for tennis.*

**party** 1 a group of people who come together to enjoy themselves. 2 an organized group who try to get certain people elected to the government.

**pass** 1 to go by. *You have to pass the school to reach the park.* 2 to give something to someone who cannot reach it.

*Please will you pass me the butter?* 3 a piece of paper that allows you to go somewhere or do something. *My grandma has a pass that allows her to go free on the buses.*

**passage** a narrow way between buildings or through a building.

**passenger** a person being taken in a car, ship or aircraft.

**Passover** a Jewish festival.

**passport** a document that travelers show when going from one country to another.

**password** a secret word that helps one to be recognized by a sentry.

**past** 1 the time before the present time. *The Sumerians lived in the distant past.* 2 up to and further than something. *You go past the school to get to the hospital.*

**paste** a soft, moist mixture.

**pasteurize** to kill germs by heating, especially milk. How to do this was discovered by Louis Pasteur.

**pastime** a game, a hobby; anything done to pass the time in a pleasant way.

**pastry** a mixture of flour, fat and water, cooked to make pie crusts.

**patch** 1 a small piece of ground. *There was a small patch of grass in the playground.* 2 a small piece of material sewn on to cover a hole.

**patchwork** bits of material sewn together in a pattern.

**patience** (say *pay-shunce*) to be able to wait calmly without complaining.

The **peacock's** train spreads like a great fan.

**patient** (say *pay-shent*) 1 someone who is looked after by a doctor. 2 able to wait a long time without getting cross.

**patrol** to go around a place to see that everything is correct. *His job is to patrol the factory at night.*

**pattern** 1 a design that is repeated on something to make it look pretty. *I have a dress with a pattern of flowers on it.* 2 anything that is copied to make something else. *Mother used my dress as a pattern to make a dress for my sister.*

**pause** (say *paws*) stopping for a short time.

**pavement** a paved surface.

**peace** freedom from war or violence; calmness.

**peacock** a large bird. *The male peacock can spread its beautiful fanned tail.*

**peak** the top of a mountain.
**peanut** a groundnut; a nut that grows in a pod under the ground.
**pear** a sweet, juicy fruit that is narrow at one end.
**pearl** a silver-white ball found in some oysters (a kind of shellfish). *Pearls are used to make jewelry.*
**peasant** a poor person who works on the land.
**pebble** a small rounded stone.
**peck** to use the beak to pick up food or cut something.
**peculiar** very strange or unusual. *The man was wearing a peculiar hat with green feathers all over it.*
**pedal** 1 a part that is pressed by the foot to make something work. *The pedals of a bicycle turn the wheel.* 2 to press pedals.
**pedestrian** a person walking in the street.
**pedigree** a record of the members of a family who have lived up to now. *Our dog has a pedigree that shows her great-grandparents.*
**peer** to look at closely, as if unable to see properly.
**pen** 1 a small fenced place for animals. 2 a tool for writing that uses ink.
**pendant** an ornament that hangs down on a chain.
**pendulum** a weighted rod that is hung so that it can swing back and forth, as on some clocks.
**penguin** an Antarctic sea bird. *Penguins swim with their wings.*

An emperor **penguin** with young.

**peninsula** area of land almost surrounded by water. *Italy is a peninsula.*
**penknife** (say *pen-nife*) a small knife that shuts into itself.
**pen pal** someone who writes to you and to whom you write although you have not met. *My pen pal is called Ali. He lives in Nigeria.*
**pension** (say *pen-shun*) money paid regularly to someone who has retired from work.
**pentagon** a five-sided figure.

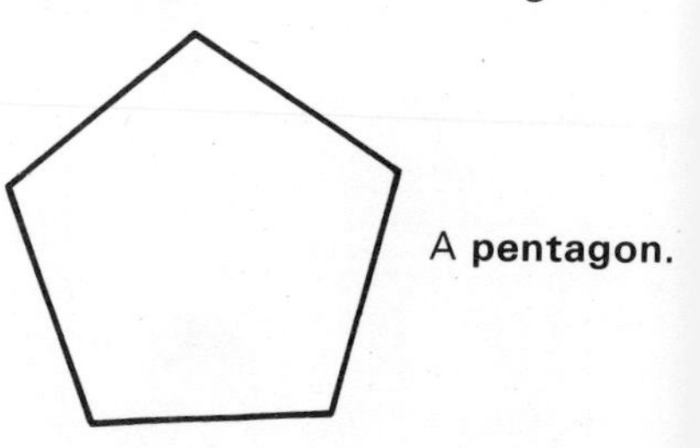
A **pentagon**.

**people** (say *peeple*) men, women and children; human beings. *All the people on our street came to the party.*
**pepper** a hot tasting powder made from dried berries. *Pepper is used to flavor food.*
**percent** a fraction written as part of 100. *50 percent is 50 parts in 100, or* $\frac{1}{2}$*; 10 percent is 10 parts in 100, or* $\frac{1}{10}$*. Percent is often written* %.
**perch** a resting place for a bird.
**percussion instrument** a musical instrument that is struck or shaken. *Drums, tambourines and triangles are percussion instruments.*
**perennial** lasting for a long time; for more than a year. *Roses and lilies of the valley are perennial flowers.*
**perfect** so good that it cannot be made better.
**perform** 1 to do something in front of other people. *We performed our play in front of the whole school.* 2 to do something. *I am sure that he will perform the task perfectly.*
**performance** something that is done so that other people can see or hear it.
**perfume** 1 a scent. 2 a sweet smelling liquid.
**perimeter** the distance around the outside of an area.
**period** a length of time.
**periscope** an instrument like a tube with mirrors in it that lets someone see over something. *We used a periscope to see over the heads of the crowd.*
**permanent** unchanging; not expected to change. *This is now our permanent address.*
**permit** 1 to allow. 2 something written to say that a certain thing can be done.
**perpetual** lasting forever.
**person** any man, woman or child. *Did a person in a brown hat come in here?*
**persuade** (say *per-swade*) to make or try to make someone change their mind.
**pest** an animal that is harmful or causes trouble. *Rats are pests on a farm because they eat grain.*
**petal** one of the leaf-like parts of a flower (see picture at **flower**).
**pew** a bench in a church.
**pharaoh** (say *faro*) a king of ancient Egypt.
**phase** 1 a stage in the development of something. 2 one of the various stages of the Moon's monthly journey around the Earth.
**philosophy** the search for knowledge; the study of ideas.
**phone** short for **telephone**.
**photograph** a picture taken by a camera.
**photostat** a copy of writing or pictures made by a special machine.
**phrase** a group of words linked together to form part of a sentence. "*Part of a sentence*" *is a phrase in the last sentence.*

**physical** 1 having to do with the body. 2 of a map, showing features like high and low ground and rivers.
**physics** the study of light, heat, sound and energy.
**piccolo** a small musical wind instrument which gives very high notes.
**pick up** 1 to lift something up with your hand. *Pick up your pencils when I say, "Now".* 2 to give someone a ride in your car. *I picked up old Mr. Brown and took him to the store.*
**pier** (say *peer*) a structure built out over water. *A pier is a landing place for ships.*
**pigeon** (say *pid-jun*) a bird that can fly back to its home; a dove.
**piglet** a young pig.
**pigsty** a building for pigs.
**pile** a number of things on top of each other. *Mother was cross about the pile of clothes on my floor.*
**pilgrim** a person who travels to visit a holy place.
**pill** a small ball of medicine.
**pilot** 1 a person who can fly an aircraft. 2 a person who is trained to take a ship through difficult waters.
**pimple** a small fiery lump on the skin.
**pinch** to grip between a finger and a thumb.
**pine** an evergreen tree with needle-like leaves.
**pineapple** a large, sweet, juicy fruit with a prickly covering.
**pioneer** 1 a person who goes to a new place or country to settle. 2 someone who is the first to do something.
**pip** the seed of a fruit.
**pirate** a sea robber.
**pistil** the seed producing part of a flower (see picture at **flower**).
**pistol** a small gun that is held in one hand.
**pit** 1 a deep hole with steep sides. 2 a coal mine.
**pitch** 1 to throw something. 2 a sticky black material like tar. 3 to put up a tent. *They will pitch the tent out of the wind.* 4 highness or lowness of a sound.
**pitchfork** a longhandled fork used for lifting hay.
**pity** a feeling of sadness for someone's troubles.
**plague** (say *play-g*) a dangerous illness which is very quick to spread.
**plain** 1 simple; ordinary; with no pattern on it. *Her dress was plain blue with a lace collar.* 2 a large flat area of country.
**plait** (rhymes with *gate*) to twist three or more strips together.
**plan** 1 a drawing that shows where things are. 2 to decide what you are going to do. *Shall we plan a walk on the weekend?*
**plane** 1 short for **airplane.** 2 a tool for making wood smooth. 3 a tall tree with large leaves and bark that peels.

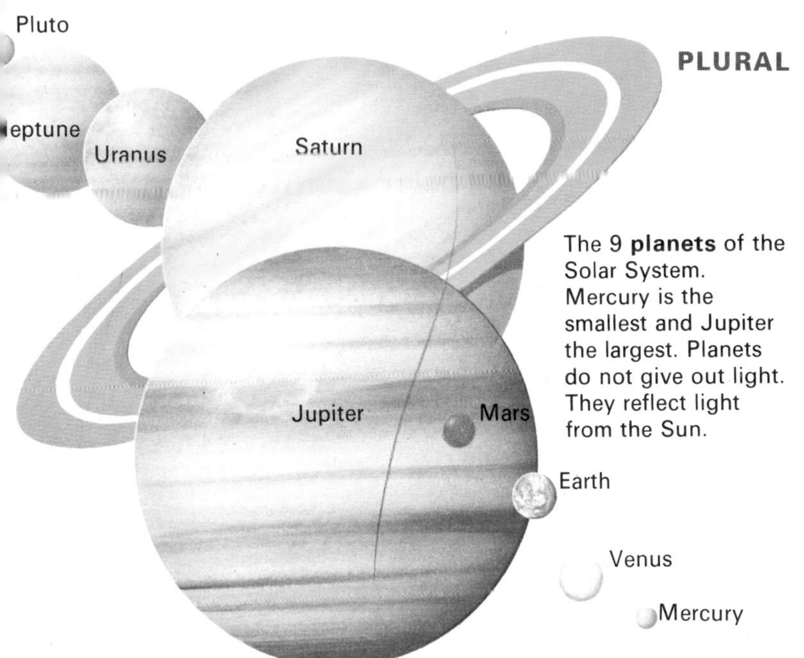


The 9 **planets** of the Solar System. Mercury is the smallest and Jupiter the largest. Planets do not give out light. They reflect light from the Sun.

**planet** one of the bodies that move around a star. *Mars, Venus and Earth are all planets that move around the Sun.*

**plank** a long flat piece of wood.

**plankton** tiny plants and animals that drift in the sea.

**plastic** a light, strong material that is manufactured. *Plastic is used to make all sorts of things, like cups, toys and buckets.*

**plateau** (say *plat-o*) level land higher than the land around it.

**platform** 1 a small, raised stage. 2 the place beside the subway lines where people wait at a station.

**play** 1 to have fun and not work. 2 a story that is told by people acting and talking to each other, usually on a stage.

**pleasure** the feeling of being happy.

**plot** 1 a secret agreement to do something, usually bad. *The police discovered a plot to rob the bank.* 2 a small piece of ground. 3 the main things that happen in a story.

**plow** (rhymes with *how*) a machine used to cut and turn over land ready for planting.

**plug** 1 a piece of wood, rubber or other material used to fill a hole. 2 a device for joining electrical equipment to the electricity supply.

**plumber** (say *plummer*) a person who fits and repairs water pipes in a building.

**plunge** to jump or fall into. *The man plunged into the canal after the drowning child.*

**plural** a word which shows that there are more than one. *Cats, kittens and children are all plural nouns.*

**plus** and; added to. *Four plus six equals ten.*
**p.m.** after midday.
**pneumatic** (say *new-matic*) worked by air under pressure; filled with air.
**pneumonia** (say *new-monia*) a serious illness of the lungs.
**pod** a long seed holder on some plants. *Peas grow in a pod.*
**poem** (say *po-em*) a piece of writing with a special rhythm. *Poems are often written in short lines with the last word in one line rhyming with the last word of another line.*
**poet** (say *po-et*) a person who writes poems.
**poetry** (say *po-etry*) poems.
**poison** a substance that makes people ill or die.
**polar** of or near the North or South Poles. *Polar bears live near the North Pole.*
**pole** 1 either the most northerly point of the Earth (the North Pole) or the most southerly point (the South Pole). 2 one of the ends of a magnet. 3 a tall, thin piece of wood or metal; a post.
**police** the people who help to keep the law and catch criminals.
**polish** to make something smooth and shiny.
**polite** well mannered.
**pollen** a fine powder on flowers which fertilizes other flowers. *Pollen is usually yellow.*
**pollute** to make dirty or spoil.
**polythene** a plastic material used for wrappings and bags.

**Polar** bears are the only bears with white fur. They spend much of their life on ice floes hunting fish and seals.

**pony** (plural *ponies*) a small horse.
**pool** a very small area of water; a pond.
**pope** the head of the Roman Catholic Church.
**popular** liked by a lot of people. *I think Andrew is the most popular boy in our class.*
**population** all the people living in a place, a country or the world. *The population of our city is 60,000.*
**porcelain** fine china.
**porch** a covered entrance to a building.
**porcupine** a rat-like animal covered with pointed spines.
**pore** a tiny opening in the skin.
**pork** the flesh of a pig.
**porpoise** a sea animal rather like a small whale.
**porridge** a soft food made of oatmeal.
**port** 1 a harbor; a town by the sea with a harbor. 2 the left side of a ship or aircraft as you are facing forward.

**porter** a person who is employed to carry things.
**porthole** a round window in a ship.
**portrait** a picture of a person.
**position** the place taken by somebody or something. *When you are all in position, the race will begin.*
**possess** to have or own. *Do you possess any money?*
**poster** a picture, usually with writing, which goes on a wall to advertise something.
**potter** a person who makes pottery.
**pottery** 1 pots and other things made of baked clay. 2 a place where pottery is made.
**poultry** hens, ducks, geese, turkeys and any other domestic fowl.
**pound** 1 a measure of weight. *There are 16 ounces in one pound.* 2 a British unit of money. *There are 100 pence in a pound.* 3 to hit heavily and often.
**poverty** being poor.
**powder** anything that is fine and dry like dust or flour.
**power** the strength or ability to do something.
**powerful** very strong or important.
**practical** able to do useful things.
**practice** 1 something you do often to get better at it. *My piano practice lasts for an hour every day.* 2 to do something often so that you can do it well. *I practice the piano every day.*

Ancient Greek **pottery** was often painted with pictures of gods and heroes.

**prairie** a wide plain with very few trees, especially in North America.
**praise** to say good things about someone.
**pray** to talk to God.
**prayer** what is said when you talk to God.
**precious** (say *preshus*) very valuable.
**predator** an animal that hunts other animals. *A tiger is a predator in the jungle.*
**predict** to say what is likely to happen in the future; to forecast.
**preface** an introduction to a book.
**prefer** to like one thing rather than another. *I prefer football to soccer.*

**pregnant** to be going to have a baby.
**prehistoric** things that happened before the time when people could write.
**prepare** to get ready.
**prescription** a doctor's order for medicine.
**present** (say **prez**-*ent*) 1 something that is given to somebody, a gift. 2 this time; now. *At present there are 20 children in my class.* 3 being in the place spoken about. *Who was present at the meeting?*
**present** (say *pree*-**zent**) 1 to give someone something in public. *The mayor presented prizes at our school open house.* 2 to show or perform. *Our class presented a play for our parents.*
**preserve** to make something last a long time. *The ancient Egyptians preserved their dead pharaohs as mummies.*
**president** the elected head of a country or organization.
**press** 1 to push on something. *The boys pressed their noses against the window of the store.* 2 to press something flat by pushing hard on it. *Father presses his pants.*
**pressure** (rhymes with *thresher*) how much one thing is pressing on another.
**prevent** to stop something happening. *The rain prevented us from going out.*
**prey** (rhymes with *ray*) an animal that is hunted by another animal. *A bird of prey is a bird that hunts animals and other birds.*
**priceless** too valuable to have a price.
**prick** to make a mark with a small sharp point.
**prickle** a sharp point in the stem of a plant, a fine thorn.
**pride** the feeling of being proud.
**priest** (rhymes with *least*) a person who is trained to perform religious acts.
**primary** first in time or importance. *The primary colors are blue, red and yellow.*
**Prime Minister** the most important person in some governments.

In 1440 Johannes Gutenberg invented type that could be used again and again. People could then **print** books much more quickly.

**prince** the son of a king or queen.
**princess** the daughter of a king or queen.
**principal** 1 the most important. 2 the leader of a school.
**principle** an important rule. *Always telling the truth is a good principle to follow.*
**print** 1 letters that you do not join together. 2 to use a machine to put letters or pictures onto paper.
**prison** a building in which people who break the law may be kept.
**prisoner** a person who is kept in prison.
**private** not open to the public; belonging to only one person or to a few people.
**prize** something that is given to someone as a reward. *I won a prize in the poetry competition.*
**probably** likely to happen, but not certain. *We will probably go to Florida next week.*
**problem** a question for which an answer is needed; a difficulty that needs to be solved. *We are having a problem with our roof.*
**process** a way of making something. *The process of making paper is a complicated one.*
**procession** a number of people and vehicles moving along together; a parade.
**produce** (say **prod**-*uce*) things that are made or grown. *His wife sold the produce from the garden.*
**produce** (say *pro*-**duce**) 1 to make. 2 to bring something out to show it. *The magician produced a rabbit from his hat.*
**producer** someone who makes or grows something.
**product** something that is produced. *The product of that factory is ice cream.*
**profit** the difference between the cost of making something and the price it is sold at.
**program** a list of events or things that are going to happen; a theater program; a TV program.
**progress** advance, improvement.
**project** a plan to be worked on. *Our class is working on a project to start a vegetable garden.*
**promise** 1 to say that you will do something. 2 what you have promised to do. *I promised to clean my room, but I did not keep my promise.*
**pronoun** a word used for a noun, like he, she, it, they, him, our.
**pronounce** to make the sound of a word.
**proof** something that shows that what is said is true. *I need some proof before I will believe it.*
**propel** to send forward.
**propeller** two or more blades that spin round. *Propellers are used to push a boat forward or to pull aircraft through the air.*

**proper** right, suitable. *She was not wearing the proper clothes for a party.*

**property** things that someone owns.

**prophet** 1 a person who tells what is going to happen in the future. 2 in the Bible, a person who speaks for God.

**protect** to keep safe from danger.

**protein** (say *pro-teen*) a body-building material in some foods, like eggs and milk.

**protest** to say or show that you think something is wrong. *We had to protest about the new school rules.*

**Protestant** a member of any Christian church which resulted from the protest against and breakaway from the Roman Catholic church.

**proud** 1 thinking that you are better than others. 2 pleased that someone else has done well. *Mother was very proud when I won a prize.*

**prove** to show that something is true. *Can you prove that you saw a ghost?*

**proverb** a short saying that gives a warning or advice. *"It is better to be safe than sorry" is a proverb.*

**provide** to give something that is needed. *Our teacher provided us with new pencils.*

**province** a large area of a country with its own government.

**prowl** to go about silently and secretly.

The **pulley** is very useful for lifting heavy things. It was invented around 800 BC.

**prune** 1 a dried plum. 2 to cut away parts of a plant to control the way it grows.

**psychology** (say *si-cology*) the study of the mind and how it works.

**pterodactyl** (say *tero-dack-til*) an extinct flying reptile.

**public** 1 known to everyone; belonging to everyone. 2 all the people.

**publish** to have a book printed for sale or to be given away.

**pull down** of buildings, to take them down on purpose.

**pulley** a wheel with a rope around it, used to lift or move heavy things more easily.

**pulse** the throbbing that you can feel in your wrist. *The pulse is caused by the blood being pumped around your body.*

**pulpit** a raised structure in a church from which the priest or minister talks.

**pump** 1 to push liquid or air through pipes. *The heart pumps blood around our bodies through tiny tubes.* 2 a machine that does this.

**punch** to hit someone with the fist.

**punctual** on time.

**punctuation** the marks used in writing like the full stop (.) and the comma (,).

**puncture** to pierce; to make a hole in something.

**punish** to do something to someone who has done wrong so that they will not want to do it again.

**pupa** (plural *pupae*) the chrysalis stage in an insect's development.

**pupil** 1 a person who is learning from a teacher. 2 the round dark opening in the colored part (the iris) of the eye.

**puppet** a kind of doll that can be made to move by pulling strings or some other method.

**purchase** to buy, or something that is bought.

**pure** 1 clean. 2 not mixed with anything.

**purple** a dark, red-blue color.

**pursue** to chase after. *The crowd pursued the thief.*

**put off** 1 to decide to do something later than planned. *We had the flu so we put off the party until next week.* 2 to feel badly about something you dislike. *I was quite put off by the way she spoke to me.*

**put up with** not to complain about something even though you do not like it. *It's not a very nice place, but my brother likes it, so I will just have to put up with it.*

**puzzle** a difficult problem.

**pyramid** a structure with a square base and sloping sides that meet at the top.

A cutaway drawing showing the inside of the Great **Pyramid.** It was built in Egypt in the 2600s BC by the Pharaoh Khufu. Inside the pyramid, the dead Pharaoh was laid to rest.

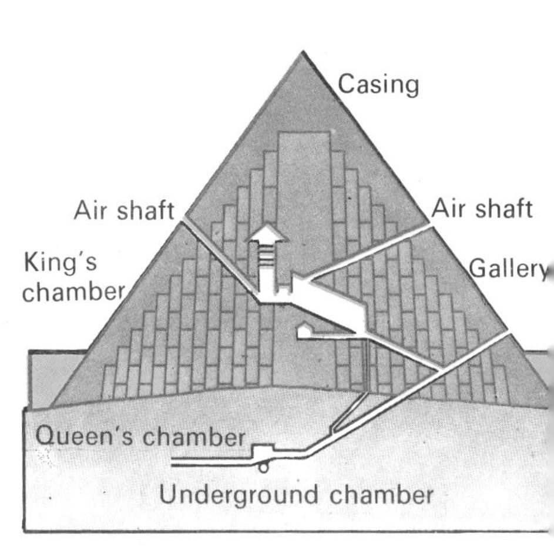

# Qq

**quadruped** a four-footed animal. *A horse is a quadruped.*
**quadruplet** one of four babies born on the same day to the same mother.
**quality** how good or bad a thing is. *We want the best quality of carpet.*
**quantity** how much; the size, weight or number of anything. *What quantity of eggs will you need?*
**quarantine** (say *kwarant-een*) a period when someone who has a disease is kept away from other people so they cannot catch it.
**quarrel** to argue angrily.
**quarry** 1 a place from which stones or gravel are dug out. 2 the prey of an animal.
**quart** (say *kwort*) a measure of liquids. *There are two pints in a quart.*
**quarter** a fourth part of a whole; $\frac{1}{4}$.
**quartet** four people doing something together, especially making music.
**quay** (say *key*) a landing place for ships.
**queen** the female ruler of a country or the wife of a king.
**queer** strange and peculiar. *This soup tastes very queer.*
**question** something that you ask when you want to find out something and get an answer.
**question mark** a punctuation mark, like this ?. It goes at the end of written questions.
**quilt** a thick padded bed covering.
**quintuplet** one of five babies born on the same day to the same mother.
**quiz** a set of questions asked to find out how much people know, usually as a competition.
**quotation marks** punctuation marks like this ". . . ." or this '. . . .'. They are mainly used in writing to show spoken words.
**quote** to repeat someone else's words. *Sandy can quote lots of poems from memory.*

# Rr

**rabbi** a teacher of Jewish law, the leader of a synagogue.
**race** 1 a group of people who are alike and have the same colored skin. 2 to run with others to find out who is fastest.

**racket** 1 a lot of noise. 2 a light bat used to hit balls in tennis, badminton or squash
**radar** an instrument that sends out radio waves. These waves are reflected back off objects like aircraft or ships, and the reflection shows where the object is.
**radiate** to give off heat and light.
**radiator** 1 a piece of equipment that sends out heat. 2 the part of a car that keeps the cooling water at the correct temperature.
**radio** an instrument that receives radio waves and uses them to produce sounds which you can hear.
**radio waves** invisible waves sent out by a transmitter and traveling very, very fast.
**radius** (plural *radii*) a straight line from the center of a circle to its edge or circumference.
**raft** logs fastened together to make a type of boat.
**rafter** one of the cross-bars of wood in a roof.
**rage** great anger.
**raid** a surprise attack.
**rail** 1 a long bar or rod. 2 one of the long metal strips that form a railroad line.
**railroad** the organization that controls a system of tracks, and the trains that run on them.
**rainbow** an arch of color in the sky. *A rainbow is caused by sun shining on rain, mist or spray.*
**rainfall** the amount of rain that falls in a period of time.
**raise** to lift up; to make higher.
**raisin** a dried black grape.
**rake** a tool like a comb on a long handle.
**ram** 1 a male sheep. 2 to hit and push hard. *The ship rammed the submarine.*
**ranch** a large farm in North America with a lot of land for grazing.

The wheels of trains and subway cars are specially shaped to run on the curved surface of a **rail**.

**rank** a name or job that shows how important someone is. *General is a very high rank in the army.*

**ransom** money paid to a kidnapper to make him or her release a prisoner.

**rap** thc sound of knocking.

**rapid** quick.

**rare** unusual; not often found.

**rash** 1 lots of red spots on the skin. 2 reckless.

**ray** line or beam of light, heat or some kind of energy.

**razor** an instrument for shaving hair from the skin.

**realize** to come to understand. *Judy realized that she must have seen a ghost.*

**rear** 1 the back part; at the back. *I like to sit at the rear of the classroom.* 2 to look after animals as they grow up. 3 of a horse, to stand up on the back legs.

**reason** anything that explains why or how something has happened.

**rebel** someone who will not obey orders.

**recall** 1 to remember; to bring back to your mind. 2 to call someone back.

**receive** (say *reseeve*) to get something that has been given to you or sent to you.

**recent** not long ago.

**recipe** (say *res-ippy*) the instructions for how to cook something.

**recite** to say aloud from memory. *Paul can recite a poem by heart.*

The safety **razor** was invented in 1880 by King C. Gillette.

**recognize** to know that you have seen somebody or something before. *I wonder if she will recognize me after all those years?*

**record** (say **reck**-*ord*) 1 a flat disk which makes sounds when it is turned on a record player. 2 the best performance known. *She scored a record number of goals.*

**record** (say *ree*-**cord**) 1 to write something down so it will be remembered. 2 to put sounds on a record or tape.

**recorder** a musical instrument made of wood or plastic, played by blowing into one end.

**record player** a machine for playing records.

**recover** 1 to get something back. *He recovered his boot from the mud.* 2 to get better. *I am glad you have recovered from your fall.*

**rectangle** a four-sided figure in which the opposite sides are equal to each other.

**reduce** to make less. *If you reduce the price I will buy it.*

**reed** tall, firm stemmed grass that grows near water.

**reef** a ridge of rock near the surface of the sea.

**referee** person who controls a game or match.

**reference book** book that is used to find particular pieces of information. You do not usually read through the whole book. *Dictionaries and encyclopedias are reference books.*

**reflect** send back light, heat, sound or radio waves from any object.

**reflection** the picture you see in a mirror or in calm water.

**refresh** to give new energy to.

**refrigerator** an appliance in which food is kept very cold so that it does not go bad.

**refuse** (say *ree-fuse*) to say that you will not do something that you are asked to do. *I refused to clean up my sister's books.*

**refuse** (say *ref-yuse*) rubbish, things that are thrown away.

**region** (say *ree-jun*) an area of the world or of a country with no particular edge. *Evergreens grow mainly in the colder regions of the world.*

**regret** to be sorry for something that has been done.

**regular** happening in the same way or at the same time again and again. *There is a regular bus service between New York and Washington.*

**rehearse** to practice, particularly for a play or concert.

**rehearsal** a practice performance.

Both the male and female **reindeer** have great branches of antlers. They live in large herds.

**reign** (rhymes with *pain*) to rule as a king or queen.

**reindeer** (say *rayn-deer*) a kind of large deer that lives in cold regions. *Reindeers are used in Lapland to carry loads.*

**reins** (rhymes with *canes*) straps fastened to a bridle to

Home **refrigerators** date back to the late 1860s. This one was made in 1927.

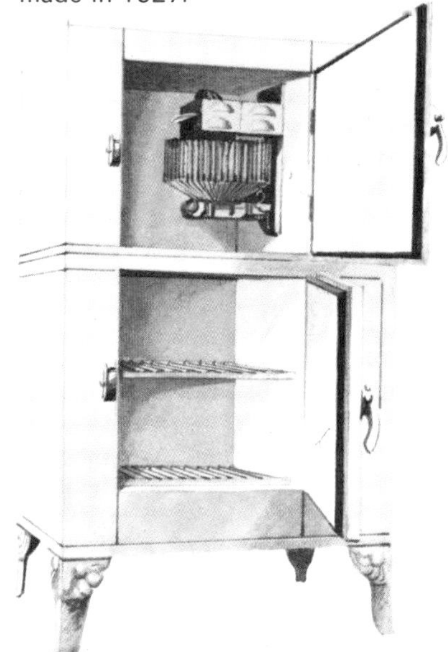

control a horse.

**reject** to throw away because it is not good enough.

**relative** someone who belongs to the same family as you. *Your aunt and uncle are your relatives.*

**relax** to become less tight; to loosen. *If you relax your muscles you will feel better.*

**relay race** a race in which each person in a team goes part of the distance.

**relief map** a map that shows where high and low areas of land are.

**religion** a belief that there is a god who created and controls the universe.

**remain** 1 to stay after others. *Sue remained in the house when the others went out.* 2 to be left over after some has been taken away. *You can have the few candies that remain.*

**remainder** what is left over when a part has gone or been taken away.

**remind** to make or help someone remember. *Sarah reminded everyone about her birthday.*

**remote** far away from other places. *We spent our vacation on a remote island.*

**remove** to take away.

**rent** a regular payment made for the use of a house or other place or thing.

**repair** to make something that is broken whole again; to mend.

**repeat** to say or do again.

**replace** to put back where it came from. *Please replace the book on the right shelf.*

**report** 1 to tell of something. 2 a written record.

**represent** to act or speak for other people. *Your senator represents you in the Senate.*

**reproduce** 1 to make something happen again; to copy. *The concert was recorded on tape and reproduced the next day.* 2 to give birth.

**reptile** a cold-blooded vertebrate animal that creeps or crawls. *Crocodiles, snakes and turtles are all reptiles.*

**republic** a country that elects a president as head of state and does not have a king or queen. *America is a republic.*

**require** to need. *She requires some help with the costumes.*

**rescue** to take from danger; to set free. *The knight will rescue the princess from the dragon.*

**resemble** to be or look like something or somebody else. *Alan resembles his grandfather.*

**reserve** 1 to keep back to use later. *Shall I reserve a chair for you if you are late?* 2 a place kept for a special purpose. *You can see some very rare birds at the bird reserve.*

**reservoir** a place where a large amount of water is stored, often in an artificial lake.

**resident** someone who lives in a particular place.

**resign** (say *res-ine*) to give up, especially to give up a job.

## RICE

The young shoots of **rice** are planted in flooded fields called paddies.

**resources** the useful things that a person or country has. *Oil is one of our country's greatest resources.*

**responsible** in charge of something. *I am responsible for the paint closet.*

**restaurant** a place where you can buy and eat food.

**restore** to put back as it was before. *Brett restores broken china.*

**result** 1 something that happens because of some action or happening. *Joe's injury was the result of a kick at football.* 2 the final score in a game.

**result from** to be the result of.

**retail** to sell goods in a shop.

**retire** 1 to give up work, usually because one is old. 2 to go back; withdraw. *He retired from the room and went to bed.*

**retreat** to go back from.

**revenge** something bad done to someone in return for something bad done to you.

**reverse** 1 to go backwards, particularly in a vehicle. 2 the opposite of something.

**revolution** 1 a time when a government is changed by force, not by an election. 2 a time when ideas and the way people live are changed by new ideas or actions, as in *the Industrial Revolution.* 3 a full turn of a wheel.

**revolver** a gun held in the hand that can fire several times without being reloaded.

**reward** a present given to someone for what they have done. *We were given a reward for helping to catch the thief.*

**rhinoceros** a large African or Asian animal with a very thick skin and one or two horns.

**rhyme** (rhymes with *time*) to use a word that sounds like another word. *Egg and beg rhyme with each other.*

**rhythm** (say *rith-em*) the pattern of beats in music and poetry.

**rib** one of the curved bones of the chest.

**rice** a grain that is used as food. *Rice grows in wet parts of India and China.*

**rid, get rid of** to throw away something that is not wanted.

**riddle** a puzzling question. *"What goes up when the rain comes down?" is a riddle. (The answer is an umbrella.)*

**ridge** a long narrow part higher than what is on either side.

**ridiculous** silly enough to be laughed at.

**rifle** a gun that is held against the shoulder when it is fired. *A rifle's barrel is grooved inside.*

**rim** 1 the edge of a container. 2 the outside edge of a wheel.

**rind** the skin of some fruits, vegetables and of cheese and bacon.

**rink** a place for skating.

**rinse** to wash out in clean water.

**rip** tear.

**ripple** small movement on the surface of water.

**risk** the chance of danger or loss.

**river** a large stream of water that flows from higher to lower ground and into another river, a lake or sea.

**roar** loud deep sound like that which a lion makes.

**roast** 1 to cook in an oven. 2 a piece of meat cooked in the oven.

**rob** to take or steal things.

**robber** a person who steals; a thief.

**robot** a machine that can be made to do things that people do.

**rock** 1 a large stone. 2 a type of popular music. 3 to move from side to side.

**rocket** 1 a firework that shoots up into the sky. 2 a device for sending missiles and spacecraft into space.

**rod** a long, straight stick.

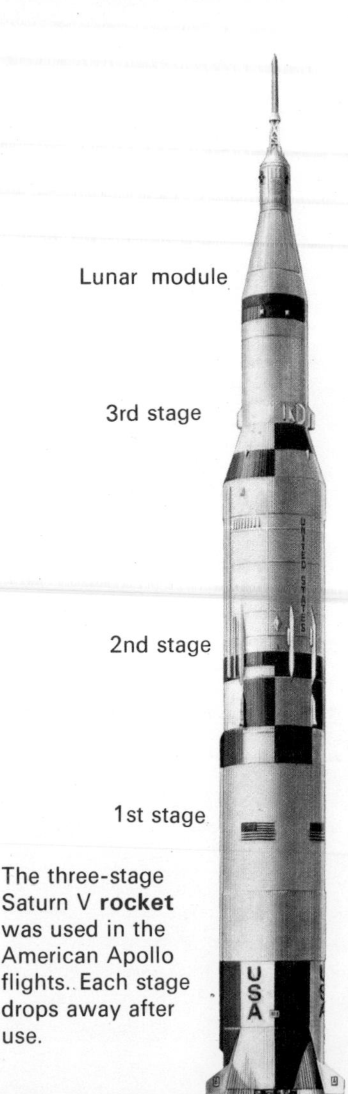


The three-stage Saturn V **rocket** was used in the American Apollo flights. Each stage drops away after use.

The squirrel (left) and the dormouse are **rodents**. All rodents have large front teeth that grow all the time.

**rodent** one of a group of mammals that gnaw things. *Rats, mice and squirrels are all rodents.*

**rodeo** performance by cowboys of riding and other skills.

**roll** 1 to turn over and over like a ball. 2 to make something into a shape like a tube. 3 a small loaf of bread.

**roller skates** set of wheels that can be attached to a shoe for skating on the ground.

**rolling pin** a long tube used for rolling out pastry to flatten it.

**Roman Catholic** a Christian who accepts the Pope in Rome, and follows the way of that church.

**roost** a resting place for birds, a perch.

**rotate** to go around and around.

**rotten** to be soft or bad. *Wasps like to eat rotten apples.*

**rough** (rhymes with *cuff*) 1 not smooth. *My dog has a rough coat.* 2 not gentle. 3 done quickly and not meant to be exact. *Can you draw me a rough plan of the town?*

**roundup** the act of collecting cattle by riding around them and driving them in.

**route** (rhymes with *boot*) the road or direction taken to get somewhere.

**row** (rhymes with *doe*) 1 to use oars to make a boat move through water. 2 a line. *She planted a row of beans in her garden.*

**royal** to do with kings and queens. *When a king is married, he has a royal wedding.*

**rubber** 1 a strong, elastic material made from the sap of a rubber tree.

**rubbish** waste matter that is thrown away.

**rucksack** a bag that can be strapped on your back for carrying; a knapsack.

**rudder** a flat, upright, moveable part at the back of a boat or aircraft used for steering.

**rude** 1 rough. 2 coarse; not polite. *The boy was very rude when he spoke out in class.*
**ruin** (say *roo-in*) 1 to spoil completely. 2 the remains of an old building. *We visited the ruins of an abbey on our field trip.*
**rule** 1 a law; something that must be obeyed. 2 to be in charge of a country. *William the Conqueror ruled England after 1066.*
**ruler** 1 a straight piece of plastic or metal used for drawing lines or measuring. 2 a person who rules a country.
**rumor** a story that is passed around, but may not be true. *There is a rumor that we are having an extra week's vacation.*
**rung** one step of a ladder.
**runway** the hard surface from which an aircraft takes off.
**rural** of or about the countryside.
**rush** 1 to go very fast. 2 a strong grass that grows near water.
**rust** the reddish-brown substance that forms on iron and some other metals when they become damp.

**sabbath** a weekly religious day of rest. The sabbath is Saturday for Jews, and Sunday for Christians.
**sabotage** to damage something on purpose.
**sack** 1 a large bag made of strong material. 2 to destroy a town captured in war.
**sacred** to do with religion and worship. *The Bible and the Koran are sacred books.*
**sacrifice** 1 to give away something precious, often to God. 2 the thing that is given away.
**saddle** the rider's seat used on a bicycle or a horse.
**safe** 1 protected from danger. 2 a special strong, locked container where money and other valuable things can be kept.
**safety pin** a pin that locks its sharp point into itself, and so cannot prick anyone.

**saga** an old story, especially one that tells of the ancient Norse heroes of Scandinavia.

**sail** 1 to travel across water in a ship or boat, especially when the travel is powered by wind. 2 a sheet of canvas tied to the mast on a ship to catch the wind.

**saint** an extremely good person, particularly one who has been recognized as holy by the church.

**salad** a mixture of uncooked vegetables such as lettuce, tomato and cucumber.

**salary** the money paid to someone for their work, sometimes called wages.

**saliva** spit; the liquid in your mouth.

**salute** to raise your stiffened hand to your forehead or hat as a greeting, as soldiers do.

**sample** an example of something, which can be used to show what the others are like.

**sanctuary** a safe place for people, or for birds and animals. *In a bird sanctuary it is against the law to hunt or kill the birds.*

**sap** the juice in the stems of plants.

**sari** a length of cloth draped around the body as a dress, and worn mainly by Indian women.

**Satan** the devil; the evil one in many religions.

**satchel** a shoulder bag used to carry books.

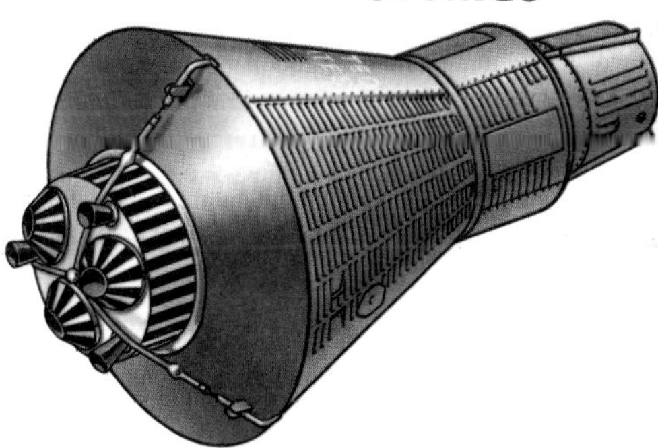

The Mercury spacecraft was the first American man-made **satellite** to carry a man.

**satellite** 1 a small planet that moves through space around the Earth or another planet. 2 an artificial object put into orbit around Earth.

**satisfactory** all right, or good enough.

**satisfy** to please, to make someone contented. *He wanted to satisfy his teacher, so he did his homework carefully.*

**sauce** a liquid mixture served with some foods.

**saucepan** a metal cooking pot with a handle and sometimes a lid.

**saucer** a small curved plate on which a cup stands.

**sauna** (say *sawna*) a kind of hot steam bath.

**sausage** a chopped meat mixture which is made into a tube-shape inside a skin.

**savage** wild and fierce.

**savanna** large areas of grassy treeless plains.

**savings** the money someone has saved, often kept in a bank.

**saxophone** a metal musical instrument, played by blowing into it.

**saying** a well-known phrase or proverb. *"Too many cooks spoil the broth" is a saying.*

**scab** the dry protective crust that grows over a wound.

**scaffolding** a structure of tubes and planks used when a building is being put up or repaired.

**scald** to burn with hot liquid or steam.

**scale** 1 one of the thin pieces of hard skin that cover the bodies of fish and reptiles. 2 a series of measuring marks on an instrument such as a ruler or thermometer.

**scales** an instrument for measuring how much things weigh.

**scalp** the skin and hair on your head.

**scar** the mark left on skin from a wound, after it has healed.

**scarce** rare, uncommon, in short supply. *Because of the fuel shortage, oil is very scarce.*

**scare** to frighten.

**scarlet** bright red.

**scatter** to go off in different directions, or to throw something so that it spreads out. *Jill scattered crumbs on the bird table.*

**scene** (sounds like *seen*) the place where something happens. *Luckily, there was a policeman at the scene of the accident.*

**scenery** (say *seenery*) 1 the natural features of a place, such as hills, fields and trees. 2 the painted curtains and screen used to make a theater stage look like a real place.

**scent** (sounds like *sent*) 1 a smell, usually a pleasant one. 2 a perfume.

**scholarship** money won by someone to pay school or university fees.

**school** 1 a place where children are taught. 2 a group of fish swimming together.

**science** 1 knowledge from studying, watching and testing. 2 a special branch of study like physics, biology or astronomy.

**science fiction** stories that are based on imagined scientific events.

**scientist** a person who studies a scientific subject.

**scissors** a tool with two blades joined together, which cut when they meet.

The **scorpion** uses its sting to stun or kill its prey.

**scold** to speak crossly to someone about what they have done or not done. *The teacher scolded them for being late to school.*

**scooter** 1 a child's toy with two wheels, a base and a handle bar. 2 a motor scooter is a light motor bike with a small engine.

**scorch** to darken the surface of something by burning it slightly.

**score** 1 to get a point in a game. *Harry tried to score a goal.* 2 the number of points each side has scored in a game. *The score was 2–3 at halftime.*

**scorpion** a small creature of the spider family, with a poisonous sting in its tail.

**scout** 1 someone who is sent out ahead of his group to look at the countryside. 2 a boy or girl who is a member of the scouting associations.

**scowl** a cross look, when the person wrinkles up his forehead in anger.

**scramble** 1 to climb or crawl up. *We managed to scramble to the top of the hill.* 2 to mix up. *We scrambled the jigsaw pieces on the table.*

**scrapbook** a book in which to stick cut out pictures or other papers.

**screen** a frame covered with wood or cloth, and used to hide something. *They put a screen around my bed in the hospital when the doctor came.*

**screw** a nail with a spiral groove down its length.

**screwdriver** a tool for driving screws into walls and other things.

**scribble** to make untidy patterns with a pen or pencil. *Our teacher scolded me for making a scribble in my book.*

**scroll** (sounds like *hole*) a roll of paper with writing or pictures on it.

**sculptor** a person who makes statues or carvings.

**sculpture** the art of making things from wood, stone or other hard materials.

**scythe** a tool with a curved blade for cutting grass or grains.

**sea** the big areas of salt water which cover most of the Earth.

**seagull** a bird that lives near the sea and eats fish.

**sea horse** a small fish with a horse-shaped head.

**seal** 1 a smoothly-furred animal that lives in or near the sea. 2 to close something by sticking its edges together. *We sealed the letter with glue.* 3 an impression stamped onto something to show that it is genuine. *The letter was stamped with the king's seal.*

**Seals** are sea mammals. The one below is a ringed seal.

**Seaweeds** provide food and shelter for many sea animals. There are green, brown and red seaweeds.

**sea level** land that is at the same level as the sea, and used to measure all other land. *The hill was 40 yards above sea level.*
**seaweed** plants that grow in or near the sea.
**seam** the line where two pieces of cloth are sewn together.
**search** to look for.
**season** a time or part, one of the four divisions of the year called spring, summer, autumn and winter.
**seashell** the hard covering of a sea-creature.
**second hand** already used, not new. *We bought my bike second hand from a neighbor.*
**secretary** an office person who types letters and makes arrangements for other people.
**section** one of the parts into which something can be divided. *The apple was cut up and I got a section of it.*
**sector** any part of a circle between two radii and the circumference.
**secure** 1 safe, out of danger. 2 to fix something so that it is safe. *The guard made sure the door lock was secure.*
**see about** to make arrangements for something to happen. *I'll see about ordering a Christmas tree.*
**see off** to go with someone to the place where they start a journey. *We will see them off at the airport tommorrow.*
**seek** to look for.
**seesaw** a long plank balanced on a central support, which rocks up and down when people sit on the ends.
**segment** one separate part of something. *Oranges can be divided into separate segments with your fingers.*

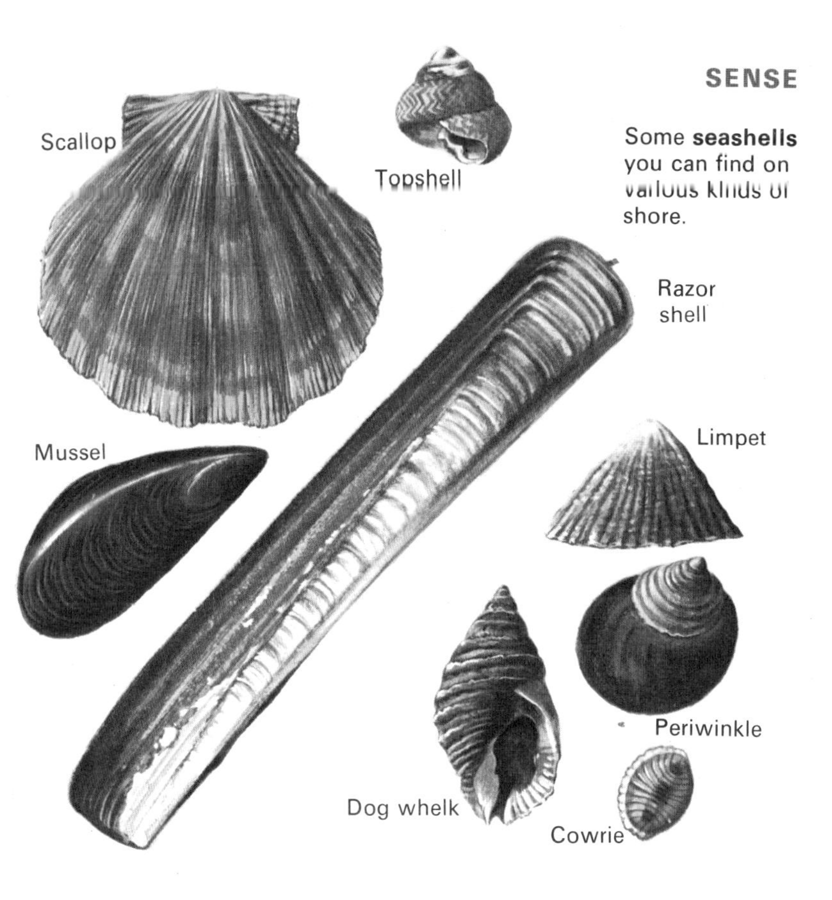


Some **seashells** you can find on various kinds of shore.

**seize** (sounds like *sneeze*) to grab something firmly.
**seldom** not often.
**select** to choose from a group. *Ben was selected from his class for the team.*
**self-defense** looking after yourself against attack.
**self-service** a shop set out and organized so that the customers can serve themselves from the shelves.
**selfish** caring too much about yourself and what you want, rather than about other people.
**semaphore** a system of sending messages with flags which you wave in the air.
**semicircle** half a circle.
**senior** older in years, or more important than others.
**sense** 1 one of the five ways your body has to tell you what is happening around you. The five senses are sight, hearing, touch, smell and taste. 2 The meaning of something. *I can't make sense of what he is saying, because he is talking too fast.*

**sentence** 1 a group of words that make sense together. 2 a punishment given to a criminal by a law court. *The burglar got a sentence of 2 years in prison.*
**sentry** someone whose job is to guard something.
**separate** 1 divided, not joined together. *The jigsaw came in 100 separate pieces.* 2 to divide something up. *She asked me to separate the peas from the beans.*
**serf** a person in history who belonged to the place where he lived, and to the lord who owned the land. A serf was a kind of slave.
**sergeant** (say *sar-jent*) a rank in the army, airforce or police.
**serial** a story that is told in parts, instead of all at one time. *We watch that serial on TV every Sunday night.*
**series** a number of things that happen one after the other, and which belong together in some way. *Peter had a series of colds last winter.*
**serious** thoughtful, not funny.
**serpent** an old-fashioned word for a snake.
**servant** a person who is paid to work in the house of another person.
**serve** 1 to work for someone. 2 to sell things in a store. 3 to give out the food at a meal.
**set** 1 a group of people or things that belong together. *We bought a set of dishes for our brother.* 2 to become hard. *The jello was left to set overnight.* 3 to arrange things in a certain way. *Will you set the table for dinner, please?*
**set about** begin to do something.
**set eyes on** to catch sight of something.
**set in motion** start something off.
**set off** to start out on a journey.
**set sail** to begin a voyage.
**settee** a sofa, a long soft seat.
**settle** 1 to go to a place and stay there. *My uncle went to Canada to settle.* 2 to decide something. *We couldn't agree which of us should eat the cake, so we asked Dad to settle the argument for us.*
**set upon** to attack someone in a violent way.
**settlement** a place where people have moved, built houses and decided to live.
**sever** to cut or break.
**several** some, usually more than three. *There were several coats left in the hall.*
**severe** strict or harsh, not gentle. *Last winter the weather was very severe.*
**sew** to join pieces of material together with a needle and thread.
**sewing machine** a machine for joining pieces of material together.
**sewer** a large drain for taking away waste from industry and bathrooms.
**sex** being male or female.

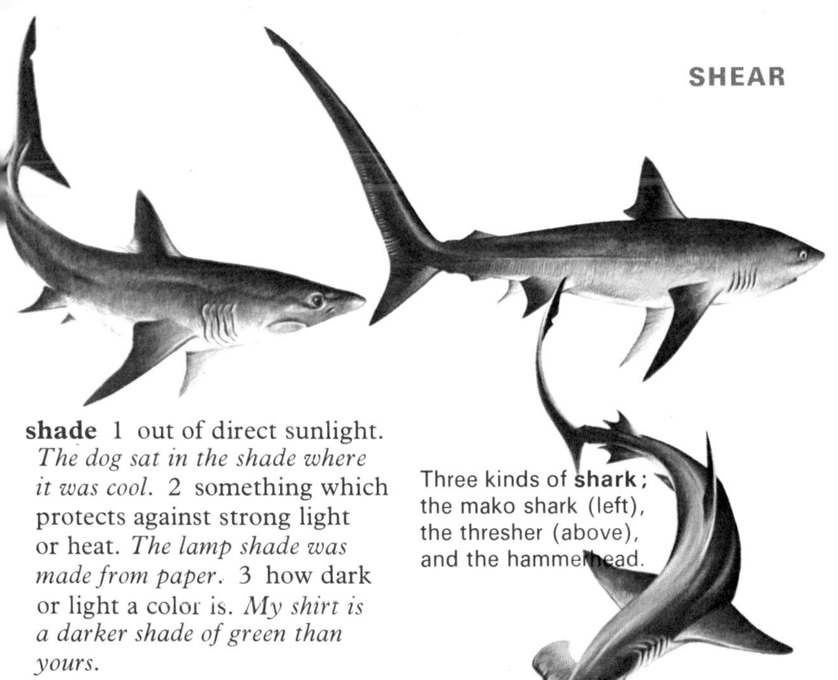

Three kinds of **shark**; the mako shark (left), the thresher (above), and the hammerhead.

**shade** 1 out of direct sunlight. *The dog sat in the shade where it was cool.* 2 something which protects against strong light or heat. *The lamp shade was made from paper.* 3 how dark or light a color is. *My shirt is a darker shade of green than yours.*

**shadow** 1 the dark shape made by an object when it is in a strong light. 2 to follow someone closely, as their shadow does.

**shaft** 1 a long handle, such as the one on a spear. 2 a narrow, deep hole that leads to a mine or pit.

**shallow** not deep. *The water was shallow and only covered my feet.*

**shame** feeling sorry and regretful for having done something wrong.

**shampoo** liquid soap for washing your hair.

**shape** the outline of something, what appearance it has. *The eraser was made in the shape of a bear.*

**share** to divide something up among a group. *Annie gave me a share of her candies.*

**shark** a large and fierce fish.

**sharp** 1 something with a pointed edge or end that cuts things easily. 2 sudden or quick. *There was a sharp bend in the road.*

**shatter** to break into small pieces.

**shave** to cut hair off parts of your body. *Most men shave their faces every day.*

**shawl** a cloth worn around your shoulders for warmth or for decoration.

**sheaf** (plural **sheaves**) a bundle of grain stalks tied together after they have been harvested.

**shear** to cut the wool from a sheep.

**shears** a pair of scissors like large blades, used for cutting plants or shearing sheep.
**sheath** a cover for a sword or a knife.
**shed** 1 a small hut. 2 to let things fall off or drop away. *Some trees shed their leaves in the autumn.*
**seep dog** a dog that herds sheep together for a farmer.
**sheer** 1 very steep, like the sides of a cliff. 2 very fine material which can be seen through.
**shell** a thin hard outer covering. *Eggs and nuts have shells.*
**shellfish** a soft-bodied water animal that lives inside a shell for protection.
**shelter** a place that protects from unpleasant weather.
**shepherd** a person who looks after sheep for a living.
**shield** a large piece of metal, wood or leather used to protect the person who carries it against attack.
**shift** to change the position of something. *Graham wants to shift the table into the corner of the room.*
**shilling** a coin used in the past in many countries before decimal currency.
**shin** the front of the leg between the knee and the ankle.
**ship** a large boat.
**shipwreck** an accident in which a ship is sunk or badly damaged at sea.
**shipyard** a place where ships are built or repaired out of the water
**shiver** to shake with cold or fear
**shoal** a group of fish swimming together.
**shock** an unpleasant surprise.
**shoot** 1 to use a gun, or a bow and arrow. 2 the tip of a young growing plant.
**shore** the land along the edge of a sea or lake.
**shorts** pants that come to

Roman soldiers carried large **shields.**

knees or above them.

**shortsighted** someone who can see clearly when things are close, but cannot see things that are further away; *nearsighted.*

**shot** the firing of a gun. *We heard a shot in the distance.*

**shoulder** the part of your body from your neck to your arm.

**shovel** a large spade with a curved blade.

**show** 1 to let something be seen by other people. 2 a kind of play or entertainment. *The artist arranged a show of his paintings.*

**shower** 1 a short period of light rain. 2 a special tap fitting for washing yourself. *People stand under the shower and it sprinkles them with water.*

**show off** to display something, or to try to make people think you do something very well.

**shriek** (say *shreek*) a scream.

**shrill** a high and loud sound.

**shrimp** a small shellfish with a long tail.

**shrink** to get smaller. *Wool often shrinks in hot water.*

**shrub** a bushy plant, like a small tree.

**shudder** to shake suddenly with cold or fear.

**shutter** 1 a cover for a window. 2 part of a camera.

**shy** 1 not liking to meet other people. 2 to turn away in sudden fear. *Horses sometimes shy away from strange objects.*

**sick** 1 ill, not well. 2 to be sick is to vomit, or to bring food back through your mouth from your stomach.

**sideways** with one side first. *Crabs move sideways along the ground.*

**siege** (say *seej*) a time when an army surrounds a town or building so that people cannot get in or out.

**sieve** (say *siv*) a frame with a stiff net, used to take small things from water, or to drain liquid from something.

**sigh** (sounds like *die*) to breathe out loudly, usually to show that you are tired or bored.

**sight** 1 the ability to see. *Sight is one of the five senses.* 2 something that is seen by someone. *We saw a very strange sight on the beach.*

**sign** 1 a board with words or pictures to give information to people. *The sign said "danger".* 2 to write your own name on something. 3 a mark or clue that has a special meaning. *The footprints were a sign that someone had been to the house.*

**signal** 1 a sound or movement that has a special meaning. *Car drivers have to signal before they turn.* 2 to send a message. *He raised his hand to signal the teacher.*

**signature** a person's name written in their own writing.

**silence** a time when there is complete quiet.

**silent** without any sound.

**silhouette** the outline or shape of something.
**silk** a soft, fine cloth made from the thread of the silkworm caterpillar.
**sill** the ledge along the bottom of a window.
**silver** 1 a valuable whitish shiny metal, or coins made from metal the same color. 2 a color that looks like the metal.
**similar** like something else, but not exactly the same. *Robyn has a similar dress to mine, but it has red bows instead of blue ones.*
**sin** breaking a religious law, or doing something that is known to be wrong.
**since** 1 from that time. *We haven't met since we were little.* 2 because. *I often meet John, since we live on the same street.*
**sincere** honest, true.
**single** 1 just one. *You have only a single chance in this game.* 2 unmarried.
**singular** one person or thing, not plural.
**sinister** frightening, something that seems evil.
**sink** 1 to drop down through liquid. *A stone will sink to the bottom of a pool.* 2 a basin for washing clothes or dishes in.
**siren** an instrument for making a loud warning signal, like a police siren.
**site** a place for buildings. *There was a bulldozer on the building site.*
**size** measurement, showing how large or small something is.

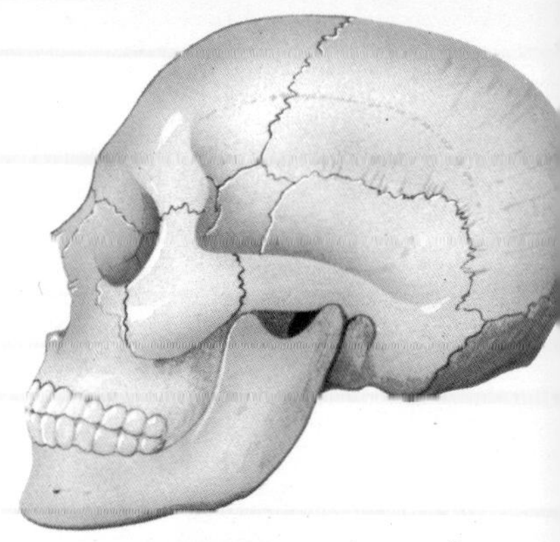

The human **skull** is made up of 22 pieces of bone. But in an adult they are all fixed tightly together except for the jaw.

**skate** a steel blade fixed to a boot for fast movement on ice.
**skeleton** the framework of bones in the body of an animal.
**sketch** to draw quickly and roughly.
**ski** long strips of wood or other material fixed to boots for fast movement over snow.
**skid** to slip by mistake. *Cars often skid on icy roads.*
**skill** the ability to do something very well.
**skull** the bony frame of the head.
**skunk** a black and white animal that gives off a very bad smell when it is frightened.
**skylight** a window in the roof of a building.
**skyline** the silhouette or outline of things against the sky.

**skyscraper** a very tall building.
**slang** a way of using words that is thought to be less correct than other ways. *"Cop" is slang for "policeman".*
**slant** a slope, like the one a ladder makes when it is up against a wall.
**slap** to hit something with a flat hand.
**slash** to make long cuts in something.
**slaughter** to kill, usually when many animals or people are killed at once.
**slave** a person who is owned by someone else, and has to work without pay, doing exactly what their owner wants.
**slay** to kill.
**sled** a small vehicle used for traveling over snow or ice. A sled has runners made from strips of wood or metal instead of wheels.
**sleeping bag** a padded bag for sleeping in, often used when camping.
**sleet** a mixture of rain and snow which falls very hard.
**sleigh** (sounds like *ray*) a large vehicle used for traveling over snow or ice. Some sleighs have engines, and others are pulled by horses.
**slender** thin, narrow.
**slide** 1 to move smoothly over something. *It's fun to slide on the ice in winter.* 2 a structure in a playgound or park, on which children climb and slide.
**slight** small, not important. *Belinda made a slight mistake.*
**slim** 1 thin, slender. 2 to eat less and try to lose weight.
**slime** unpleasantly wet, slippery material.

The **skyscraper** was only possible because of steel girders, special concrete and safe elevators.

The garden **snail** carries its home on its back. When threatened, it can pull its body into its shell.

**sling** 1 a piece of cloth used to support an injured arm. 2 a loop of leather used for throwing stones, sometimes also called a slingshot.

**slipper** a soft shoe worn in the house.

**slit** 1 a long narrow hole. 2 to make a hole or an opening in something.

**slope** a slanting place.

**sloppy** messy, untidy.

**slot** a narrow opening in something that smaller things can be pushed through. *Some front doors have slots for letters.*

**slum** an area with old and damaged houses in which too many people have to live.

**sly** clever at tricking people in secret, cunning.

**smack** to hit hard with the flat part of your hand.

**smart** 1 clever. 2 well-dressed, neat. 3 a sharp stinging pain.

**smith** someone who makes things from metal. *A goldsmith makes jewelry and ornaments.*

**smoulder** to burn very slowly.

**smuggle** to take things into a country secretly, by hiding them. *Smuggling is against the law.*

**snack** a small quick meal.

**snail** a small animal with a soft body and a hard protective shell. There are water snails and land snails.

**snake** a long, thin reptile without legs. *Some snakes are poisonous.*

**snap** 1 to break suddenly. 2 to bite at someone suddenly. *Dogs sometimes snap at unfriendly people.*

**snare** a trap for animals.

**snarl** to growl like a dog does when it is angry or frightened.

**snatch** to take away quickly. *The cat tried to snatch the fish from the plate.*

**sniff** to draw in air quickly and noisily through your nose.

**snob** someone who admires people only if they are rich or important.

**snore** to make a noise through your nose or mouth when you are asleep.

**snorkel** a tube for breathing air through when you are under the water.

**snout** an animal's nose.
**snow** flakes of frozen water that fall from the sky in very cold weather.
**snug** warm and cozy.
**soak** to leave something in liquid for a very long time.
**soar** (sounds like *door*) to fly high in the sky.
**sob** to cry noisily.
**soccer** a world-wide game played with a round ball between two teams, each with 11 players.
**social** 1 living together in groups. *Ants are social insects.* 2 to do with people and how they live. *My aunt works in the social services office in our town.*
**society** all the people who live in a group or country, and the way they live and meet.
**socket** a hole into which something fits. *Jack put the bulb into the electric light socket.*
**sofa** a soft seat for two or more people.
**soil** the earth in which plants live and grow.
**solar** to do with the sun. *Some people heat water with solar energy.*
**soldier** a member of an army.
**sole** 1 the flat part underneath your foot, or your shoe. 2 a flat sea fish. 3 just one thing or person. *He was the sole member of the class to fail the test.*
**solemn** serious, thoughtful.
**solid** 1 anything that can be touched, and is not a liquid or a gas. 2 not hollow, with no space inside. *The ball was made of solid rubber.*

A single large **snowflake** may be made up of thousands of tiny ice crystals.

**solitary** alone, lonely.
**solo** on your own. *Jane gave a solo performance on her guitar.*
**solve** to find the answer to a problem or puzzle.
**somersault** (say *sumer-solt*) to turn head over heels.
**soothe** to make someone calm when they are upset or angry.
**sore** something that hurts when it's touched, like a bruise.
**sorrow** sadness, grief.
**sort** 1 a type or group of things or people. *What sort of car did your father buy?* 2 to arrange things in sets or groups. *Pat tried to sort out her clothes from Jan's.*
**soul** (sounds like *hole*) the part of a person that is thought to live forever, especially by religious people.
**sound** anything that you can hear.
**sound barrier** the speed of sound. When a plane travels faster than sound, it goes through the sound barrier.

**soup** (sounds like *loop*) a liquid food made from meat or vegetables mixed together.

**sour** sharp-tasting like lemons, not sweet.

**source** the starting point, the beginning. *This river's source is in that mountain.*

**south** the direction opposite north on a compass.

**souvenir** something that you keep to remind you of a place, person or a event.

**sovereign** a king or queen.

**sow** (sounds like *how*) a female pig.

**sow** (sounds like *so*) to put seeds in the ground so they grow.

**space** 1 the distance between things. *There is very little space left on the bookshelf.* 2 a place with nothing in it. *Tony took the empty space on the platform.* 3 all the places beyond the Earth in the universe. *The Sun, moon and stars are all in space.*

**spacecraft** a machine that carries people and things out into space, away from Earth.

**span** to reach from one side of something to the other. *The bridge had to span a very wide river.*

**spank** to hit, usually on someone's bottom, as a punishment.

**spare** extra to what is needed. *You can use my spare pen.*

**spark** a tiny glowing bit from a fire.

**sparkle** to flash with light.

**sparrow** a common small grey-brown bird.

**spawn** the eggs of fish and other water animals, such as frogs.

**spear** a weapon made from a long pole with a sharp point on the end.

**special** different from others, and usually better than them. *My birthday is a very special day for me.*

**species** a group of animals or plants that are alike in some way. *Mice are a species of rodent, and so are rats.*

**specimen** a sample, a small

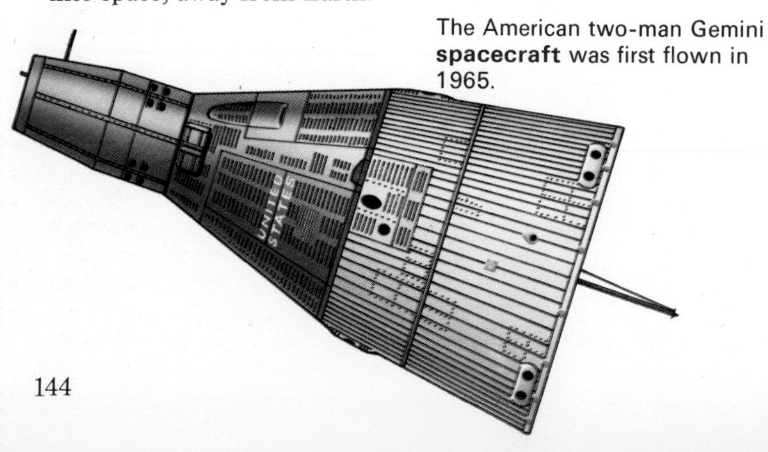


The American two-man Gemini **spacecraft** was first flown in 1965.

amount or an example of something that shows what the rest are like.

**speck** a tiny amount of something, usually dust.

**spectacles** a pair of glasses worn in front of your eyes to help you see better.

**spectator** someone watching a game or other entertainment. *The spectators cheered when Kevin scored a goal.*

**spectrum** when a ray of light passes through a special kind of glass, it splits up into a band of colors called a spectrum. It looks like a rainbow.

**speech** 1 speaking. 2 a talk given to a group of people.

**speed** how fast something or someone moves. *My car can reach a speed of 100 miles an hour.*

**speedometer** an instrument for measuring how fast something is moving.

**spell** 1 to write the letters of a word in the correct order. 2 magic words that make something happen in a strange way. *The witch's spell turned the prince into a piglet.*

**sphere** a round object like a ball.

**spice** part of certain plants used to flavor and preserve food. *Ginger and pepper are both spices.*

**spider** a small animal with eight legs. *Some spiders make webs to catch insects.*

**spill** to let something fall out of its container. *Did you spill the salt on the table?*

**spin** 1 to turn around quickly in one place. 2 to make thread by twisting fibers together.

**spine** the long line of bones down the middle of your back, the backbone.

**spiral** the shape a line makes when it circles around, like a screw.

**spire** the tall pointed part of a church or other building.

**spirit** 1 the same thing as a soul. 2 a ghost.

**spit** saliva, the liquid in your mouth.

**splash** to throw water about.

**splendid** very good, or very impressive in some way. *We saw a splendid view on our trip to the sea.*

**splinter** a small sharp piece of wood or other material.

**split** to break something into parts. *The class split up and went off in different directions.*

**sponge** 1 a sea animal with a very light, soft body. 2 a soft piece of plastic that looks like the sea animal, but is used for washing.

Although **spiders** look like insects, they are not. Insects have 6 legs, spiders have 8.

**spore** the tiny dust-like thing from which some plants grow. *Ferns and mushrooms have spores instead of seeds.*

**sport** games and other activities, usually ones that happen outside. *Football and tennis are sports.*

**spotlight** a strong beam of light that can be moved around.

**spring** 1 to move suddenly upward. *The tiger made a quick spring at the goat.* 2 one of the seasons of the year, when plants begin to grow again after winter. 3 a place where water comes out of the ground. 4 a spiral-shaped coil of metal.

**sprout** to start to grow.

**spy** (plural **spies**) 1 to find out something by secret methods. 2 a person who does that, usually for a government.

**square** an area with four equal sides.

**squash** 1 to press something so that its shape flattens out. 2 a game played in a special room with a ball and racket.

**squat** to crouch on the ground with your knees bent.

**Squirrels** have sharp claws for climbing and bushy tails that help them keep their balance.

**squeal** a long shrill sound.

**squeeze** to press something very tightly.

**squint** to look with eyes partly closed.

**squirrel** a small gray or red animal with a bushy tail.

**St.** 1 an abbreviation for saint, as when you write "St. Francis of Assisi". 2 an abbreviation for street, as when you write "Chestnut St.".

**stab** to wound someone with a knife or another sharp weapon.

**stable** a building for horses and cattle.

**stack** to arrange things on top of each other in a pile.

**stadium** a large building where people can gather to play or watch sports, or to have meetings. They are usually open to the air in the middle.

**staff** 1 a group of people who work together. *There are four teachers on the staff of this school.* 2 a thick stick.

**stag** a male deer.

**stage** 1 the raised platform in a theater on which people perform plays. 2 a point in the development of something. *What stage have you reached with your project?*

**stagger** to walk unsteadily.

**stale** not fresh, old.

**stalk** (say *stawk*) 1 the stem of a plant. 2 to follow something or someone so quietly that your presence is a secret.

**stall** 1 a table or stand in a flea market. 2 a division of a

The Penny Black of 1840 was the first postage **stamp** with a sticky back.

barn or stable for one animal. 3 stopping a car engine by mistake.

**stallion** a male horse.

**stamen** the male part of the flower that holds the pollen.

**stammer** a speech fault in which the person repeats the sounds at the beginning of words, like this: "I c-c-can't s-s-see."

**stamp** 1 to bang your foot on the ground. 2 a small label bought at a post office, which has to go on letters and parcels.

**stand** 1 to be upright, in place. *The statue stands in the middle of the square.* 2 something on which things can be displayed, like a small high table.

**standard** 1 something by which things can be compared or measured. *This ruler is not the standard size, it's much too short.* 2 a flag on a pole, usually raised to show loyalty to a country or its government.

**stand-in** someone who acts for another person when that person cannot be there.

**star** 1 one of the tiny shining lights you see in the sky at night. Stars are really very large, and most of them are millions of miles away. 2 a famous singer or actor.

**starboard** the right hand side of a ship when you are facing towards the front, or bow.

**stare** to look hard at something for a long time.

**startle** to surprise someone.

**starve** to grow ill from not having enough food, or from not having any at all.

**state** 1 how something or someone is. *The garden is in an untidy state.* 2 a country, or a division of a country. *There are 50 states in the United States of America.* 3 to say that something is true. *This book states that the king is dead.*

**stationary** standing still, not moving.

**stationery** the paper, pens, pencils, ink and other materials used for writing.

**steak** (sounds like *break*) a thick slice of meat or fish.

**steam** water that is so hot it has turned into water vapor, or gas.

**steamer** a boat driven by steam engine power.

**steel** a strong metal made from iron in a furnace.

**steep** sloping sharply.

**steeple** a tall pointed tower on a church or other building.

**stem** the stalk of a plant, the part that grows up from the ground.

**step** 1 one of the movements you make when you walk, run or dance. 2 the flat parts of a stair or ladder, where you put your feet when you climb them.

**stepfather** the husband of your mother who is not your own father.

**stepmother** the wife of your father who is not your own mother.

**stereo** or **stereophonic sound** sound that is put through two or more loudspeakers.

**sterilize** to destroy all germs with heat or strong antiseptic.

**stern** 1 strict or severe. 2 the back end of a boat or ship.

**stethoscope** an instrument used to listen to people's heart beats and the sound of their breathing.

**stew** a meat and vegetable mixture, usually cooked for a long time.

**steward** a man who looks after people, often on a train or airplane.

**stewardess** a woman who looks after people, often on a train or airplane.

**stick up for** to support someone who is in trouble. *I knew it wasn't Ray's fault, so I tried to stick up for him when the others blamed him.*

**stiff** not easily bent, rigid.

**stilts** a pair of poles which you can stand on and walk above the ground, balanced on them.

**sting** a sharp defense that some animals and plants have to protect themselves with. *Wasp stings hurt.*

**stink** to smell bad.

**stir** to move liquid around with something. *Steve forgot to stir the soup, and it burned.*

**stirrup** a metal holder which hangs on each side of a horse's saddle, in which the rider puts his feet.

**stitch** (plural **stitches**) 1 one of the loops made in cloth when you are sewing. 2 one of the loops made in wool when you are knitting.

**stock** goods kept to be used or sold. *I keep a large stock of paper in that closet.*

**stomach** the middle part of your body, to which food goes after it is swallowed and where digestion begins.

**stone** 1 a kind of rock. *The statue was made from stone.* 2 a small piece of rock. *I've got a stone in my shoe.* 3 the hard seed of some fruits, like plums. 4 a gem, a precious stone.

**store** 1 a large shop. 2 to keep things until they are needed. *Squirrels store nut.*

**stork** a tall white bird with a long beak and wide wings.

**storm** a very strong wind with rain or snow.

**story** one floor of a building. *My bedroom is on the third story of the house.*

**stowaway** someone who hides on a ship, or some other vehicle, in order to travel in secret or without paying.

**straight away** at once, immediately.
**straighten** to make something right or correct. *Henry asked me to help him straighten the carpet.*
**strain** 1 to push, stretch, or to try too hard. *Betty found it a strain to play tennis all day.* 2 to take the liquid out of something. *Max strained the water out of the vegetables.*
**strait** a narrow channel of water joining two larger bits of water.
**stranger** someone you don't know.
**strap** a strip of leather or some other material used to fasten or hold things.
**straw** 1 dry stalks of corn. 2 a thin tube for drinking through.
**stray** to wander away. *The fence was broken and so the cows could stray onto the road.*
**strength** how strong something or someone is. *Walter did not have the strength to lift the barrel by himself.*

In parts of Europe white **storks** nest on chimneys.

**stretch** 1 to pull something out so as to make it bigger. 2 a length of time or a distance. *Janet could see a long stretch of road ahead of the car.*
**stretcher** a movable bed for carrying sick or injured people.
**strict** stern, severe, unkind.
**strike** 1 to hit hard. 2 to stop work as a protest against the people who employ you.
**strip** 1 a long narrow piece of material. 2 to take off all your clothes.
**stroke** to move your hand gently over something. *Carol liked to stroke her cat's soft fur.*
**stroll** (sounds like *pole*) to walk along slowly.
**structure** 1 anything that has been built. *A house is a structure, and so is a table.*
**struggle** to fight, usually when you use your whole body. *Jenny had to struggle to free herself from the rope.*
**stubborn** not willing to change, or to do what other people want.
**student** someone who is studying, usually at a school or a college.
**study** 1 to read and learn to look at something hard. *He had to study the map for a long time before he made the journey.* 2 a room in which someone works by himself.
**stuff** 1 to fill something with some kind of material. *My*

*teddybear is stuffed with wool.* 2 anything you don't know the name of, or what it is called. *What's that stuff your dad mended the cup with?*

**stuffy** having no fresh air, smelling stale and airless.

**stutter** to stammer.

**style** the way in which something is done or made. *Tim's shirt is the latest style, but he doesn't like it.*

**subject** 1 the thing that is being talked about or written about. *John is the subject of everyone's interest.* 2 someone who is ruled by a government, or a king or queen.

**submarine** a kind of boat that can move under the water instead of on the surface.

**substance** anything that can be seen or touched.

**substitute** 1 to put in place of something else. *Peter used oil as a substitute for butter when he cooked the onions.* 2 a player in a game who joins in for someone else. *Paul was only the substitute but he scored the winning goal.*

**subtract** to take something away.

**suburb** the outside parts of a city, usually where people live.

**subway** an underground tunnel, or an underground railroad.

**successful** able to do what you want to do or try to do.

**suck** to take in air or liquid. *We had straws to suck our milkshakes through.*

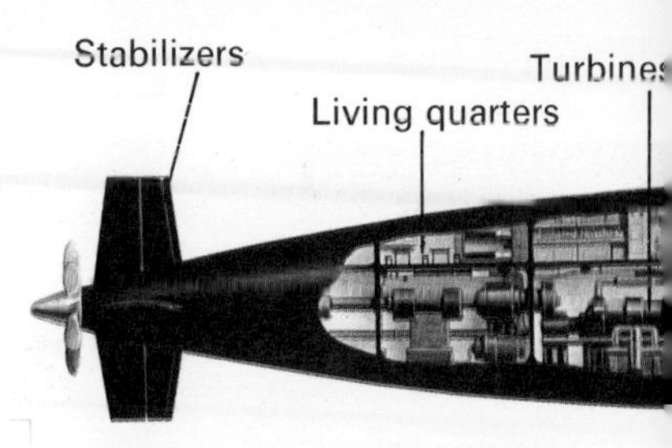


A cutaway diagram of a nuclear **submarine.** Guided missiles can be fired from underwater.

**sufficient** enough, just right, not too much.

**suffocate** when someone is stopped from breathing, they suffocate.

**suggest** to put forward an idea. *I suggest we go swimming today.*

**suicide** (say *soo-i-side*) to die by killing yourself on purpose.

**suit** 1 a jacket with pants or a skirt that are made to be worn together. 2 to be right for a certain purpose. *It will suit me to go now, because I am not busy.*

**suitable** correct, right for what is needed. *That dress will be suitable for traveling.*

**sum** 1 the whole amount. 2 answer to an addition problem.

**sundial** a kind of clock that shows the time by the shadow of the sun on a dial.

**sunrise** dawn, morning, the time when the sun comes up.

**sunset** dusk, evening, the time when the sun goes down.

**superior** better than others. *This tape player is a superior model.*

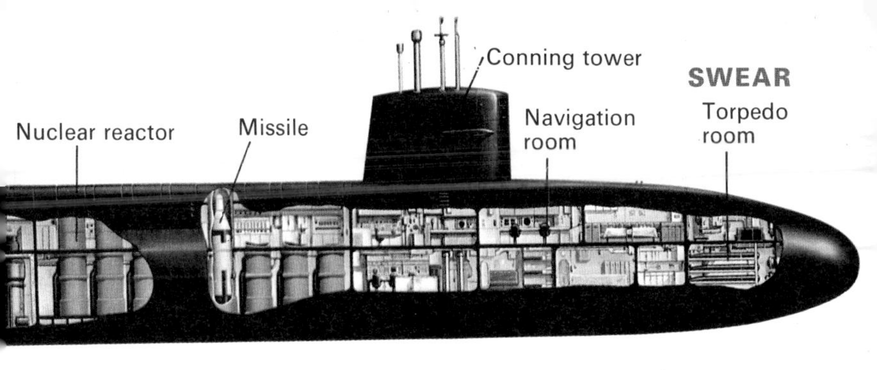


**supermarket** a large self-service shop where customers can buy many different sorts of goods.

**supernatural** something that does not have an ordinary explanation, unnatural.

**supersonic** faster than the speed of sound, or a machine that travels at that speed.

**superstitious** someone who believes in luck, chance and magic happenings.

**supply** 1 to give what is needed. *I will supply you with a book.* 2 things that are kept to be used later. *We have a large supply of pencils.*

**support** to hold up or to help.

**suppose** to think that something is true, although it may not be. *Let's suppose that cup is empty.*

**surf** large waves breaking on the shore of a beach.

**surface** the all-over covering of something, the outside. *The astronauts landed on the surface of the moon.*

**surgeon** a doctor who operates on people.

**surgery** an operation; work done by a surgeon.

**surname** your family name. *My name is Anne Bell, so my surname is Bell.*

**surprise** something that happens unexpectedly. *The party was a lovely surprise.*

**surrender** to give in. *The soldiers had to surrender when they lost the battle.*

**surround** to enclose, or to be all around. *Flower gardens surround our house.*

**survive** to live through changes or difficult times.

**suspect** to have a feeling that something is true, although you are not sure. *I suspect that someone has worn my bathing suit because it seems damp.*

**swallow** 1 to make food go down your throat. 2 a bird with pointed wings and a long, curved tail.

**swap** (or **swop**) to exchange one thing for something else. *Will you swap your lunch for mine?*

**sway** to move gently from side to side.

**swear** 1 to use bad language, words that many people do not think right. 2 to make a solemn promise.

**sweat** (sounds like *wet*) the liquid that comes out of your skin when you are hot or nervous.
**sweater** a garment for the top of your body.
**sweep** to clean with a brush.
**swell** to get bigger, to increase.
**swift** 1 fast, quick. 2 a fast flying bird with long wings.
**switch** 1 to change from one thing to another. *Brenda didn't like her teacher so she asked to switch to a different group.* 2 a piece of equipment for turning power on and off.
**sword** a hand weapon with a long blade.
**syllable** one section or part of a word, which can be said by itself. *Ambulance has three syllables : am-bu-lance.*
**symbol** a sign. *In arithmetic the symbol + means "add".*
**symmetrical** the same, even, balanced. *The letter "T" is symmetrical at the top.*
**synagogue** a meeting place for Jewish religious worship and teaching.
**synonym** a word that has the same meaning as another word. *Looking glass is a synonyn for mirror.*
**syringe** an instrument for sucking a liquid in, and forcing it out again, in a thin stream.
**syrup** a sweet liquid.

# Tt

**table** 1 a piece of furniture with a flat top supported by legs. 2 a way of arranging figures, such as a multiplication table.
**tack** 1 a small flat-headed nail. 2 to sew something with long loose stitches.
**tackle** 1 equipment for a sport or some other activity. *Dad keeps his fishing tackle in the garage.* 2 to start work on a problem. *John decided to tackle the spring cleaning alone.*
**tadpole** a young frog or toad, at the stage between the egg and the adult.
**tag** 1 a small label. 2 a game in which one person chases the others, and catches them by touching or "tagging" them.
**tailor** a person who makes suits, coats and other clothes.
**take in** 1 to be tricked. *I was taken in by what he said, but it was really a lie.* 2 to bring someone into your house. *The hotel was full, so the manager*

*found a motel to take us in.* 3 to understand. *I'm sorry, but I didn't quite take in what you said.* 4 to make something narrower. *The skirt was too big, but I took it in at the waist.*

**take up** to start doing something which is new to you. *My father has decided to take up pottery at night school.*

**tale** a story.

**talent** an ability to do something well. *Nell has a natural talent for skating.*

**talon** the long claw of a bird of prey, such as a hawk.

**tambourine** a musical instrument shaped like a shallow drum, with disks around it. It is shaken, and beaten with your hand.

**tame** an animal that isn't wild, and is used to being with humans.

**tan** 1 a light brown color. 2 to go brown in the sun. 3 to make animal skins into leather.

**tangled** confused and mixed-up.

**tank** 1 a large container for liquids. 2 an armored vehicle with guns which moves on tracks instead of wheels.

**tanker** a ship used to carry liquids, such as oil.

**tape** 1 a narrow length of material. 2 a strip of plastic used to record sound.

**tape recorder** an instrument for recording sounds on tape and playing the sounds back again.

**tapestry** a picture on cloth, made by sewing or weaving in colored threads.

**tar** a thick, sticky, black substance that comes from oil.

**tart** 1 sharp or sour tasting. 2 a pie with pastry underneath the filling but not on top of it.

**task** a job, a piece of work. *It was her task to make the beds in the morning.*

**tavern** an old-fashioned word for an inn or hotel where food and drink are served.

**tax** (plural **taxes**) money paid to the government by people and organizations. *Taxes are used to pay for roads to be built.*

**taxi** a car with a driver that can be hired for short journeys.

**tea** the dried leaves of an evergreen shrub. The leaves are soaked in boiling water to make the drink called tea.

Giant **tankers** can measure up to 1500 feet in length.

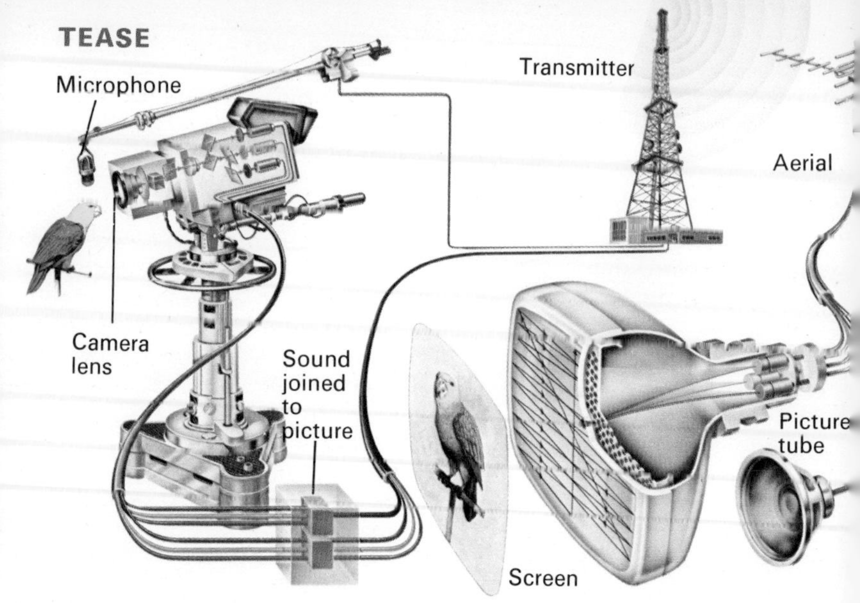


The **television** camera changes light waves into electrical "vision" signals. With sound signals from the microphone, these are sent out on radio waves. The receiver changes the signals back to pictures and sounds.

**tease** to make fun of someone, often unkindly.
**technical** to do with machinery or how things work.
**technology** the study of technical ideas.
**teethe** the stage when babies get their first teeth.
**telecommunications** to do with long-distance signals by telephone, radio, telegraph and television.
**telegram** a word message sent by telegraph or radio.
**telegraph** a system of sending long-distance messages by electric current.
**telephone** an instrument for talking to people by long-distance.
**telescope** a tube-like instrument with special lenses, which makes distant things clear and large.
**television** a way of sending and receiving pictures and sounds by radio waves.
**temperate** a climate that is neither very hot nor very cold. *New Zealand has a temperate climate.*
**temperature** how hot or cold it is. *Temperature can be measured with a thermometer.*
**temple** a building used for meeting and worship in some religions.
**temporary** lasting for a short time, not permanent. *A cold is a temporary condition. It doesn't last long.*

**tend** 1 to be likely to do something. *This boat tends to steer to the left.* 2 to look after. *Shepherds tend their sheep in the fields.*
**tender** delicate, soft, easily hurt.
**tennis** a ball and racket game for two or four people, which is played on a special court.
**tent** a shelter made from waterproof material and held up with ropes and poles.
**tentacle** a long, thin, snakelike part of animals such as on the octopus.
**term** a period of time. *The spring term lasts for ten weeks.*
**terminal** an end station on a bus, train or air route.
**termite** an insect like an ant that builds large hills of earth and mud.
**terrible** very bad, frightening, dreadful.
**terrify** to make someone very frightened.
**territory** an area of land.
**terror** great fear.
**test** 1 to try out something. *I want to test the car before I buy it.* 2 a set of questions to be answered, a kind of small exam.
**text** the main part of a printed book.
**textbook** a book used for study in a school or college.
**textile** woven cloth of any sort.
**texture** how the surface of something feels when you touch it. *The dog's coat had a rough texture.*
**thatch** a roof covering made from layers of straw or reeds.
**theater** a building where plays are performed.
**theory** (say *thee-o-ri*) an idea to explain something. *I have a theory about why he ran away.*
**therefore** for that reason, and so.
**thermometer** an instrument for measuring the temperature of something.
**thermos** a container for keeping things like drinks and soup at the same temperature.
**thermostat** an instrument that automatically controls the amount of heat.
**thief** a person who steals.
**thigh** (sounds like *my*) the part of your leg between your hip and your knee.
**third** 1 next after the second. 2 one of three pieces that make one whole thing. *There were three of us, so we each had one third of the cake.*
**thorough** properly and carefully. *Fred gave his room a thorough cleaning.*
**thought** an idea or an opinion.
**thread** (sounds like *bed*) 1 a length of spun fiber. 2 to put a thread through a hole, such as the eye of a needle.
**threaten** to warn that you will do something bad. *Michael tried to threaten his sister with a punch.*
**thresh** to beat the seeds from stalks of grain.
**thrill** to make someone excited.

**throat** the front of your neck, and the tubes inside that take food and air into your body.
**throne** a special chair for a king or queen, or some other important person.
**throw up** to be sick, to vomit.
**thunder** the noise that follows lightning in a storm
**tick** 1 to make a light, repeated sound like a clock. 2 a small animal that burrows into the skin of animals and sucks their blood.
**tide** the regular rise and fall of the sea, caused by the pull of gravity on the Earth's surface.
**tidy** neat, in order.
**tie** 1 to fasten something with string or rope. 2 a thin piece of cloth worn knotted around the neck of a shirt.
**tights** a close-fitting piece of clothing that covers your feet, legs and body up to your waist.
**tile** a flat piece of hard material used to cover floors, walls or roofs.
**till** to dig the land.
**timber** the sawn and prepared wood from trees, ready to be used for building.
**timetable** a list of times at which certain things will happen. *The timetable showed us when the music lesson would begin.*
**timid** shy, not brave.
**tin** 1 a soft, pale metal which is mixed with other metals, or sometimes used to coat metal objects. 2 a container for food, a can.
**tiny** very small.
**tip** 1 the point of something. 2 a garbage dump.
**tipup** to make something slant upwards or fall over.
**tire** a rim of metal or rubber around the edge of a wheel.
**tissue** 1 any kind of very fine fabric or material. 2 a paper handkerchief. 3 the mass of cells that make up an animal's body.
**title** 1 the name of a book, play, film and so on. 2 the words used to show a person's rank, such as "lord".
**toad** a frog-like animal that lives near water.
**toadstool** a kind of fungus

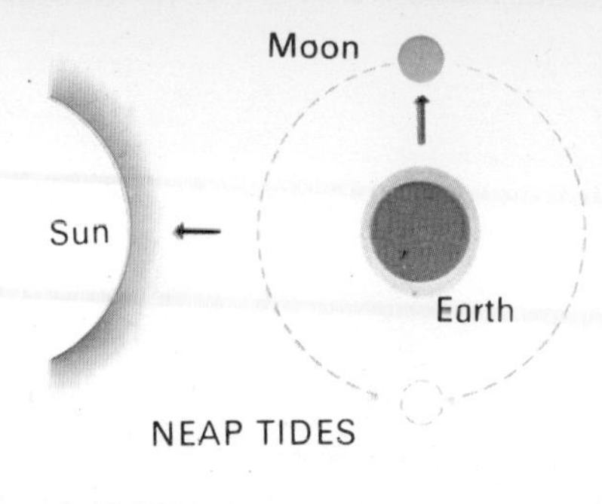


NEAP TIDES

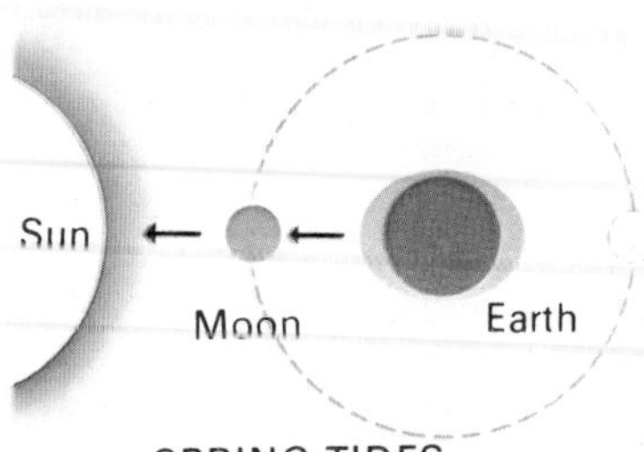


SPRING TIDES

Spring **tides** are caused by the Sun and Moon pulling together. Neap tides occur when the Sun and Moon are at right angles to one another.

like a mushroom, some of which are poisonous.

**toast** 1 slices of bread cooked on both sides. 2 to drink to someone's success or happiness. *We drank a toast to Rob on his birthday.*

**tobacco** a plant, the leaves of which are dried and used in cigarettes, pipes and cigars.

**toboggan** a long flat sled for sliding down snowy hills.

**toilet** a lavatory, or the room in which the lavatory is.

**tomato** (plural **tomatoes**) a red juicy fruit eaten as a vegetable.

**tomb** (sounds like *room*) a place where dead bodies are buried, or a stone which marks where that is.

**ton** a measure of weight (2000 pounds).

**tonight** the night of this day.

**tonne** a metric measure of weight (1000 kilogrammes).

**top** 1 the highest point of something. 2 a spinning toy.

**torch** a portable light, often electric.

**tornado** a violent storm, usually with heavy rain.

**tortoise** a slow moving land animal, which has a hard shell.

**torture** very cruel treatment done to someone on purpose.

**toss** to throw into the air.

**total** 1 complete, all of something. 2 the answer when a series of numbers is added together. *The total of 7+6+3 is 16.*

**touch** to be close enough to feel something. *I reached out until I could just touch the wall.*

**tough** not easily cut, strong and rough. *You need tough boots for climbing.*

**tour** a journey on which you visit a number of places.

**tower** a kind of tall building, or the tall part of a building such as a church.

**trace** 1 to copy something by covering it with very thin paper and drawing around the outline that shows through. 2 a small sign or mark left by something.

**track** 1 a series of marks left by an animal or a vehicle. 2 a railroad line. 3 very strong, flat chains of steel which are used instead of wheels on tanks and some kinds of tractor. 4 to follow something by watching for the signs, or tracks, it has left behind.

**tractor** a strong motor vehicle used to pull farm machinery.

The African leopard **tortoise** (above) is a land reptile. The snapping turtle (below) is a meat-eater.

**trade** to buy and sell, or to exchange.

**trademark** a special mark or sign used to show who made something.

**trade union** an organized group of people who work in the same sort of job.

**traffic** vehicles like cars and trucks moving along roads. *The traffic is very heavy today because lots of people are driving out into the country.*

**tragedy** (plural **tragedies**) a very sad happening, or a play about one.

**trail** 1 a series of marks left to show the way to somewhere. 2 to pull something along behind you.

**trailer** a vehicle that is towed along behind another one.

**train** 1 a group of carriages or wagons joined together and pulled along a track by an engine. 2 to practise something. *The team trains three times a week.*

**traitor** someone who betrays his country or his friends.

**tramp** 1 to walk heavily. 2 a long walk, a hike. 3 a homeless person who wanders, or tramps, from place to place.

**trample** to tread heavily on something.

**transfer** to move from one job or place to another.

**transistor** 1 a very small electronic device that is used in radios and other electrical equipment. 2 a radio that uses transistors.

**translate** to change from one language into another. *Pam had to translate a poem from French into English.*

**transparent** something that is clear enough to see through.

**transplant** to move a plant from one bit of soil to another.

**transport** 1 to carry people or goods from one place to another. 2 the vehicles in which people or goods are carried.

**trap** a device for catching animals.

**trapeze** a bar hung on ropes far above the ground, and from which people swing.

**trapezoid** a four-sided figure with two sides parallel.

**trawler** a fishing boat that drags (or trawls) nets along the bottom of the sea to catch fish.

**tread** 1 to put your feet down on the ground. 2 the rubber and its raised pattern on the outside of a tire.

**treason** giving away important information to an enemy, especially in wartime.

This freezer **trawler** can quick-freeze hundreds of tons of fish while still at sea.

Engine room

Three different kinds of **triangle.**

**treasure** 1 a store of valuable things, such as gold and jewels. 2 to value something very highly. *Alan treasures a signed photo of his favorite rock star.*

**treat** 1 to behave towards someone in a certain way. *Caroline treats her baby brother very kindly.* 2 to put something right. *You can treat that stain with salt.* 3 something that gives you special pleasure. *My aunt took us to the play for a treat.*

**treaty** a written agreement between countries.

**tremble** to shake gently all over.

**trendy** following the latest fashions.

**trial** 1 an examination in a court of law. 2 a test of something to see how good it is. *We watched the trial of the new helicopter.*

**triangle** 1 a flat shape with three sides. 2 a musical instrument, like a triangle of metal, that is hit with a stick.

**tribe** a group of people who have the same customs and language.

**tributary** a small stream or river that flows into a larger one.

**tricycle** a three-wheeled cycle.

**trifle** 1 an unimportant thing. 2 a sweet pudding made from cake, custard, fruit and cream.

**trigger** the lever on a gun that is used to fire it.

**trim** 1 neat and tidy. 2 to cut something so as to make it neat and tidy. *The barber was asked to trim my hair.*

**trio** (say *tree-o*) three people working together, especially musicians.

**triple** made of three parts.

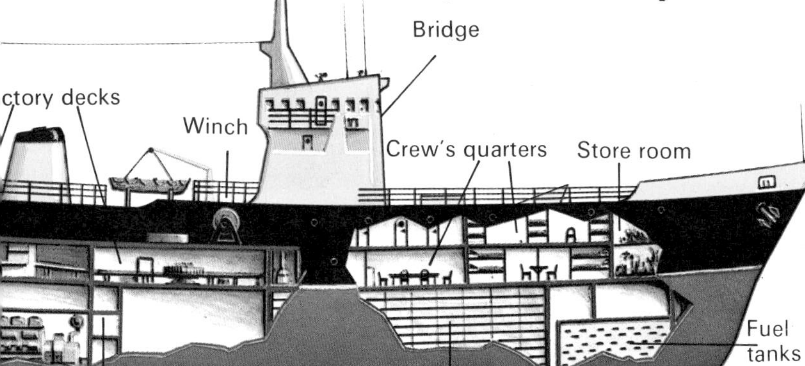

**triplet** one of three babies born to the same mother at the same time.

**trolley** a small hand cart.

**trombone** a musical wind instrument made of brass.

**tropics** the areas of land around the equator.

**trot** to run with short steps, like the slow run of a horse.

**truant** a child who stays away from school when he is supposed to be there.

**truck** a wheeled vehicle used to move heavy objects.

**trumpet** a musical wind instrument made of brass.

**trunk** 1 the main stem of a tree. 2 a large box. 3 the long nose of an elephant. 4 the back part of an automobile.

**trust** to believe that something or somebody is good, or will tell the truth.

**tuba** a large musical wind instrument that gives a low note.

**tube** a long, hollow cylinder.

**tuber** the large part of an underground stem, from which new plants grow. *A potato grows from a tuber.*

**tug** 1 to pull hard. 2 a small boat that tows larger ships in and out of ports.

**tumble** to fall down suddenly.

**tundra** the cold treeless plains in the northern parts of the world.

**tunic** a close-fitting jacket, often part of a uniform.

**tunnel** 1 an underground passage. 2 to dig under the ground.

**turbine** an engine with a driving wheel which is turned by water, steam or air.

**turkey** a large bird farmed for food.

**turn up** 1 to arrive, usually unexpectedly. *Emma turned up just before dinner.* 2 to increase something by using a control. *That knob on the radio turns up the sound.*

**turn down** to refuse an offer or an idea. *I wanted to turn down the job, but I needed the money so I agreed to do it.*

**turtle** a sea or land reptile with a hard shell.

**tusk** a long pointed tooth.

This early **typewriter** was made in 1876. It can write only capital letters.

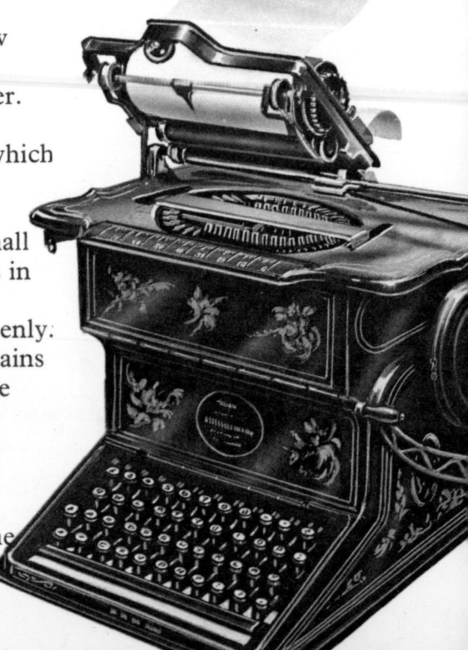

**twilight** the dim light between sunset and night time.
**twin** one of two children born to the same mother at the same time.
**twinkle** to send out little flashes of light.
**twist** to wind around, to turn and curve.
**type** 1 a kind, a sort. *Tulips are a type of flower.* 2 to use a typewriter. 3 the letters used to print words.
**typewriter** a machine that prints letters.
**typical** a good example of its kind.
**tyrant** a cruel, unfair ruler.

**udder** the bag-like part of a female animal from which milk comes.
**umpire** the person who sees that the rules are obeyed in certain games. *Important tennis matches have an umpire to referee them.*
**unanimous** when everyone agrees.
**unconscious** not conscious, not knowing what is happening around you.
**uncover** to take the cover off something, or to show it.
**underline** to draw a line under words on a page to make them stand out, like this: Danger!
**underpass** a place where one road passes under another one.
**unearth** to dig up or to discover something. *Granny managed to unearth some old family photos from her desk.*
**unemployed** without a paid job.
**unfortunate** unlucky.
**unicorn** a mythical animal in fairy stories, which looks like a horse but has a horn on its head.
**uniform** matching clothes worn by all the members of a group of people.
**union** joining together of a number of things or people.
**unique** (say *yoo-neek*) the only one of its kind.
**unit** a single thing, or a group of things that are thought of as being one thing. *A foot is a unit of length, made up of 12 inches.*
**unite** to join together.

**universal** general, common, done by most people. *Listening to the radio is a universal habit.*
**universe** everything that is known to exist, including the Earth, sun, stars and moon.
**university** a place where people can go on studying after they have finished high school.
**upholstery** the padding and covering of chairs and sofas.
**upper** above, in a higher place.
**upright** standing straight. *We put the pole upright in the sand.*
**uproar** a violent noise or disturbance.
**upset** 1 to knock something over. *Mark upset the milk.* 2 to make someone unhappy. *Jan was very upset by the bad news.*
**urban** to do with towns or cities. *A city is an urban area.*
**urgent** so important that it needs to be attended to at once.
**used** not new, secondhand.
**used to** 1 to know something well because it has often happened. *We are used to waiting a long time for the bus.* 2 something that belongs to the past. *Her parents used to live in Australia but then they moved to New York.*
**useful** helpful, valuable, something that works well. *A hammer is a very useful tool.*
**useless** not useful, no good to anyone. *A broken watch is useless.*
**usual** the way in which something happens, or is done, most of the time. *Adam wore his usual clothes to the party.*
**usually** in an ordinary or a normal way. *We usually go to school together.*
**utensil** a tool or instrument, especially one that is used in cooking. *An egg beater is a very handy utensil.*
**utter** 1 complete or total, especially something bad. *The room was an utter mess.* 2 to say something, to make a sound. *The kitten tried to utter a faint mew.*

# V v

**vacant** empty; not filled.
**vaccinate** (say *vak-sin-ate*) inoculate against a disease, usually measles.
**acuum** (say *va-kyoo-um*) an empty space; empty of air.
**vague** not clear.
**vain** 1 showing too much pride. 2 unsuccessful. *They searched for the dog in vain.*
**valley** a hollow between hills, often with a river flowing along it.

**valuable** of great value.
**value** the amount of money that something is worth.
**valve** something that allows a liquid or gas to flow in one direction and not in the other.
**vampire** a story creature that is supposed to suck people's blood.
**van** an enclosed wagon or truck.
**vandal** a person who stupidly destroys or damages things belonging to other people.
**vanish** to disappear suddenly.
**varnish** a kind of shiny, transparent liquid which is used like paint.
**vase** a glass, china or pottery container, often used to hold flowers.
**vast** very large in size. *The circus tent covered a vast area.*
**vat** a large container for holding liquids.
**vault** 1 to jump with your hands resting on something for support. *Denise tried to vault over the fence.* 2 an underground room, often used to store valuable things. 3 an arched roof.

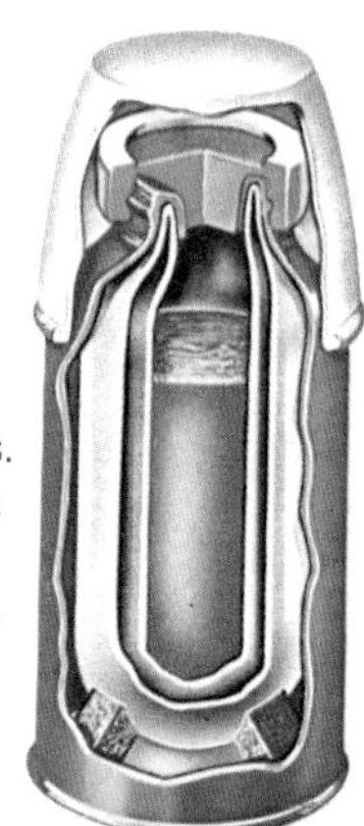

A **vacuum** flask has double walls. Between them is a vacuum to keep the heat in.

**vegetarian** a person who does not eat meat or fish. *Some vegetarians do not eat milk or eggs either.*
**vegetation** all the plants that grow in a certain place.
**vehicle** anything that is used to transport people or things from one place to another. *Trains, cars and carts are all vehicles.*
**vein** (sounds like *lane*) one of the small tubes that carry blood from your body back to your heart.
**venom** the poison of snakes and other poisonous animals.
**verb** a word for something that is done, or happens. *In "the cat ate the rat", the verb word is "ate".*
**verse** one section or part of a song or poem.
**versus** a Latin word that means "against". It is shortened to vs. in the results of sporting events, such as Harvard vs. Yale.
**vertebra** (plural **vertebrae**) the small bones in the backbone.
**vertebrate** any animal that has a backbone.
**vertical** straight up and down.
**vessel** 1 a container, especially one for liquids. 2 a large ship or boat.
**vet** short for veterinarian.
**veterinarian** a doctor for animals.
**viaduct** a long bridge that is built across a valley.

**vibrate** to move very quickly back and forth, to throb.
**vice** a very bad habit.
**vicious** (rhyme with *wish us*) fierce, bad, cruel.
**victim** someone who suffers harm or danger.
**victory** success, winning.
**videotape** a special kind of tape used to record the pictures and sound from films and television programs.
**villa** 1 a country house in Roman times. 2 a house.
**villain** a wicked or evil person.
**vine** a climbing plant.
**viola** a stringed musical instrument that looks like a large violin.
**violet** 1 a color, like a mixture of blue and purple. 2 a small plant with violet-colored or white flowers.
**violin** a wooden musical instrument with strings, played with a bow.
**viper** one of a group of poisonous snakes.
**virus** a tiny living particle that can carry and cause diseases.
**vise** a tool that holds things steady in one place, so they can be worked on.
**vital** 1 of great importance, essential. 2 lively, energetic.
**vitamin** a chemical in food that is important to growth and health.
**vixen** a female fox.
**vocabulary** all the words known or used in a certain language.
**volcano** (plural **volcanoes**) a mountain through which lava and gas blow up from deep under the ground.
**volume** 1 the amount of space within something, its capacity. 2 one of a set of books. *This encyclopedia has 12 different volumes.* 3 how loud a sound is. *Please turn up the volume on the television so that I can hear the program.*
**vomit** to be sick, to throw up food from your stomach through your mouth.
**vote** to show what you want from a group of choices by supporting one of them. *Our class was asked to vote for a leader.*
**vow** to make a solemn promise.
**vowel** the letters a, e, i, o, u and (sometimes) y are called vowels.

Three kinds of **volcano**. Hawaiian volcano (top); explosive volcano (center); and intermediate Vesuvian volcano (bottom).

**wage** the money you get for working; your salary.
**wagon** an open cart with wheels.
**wail** a cry, usually loud and shrill.
**waist** the narrow part of your body between your chest and your hips.
**wait** to stay in one place, expecting something to happen. *We will wait here until you come back.*
**waiter** a man who serves food in a restaurant.
**waitress** (plural **waitresses**) a woman who serves food in a restaurant.
**wake** 1 to stop sleeping. 2 the track left in water by a ship.
**wallet** a folding purse in which money or papers are kept.
**walrus** (plural **walruses**) a large sea animal with long tusks, which lives in the Arctic.
**wand** a slender stick used in stories by fairies and magicians.
**wander** to go from place to place without having a plan or a purpose.
**war** a very serious fight between the armies of two or more countries or groups of people.
**ward** a room in a hospital where sick people stay until they are well again.
**wardrobe** a closet where clothes are hung and stored.
**warehouse** a large building where goods of all sorts are kept.
**warn** to tell people about danger.
**warning** something that tells you about danger. *There was a warning light by the bridge, so we stopped the car.*
**warp** 1 to become twisted or bent. 2 the vertical threads on a loom, used for weaving.
**warren** a place where there is a group of rabbits living together in burrows.
**warrior** a fighter.
**washer** a small flat ring used to make a joint tight, such as on a faucet.
**wasp** a flying insect with a striped body and a stinger in its tail.
**waste** to use more than you need of something, or to throw something away although you could have used it.
**waterfall** a rush of water which falls from a high place in a river or stream.
**waterproof** a material that does not let water through it.
**watt** a unit of electric power.

**wax** a soft, yellowish material made by bees, or from oil.
**weak** fragile, easy to break, not strong.
**wealth** a great amount of money or property.
**wealthy** rich.
**wean** to change a baby animal from drinking its mother's milk to eating solid foods.
**wear** 1 to be dressed in, to have on your body. *Penny wanted to wear her new dress and her pearl necklace to the party.* 2 to become less good through being used. *The car tires have begun to wear out.*
**weary** tired.
**weave** to make cloth on a loom with a pattern of threads.
**web** a loose net of threads. *A spider makes a web with threads from its body.*
**webfoot** a foot, like the ones on ducks and frogs, which have skin joining the toes together.
**weed** a wild plant that grows where it is not wanted, such as a flower bed.
**weep** to cry with tears coming from your eyes.
**weft** the horizontal threads on a loom, used for weaving.
**weird** strange, peculiar, odd.
**welcome** to do or say things which show you are pleased when someone arrives.
**welfare** people's health and happiness.
**well** 1 healthy. 2 to do something in a good or successful way. *Emma swims very well.* 3 a deep hole for underground water.
**west** one of the points on a compass; the direction in which the sun sets.
**whale** a very large mammal that looks like a fish.
**wharf** a place where ships are loaded and unloaded.
**wheat** the grain from which most flour is made.
**whip** 1 a long rope or strip of leather joined to a handle, and used to hit animals. 2 to beat cream or other liquids very hard until they are thick.
**whirl** to turn around fast in circles.
**whirlpool** a place in a river or ocean where the water spins around.
**whirlwind** a fierce wind that blows in circles.
**whisker** a hair that grows on your face.
**whistle** 1 to make a shrill sound by blowing through your tightened lips. 2 an instrument for blowing through to make a shrill sound.
**whole** (sounds like *hole*) all of something, a complete thing.

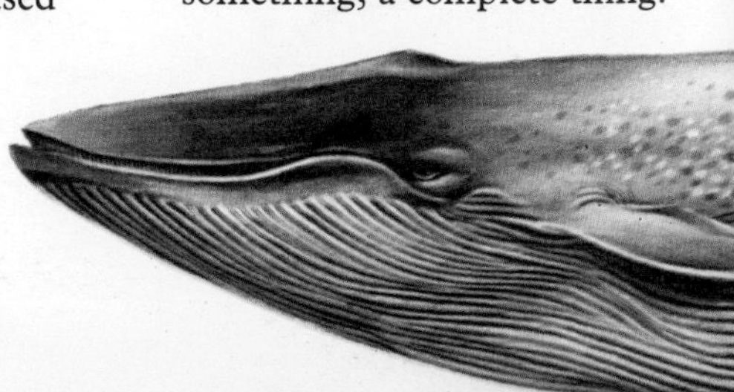

The blue **whale** is probably the largest animal that has ever lived.

**wholesale** selling things in large quantities, usually to be sold again.
**whooping cough** an illness that makes you cough in a strange way.
**wick** the thread or material put into a candle or a lamp which is lit with a flame.
**wicked** very bad, evil.
**widow** a woman whose husband is dead.
**widower** a man whose wife is dead.
**width** how wide something is, the distance from one side to the other.
**wig** false hair to cover a bald head, or to cover your own hair with different hair.
**wigwam** a tent used by North American Indians, made of a frame covered with cloth or skin.
**wild** not tame, living in a natural way.
**willing** ready to do what is wanted or needed
**wilt** to droop like a plant without water, to be limp.
**wind** (sounds like *kind*) 1 to turn the handle of a clock so that it will work. 2 to wrap thread or wool around something.
**wind instrument** a musical instrument that is played by blowing into it.
**windshield** the front window of a car.
**wine** an alcoholic drink, usually made from grapes.
**wing** 1 the part of a bird or insect used for flying. 2 the main part of an aircraft.
**wipe out** to destroy completely. *A bad earthquake can wipe out a whole village.*
**wire** a long thread of metal that can be bent and twisted.
**wisdom** knowledge and understanding.
**wise** able to understand many things.
**witch** (plural **witches**) a woman in stories who uses magic to make things happen.
**witchcraft** the magic skills of a witch.
**withdraw** to pull back from something, or to take back. *Sally is going to withdraw from the match.*
**witness** a person who sees something happen.
**wizard** a man in stories who uses magic to make things happen.
**wolf** (plural **wolves**) a wild animal of the dog family.
**woman** a grown up female human.
**wonder** to ask yourself something, to feel surprised.
**wonderful** a happening that is so good that it surprises you.

**wood** 1 a lot of trees growing together in one place, a small forest. 2 the trunk and branches of trees cut up and used to make things, timber.
**wooden** made of wood.
**woodwork** making things out of wood.
**wool** 1 the hair of sheep and goats. 2 long fibers which are spun from the hair of sheep and goats.
**woolen** made from wool.
**worker** a person who works for their living.
**workshop** a place where things are made or mended.
**world** the Earth and everything on it.
**worm** a long, thin animal that moves by wriggling its body along. *Earthworms live in the soil.*
**worn** showing signs of having been used.
**worry** to be upset or anxious about something or someone.
**worse** not as good as.
**worship** to praise God, to do with religion.
**worst** the least good.
**worth** the value of something.
**worthless** something that has no value.
**wound** an injury or a cut.
**woven** something that is made by weaving.
**wrap** to cover something completely, to make a package.
**wreath** an arrangement of flowers or leaves tied together in a circle.
**wreck** 1 to damage something so badly that it cannot be used again. 2 a ship or building that has been badly damaged.
**wrestle** to fight using your body as a weapon.
**wretched** very miserable or sad.
**wriggle** to twist and turn your body around.
**wrist** the joint between your arm and your hand.
**written** something that has been put down in words on paper.

**X ray** a special kind of photograph taken outside your body which shows the bones inside.
**xylophone** (say *zeye-lo-fone*) a musical instrument made of wooden or metal bars which are played with a stick.

Yaks are among the largest of wild cattle, but they climb as nimbly as goats.

# Yy

**yacht** a light sailing boat.
**yak** a long-haired animal of the cattle family, that comes from Asia.
**yap** a short shrill bark, like the sound small dogs make.
**yard** 1 a measurement of length (36 inches). 2 an open space.
**yarn** 1 fibers of wool used in knitting and sewing. 2 a story, a tale.
**yawn** to open your mouth wide when you are bored or sleepy.
**yearly** every year, once a year.
**yeast** a substance used to make bread and beer rise.

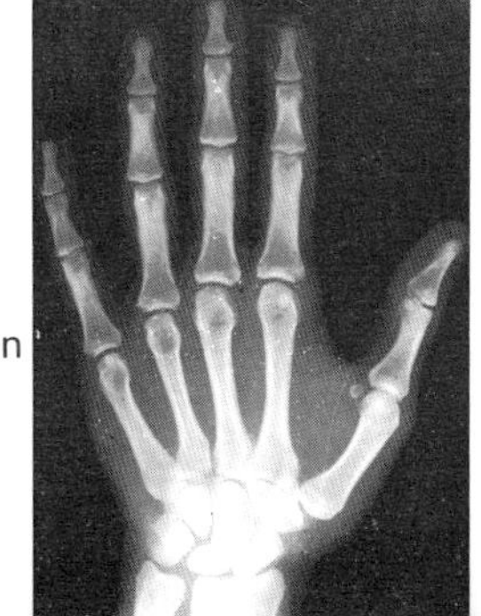

An **X ray** of a human hand.

**yell** to shout loudly.
**Yiddish** the international language used by Jewish people.
**yield** 1 to give in, or give up. 2 the amount of grain or fruit on a plant or within an area of a farm. *We got a good yield of plums from that tree.*
**yogurt** a liquid food made from soured milk.
**yolk** the yellow part of an egg.
**young** 1 not old; recently started. 2 the offspring of an animal.
**youth** 1 the time when one is young. 2 a young man.

# Zz

**zebra** an African animal like a horse. It has dark stripes on a light body.
**zero** nothing; the figure 0.
**zigzag** going one way and then another, like the letter Z.
**zinc** a hard bluish-white metal.
**zipper** a fastener with two sets of teeth that lock together.
**zone** part of a town or larger area that is special in some way.
**zoology** the study of animals.

# SPELLING LIST

*If you are not sure how to spell a word, look it up in this alphabetical list. Words marked with an asterisk, like this,* nothing*, *are not in the main part of your dictionary.*

**A**
abacus
abandon
abbey
abbreviation
able*
aboard
aborigines
about*
above*
abroad
absent
absorb
accelerate
accept
accident
accurate
ache
acid
acorn
acre
acrobat
across*
act
active
actor
actress
add
address
adjective
admire
admission
adopt
advance
adventure
adverb
advertise
advertisement
advice
advise
aerial
affect
afford
after*
afternoon*
afterwards
again*
against*
age
ago*
agree
agriculture
ahead
aid
aim
air
aircraft
air force*
airline
airplane
airport
airtight
alarm
alike
alive
all*
Allah
alligator
allow
alloy
all right*
ally
almost*
alone
aloud
alphabet
already*
altar
alter
although*
altitude
aluminum
always*
a.m.
ambassador
ambulance
ambush
ammunition
among*
amongst*
amount
amphibian
amplifier
anesthetic
anchor
ancestor
ancient
angel
anger*
angle
angry*
animal
ankle
anniversary
annual
another*
answer*
ant
antelope
antenna
antibiotic
antique
antler
any*
anyhow*
anyone*
anything*
anywhere*
apart
ape
apostle
apostrophe
appear
appointment
apricot
April*
apron
aquarium
aqueduct
arc
arch
archer
archery
architect
architecture
area
argue
arithmetic
arm
armor
army
around*
arrange
arrive
arrow
art
artery
artificial
artist
ash
aside*
ask*
asleep*
aspirin
ass
association
astronaut
astronomy
ate*
athlete
atlas
atmosphere
atom
attach
attack
attempt
attend
attic

attract
audience
August*
aunt
author
autobiography
autograph
automatic
autumn
avalanche
avenue
average
awake
away*
awful*
ax
axle

**B**

baboon
baby*
back
backbone
background
backward
backwards
bacon
bad*
badge
badger
bag*
bagpipes
bait
bake
baker
bakery
balance
bald
ball*
ballad
ballerina
ballet
balloon
banana*
band
bandage
bandit
bang*
bannisters
bank
banquet
bar
barber
bare
barge
bark
barn
barometer
barracks
barrel
base
baseball*
basement
basket*
basketball*
bassoon
bat
batch
bath*
bathe
bathroom*
baton
batter
battery
battle
bay
B.C.
beach
bead
beak
beam
bean*
bear*
beard
beast
beat
beautiful*
beauty*
beaver
became
because*
become
bed
bedroom*
bedtime*
bee
beef
beetle
before*
beg
began*
beggar
begin*
behave
behind*
believe
bell*
belong*
below*
belt*
bench*
bend
beneath*
bent
berry
berth
beside*
besides
best*
better*
between*
beware
beyond
bib*
Bible*
bicycle
big*
bill
billion
binary
binoculars
biography
biology
biplane
bird*
birth
birthday*
biscuit*
bison
bit
bitch
bite*
bitter
black*
blackboard*
blackmail
blacksmith
bladder
blade
blame
blank
blanket*
blaze
bleach
bleat
bleed*
bless
blessing*
blew
blind
blister
blizzard
block
blood
blossom
blow
blue*
blunder
blunt
blush
boar
board
boast
boat*
boil
bold
bolt
bomb
bone*
bonfire
bonnet*
boomerang
boot
border
borrow
boss*
both
bottle*
bottom*
bought*
bounce
boundary
bout*
bow
bowels
bowl
box*
boxer*
boy*
bracelet
braille
brain
brake
branch
brass
brave
bread*
break*
breakfast*
breast
breath*
breathe
breed
breeze
brick*
bride
bridegroom
bridesmaid
bridge*

bridle
bright
brilliant
brim
bring*
broad
broadcast
broke*
broken*
bronze
Bronze Age
brooch
broom
brother*
brought*
brown*
brownie
bruise
brush*
bubble
buck
bucket*
buckle
bud
budgerigar*
buffalo
bug
build
building
building site
built
bulb
bull
bulldozer
bullet
bully
bulrush
bumblebee
bump*
bun*
bunch
bundle
bungalow
bunk
buoy
burglar
buried
burn*
burrow
burst
bury
bus*
bush
business
busy
but*
butcher
butt
butter*
butterfly
button*
buttonhole*
buy*
by*

**C**

cabbage
cabin
cactus
cafe
cage
cake*
calculator
calendar
calf
call*
calm
came*
camel
camera
camouflage
camp
campfire*
can
canal
candle
candlestick
cane*
cannon
cannot*
canoe
canter
canvas
canvass
cap*
cape
capital
captain
caption
captive
capture
car*
caravan
card*
cardboard
cardigan
care
careful*
careless
carelessness*
cargo
carnival
carnivore
carpenter*
carpet*
carriage
carrot*
carry*
cart
cartoon
cartridge
carve
case
cash
cashier
cassette
castanets*
castle
cat
catalog
catamaran
catapult
catch*
caterpillar
cathedral
cattle
caught*
cause
cavalry
cave
caveman
cease
ceiling
cell
cellar
cello
cement
cemetery
census
cent
centaur
centennial
centigrade
centimeter
centipede
central
center
century
cereal
ceremony
certain
certificate
chain
chair*
chalk
champion
championship
chance
change
channel
chapel
chapter
character
charge
chariot
charity
charm
charming
chart
chase
chatter*
cheap*
cheat
check
checked*
cheek
cheer
cheerful
cheese*
chef
chemical
chemist
chemistry
cherry*
chess
chest
chew
chicken
chicken pox
chief
child*
children*
chimney*
chimpanzee
chin*
china
chip
chips
chocolate
choice
choir
choke
choose*
chop
chorus
chose*
christen
Christian
Christianity

Christmas*
chrysalis
church
cigar
cigarette
cine-camera
cinema
circle
circumference
circus*
citizen
city
civilian
civilization
civilized
claim
clap*
clarinet
class
classroom*
claw
clay
clean*
clear
clerk
clever*
cliff
climate
climb*
clinic
cloak
cloakroom
clock*
clockwise
clockwork
close*
closed*
cloth*
clothes*
clothing*
cloud*
clown
club
clue
clumsy*
coach
coal
coarse
coast
coat*
cobbler
cobweb
cock
cocoa
cocoon
code
coffee
coffin
cog
coil
coin
cold*
collage
collar
collect
college
collide
colony
color*
colt
column
comb*
combine
come*
comedy
comet
comfort
comfortable*
comic
comma
command
committee
common
communicate
communication
community
commuter
company
companion
compare
compass
compasses
compete
competition
complain
complete
complicated
compose
composed
composer
compound
computer
concave
concert
concrete
condense
conductor
cone
congratulate
conifer
conjuror
connect
conquer
conservation
conserve
consider
consonant
constable
constant
constellation
construct
contain
container
contented
contents
continent
continue
control
convenient
convent
convex
conversation
convict
convoy
cook*
cool*
cooperate
copper
copy
coral
core
cork
corkscrew
corm
corn
cornflakes*
corner*
coronation
correct
corridor
cosmonaut
cost
costume
cot*
cottage
cotton
couch
cough*
count*
counter
country
county
couple
courage
course
court
cousin
cover
covering
cow
coward
cowboy
crab
crack*
cradle
craft
craftsman
crane
crate
crater
crawl*
crayon*
crazy*
cream*
create
creator
creature
creep
crêpe paper
crept
crescent
crew
cricket
cried*
crime
criminal
crimson
cripple
crisp
crocodile
crook
crooked
crop
cross*
crossing
crossroad
crow
crowd
crown
cruel
crumb
crumble
crush
crust
crutch
cry*
crystal
cub
cube
cucumber*

cuff
cultivate
cunning
cup*
cupboard*
cure
curious
curly
currant
currency
current
curry
curtain*
curve
cushion*
custard*
custom
customer
cut*
cutlery
cygnet
cylinder
cymbals

**D**
dagger
daily
dairy
daisy*
dam
damage
damp*
dance*
danger
dare
dark*
darling*
darn
dart
date
daughter*
dawn
day*
dead*
deaf
deal
dear*
death
debate
debt
decade
decay
deceive
December*
decide
deciduous
decimal
deck
declare
decorate
decrease
deed
deep
deer
defeat
defend
defense
definite
degree
dehydrate
delay
delicate
delicious
delight*
deliver
delta
demand
democracy
den
denied
dense
dentist*
deny
depart*
depend
depth
descend
describe
desert
deserve
design
desire*
desk*
despair
dessert
destroy
detail
detect
detective
detergent
determined
develop
device*
devil
dew
diagonal
diagram
dial
diameter
diamond
diary
dice
dictionary
did*
didn't*
die*
diesel
diet
difference*
different*
difficult*
dig*
digest
digestion*
dike
dim
dinghy
dinner*
dinosaur
dip
direct
direction
dirt*
dirty*
disagree
disappear
disappoin
disaster
disciple
discover
discuss
disease
disguise
dish*
disinfect
disk
dislike*
dismiss
dismount*
disobedient
display
dissolve
distance
distant
district
disturb
ditch
dive
diver
divide
do
dock
doctor*
doe
dog*
doll*
dolphin
dome
domestic
domesticated
done*
donkey
door*
dot*
double
doubt
dough
down
downstairs*
downward
doze*
dozen
draft
drag
dragon
dragonfly
drain
drake
drank
draughts
draw
drawbridge
drawer*
drawing*
dream*
dress
dresser
drew*
drift
drill
drink*
drip
drive*
driver*
dromedary
drop*
drove*
drought
drown
drug
drum
dry*
duck
dug*
dugout*
duke
dull
dumb
dune
dungeon

during
dusk
dust*
dustbin*
duty
dwarf
dwell
dye
dyke
dynamite

E
each*
ear*
early*
earn
earth
earthen*
earthquake
earthworm*
easel
east
Easter*
easy*
eat*
ebb
echo
eclipse
ecology
edge
educate
effect*
effort
egg
either*
elastic
elbow
elder
eldest
election
electric
electricity
electronics
element
elephant
elf
else*
elsewhere*
embroidery
embryo
emerald
emergency
emigrate
emperor
empire
employ
empty*
enamel
enchant
encourage
encyclopedia
end*
enemy*
energy
engine
engineer
enjoy
enormous
enough*
enter
entertain
entire
entrance
envelope
environment
envy
equal
Equator
equinox
equipment
era*
erase
errand
error
escalator
escape
especially
estimate
estuary
etcetera
eternal
eternity
evaporate
eve*
even*
evening
event
eventually
ever*
evergreen
every*
everybody*
everyone*
everything*
everywhere*
evil
evolution
ewe
exact
exaggerate
exam
examination
examine
example
excavate
excellent
except*
exciting*
exercise
exhaust
exhibit
exhibition
exist
exit
expect
expedition
expensive
experience
experiment
expert
explain
explode
explore
explorer
explosion
explosive
export
exports
extinct
extra
extraordinary
extreme
eye*
eyebrow*
eyelash*
eyelid*
eye-opener
eyesight

F
fable
fabric
face*
fact
factor*
factory
fade
Fahrenheit
fail
faint
fair
fairy
faith
fake
fall*
false
familiar
family*
famine
famous*
fan
fang
far*
fare
farm
farmer
farmyard*
fashion
fast
farther
farthest
fasten
fastener*
fat*
father*
fault
favor
favorite
fawn
fear
feast
feather
feature
February*
fed*
feed*
feel*
feeler
feeling
feet
fell*
felt
female
fence
fern
ferret
ferry
fertile
fertilize
festival
fetch*
fête
fever
few*
fiber
fiction
field*
field glasses*
fierce

fight*
figure
file
fill*
film
fin
final
finally
find*
fine
finger*
fingerprint
finish*
fir
fire
fire engine*
fireman
fire place
firework
firm
first*
fish*
fisherman
fist
fit
fix
flag
flake
flame
flap
flash
flat
flatter
flavor
flea
fledgling
flee
fleece
fleet
flesh
flew*
flight
flipper

float
flock
flood
floor
flour
flow
flower
flu
fluid
flute
fly*
foal
foam
foe
fog
fold
foliage
folk
follow*
food*
foolish
foot*
football*
footprint
for*
force
ford
forecast
forehead
foreign
foreigner
forest
forgave
forgery
forget*
forgive
forgot*
fork
form
fort
fortify
fortunate
fortune

forward*
forwards*
fossil
foster mother
fought*
found*
foundations
foundry
fountain*
fowl
fox
fraction
fracture
fragment
fragrant
frame
frank
free
freedom
freeze
freight
freighter
frequent
fresh*
friction
fridge
Friday*
friend*
friendship
fright
frighten
frog
from*
front*
frontier
frost
frown
froze
fruit
fry*
frying pan*
fuel
full*
fun*

funeral
function
fungus
funnel
funny*
fur
furniture
furrow
furry*
further*
future

**G**

gadget
gag
gain
galaxy
gale
galleon
gallery
gallon
gallop
game
gander
gang
gangster
gap
garage
garbage
garden*
gargle
garment
gas
gasoline
gasp
gate*
gather
gauge
gave*
gay
gaze
gear

geese
gem
general
generate
generation
generator
generous
genius
gentle
gentleman*
genuine
geography
geology
geometry
germ
germinate
gesture
get*
ghost
giant
gift
gigantic
giggle
gill
gipsy
giraffe
girl*
give*
glacier
glad*
glass*
glasses
glaze
glide
glider
glitter
globe
glossary
glove*
glue
gnaw
gnome
goal
goat

goblin
god
goggles
gold
goldfish*
gone*
good*
goods
goose
gorilla
gosling
gossip
got*
govern
government
gown
grab
graceful
gradual
graft
grain
gram
granary
grand
grandchild*
grandfather*
grandmother*
grandparent*
grandstand
grape
graph
grasp
grasshopper
grateful
grave
gravel
graveyard
gravity
gravy
gray
graze
grease
great*
greedy
green
greenhouse
greet
grew
grief
grin
grind
grip
groan
grocer
groom
groove
ground
group
grown-up
growl
grub
grumble
grunt
guarantee
guard
guerrilla
guest
guide
guilty
guitar
gulf
gull
gum
gunpowder
guts
gutter
guy
gym
gymkhana
gymnasium
gymnast
gymnastics

**H**

habit
hail
hair*
hairdresser
half*
hall
Halloween*
halo
halt
halve
ham
hamburger
hammer
hamster
hand
handcuffs
handicap
handkerchief*
handle
handlebar*
handsome
hang
hangar
happen
happening
happiness*
happy*
harbor
hard*
hardly
hardy
hare
harm
harness
harp
harpoon
harvest
haste
hatch
hate*
haul
haunt
hawk
hay
haystack
hazel
head*
headache*
headdress*
headlight
headline
headquarters
heal
health
healthy
heap
hear*
heard*
heart
heat
heaven
heavy*
hectare
hedge
hedgehog
heel
heifer
height
heir
held*
helicopter
hell
helmet
help*
helpless
hem
hemisphere
hen
herb
herd
hermit
hero
heroine
heron
hesitate
hexagon
hibernate
hiccup*
hid*
hide
hieroglyphics
high*
highway
highwayman
hijack
hinge
hint
hip
hippopotamus
hire
historic
history
hit*
hive
hoarse
hobby
hockey
hoe
hold
hole*
hollow
homesick
homework
honest
honey
honeycomb
honeymoon
hood
hoof
hook
hop
hope*
hopeful
hopeless
horizon
horizontal
horn
horse*
horsepower
hose
hospital
host
hostage
hostel*
hostess

hotel
hour*
houseboat
household
housekeeper
housewife
housework
hovel
hover
hovercraft
howl
hug*
hull
hum*
human
humor
hump
hundred*
hung*
hunger
hungry*
hunt
hunter
hurrah*
hurricane
hurried*
hurry*
hurt*
husband*
hut*
hutch
hydroelectric
hydrofoil
hydrogen
hymn
hyphen
hypnosis
hypodermic
hysterical

**I**
ice
iceberg
ice cream*
icicle
icing
idea
ideal
identical
idiot
igloo
ignorant
ignore
ill*
illegal
illustrate
illustration
imaginery
imagine
imitate
immediately
immigrate
immigrant
immunize
imp
impatient
implement
import
important*
impossible
improve
incense
inch*
include*
income
increase
incredible
incubate
indeed
independent
index
Indian
indigestion
individual
indoors*
industry
industrial
infant
infection
infinity
inflate
influenza
information
inhabit
inhabitant
inherit
initial
injection
injure
ink*
inland
inn
innings*
innocent
inquire
inquisitive
insect
insecticide
inside*
inspect
instant
instantly
instead*
instinct
instrument
insult
intelligent
interested
interesting*
interfere
international
interpret
interrupt
intestine
introduce
introduction
invade
invalid
invent
invention
inventor
invertebrate
invisible
invitation
invite
iris
iron
ironmonger
irrigate
Islam
island
isolate
isthmus
italics
itch*
item
ivory

**J**
jack
jacket*
jail
jam
January*
jar*
jaw
jealous
jeans*
jelly*
jellyfish
jersey
jet
jewel
jeweler
jewelry
job*
jockey
jog
join
joint
joke*
jolly*
journalist
journey
joy
judge
jug*
juggler
juice
July*
jump*
June*
jungle
junior
junk
jury
just*
juvenile

**K**
kaleidoscope
kangaroo
kayak
keel
keen
keep
kennel
kept
kerb
kernel
kerosene
ketchup
kettle*
key
kick*
kid
kidnap
kidney
kill*
kiln
kilogram
kilometer
kilt
kimono
kind*
king*
kingdom
kiss*
kitchen*
kite
kitten*

kiwi
knead
knee*
kneel
knife*
knight
knit*
knitting*
knob
knock*
knot*
know*
knowledge
knuckle
koala
Koran
kosher

**L**

label
laboratory
labor
lace
lacrosse
lad*
ladder
ladies*
ladle
lady*
lagoon
lair
lake
lamb
lame
lamp*
land
landmark
landscape
language
lantern
lap
larder
large*
larva
larvae
laser
lash
lasso
last*
late*
lathe
lather
latitude
laugh*
laughter
launch
laundromat
laundry
lava
lavatory
law
lawn
lay
lay off
layer
lazy
lead
leader
leaf
league
leak
lean
leap
leaped
learn*
least
leather
leave*
leaves
led
ledge
left*
leg*
legal
legend
legendary
leisure
lemon*
lemonade*
lend
length
lens
Lent
lent
leopard
leotard
leprechaun
less
lesson*
let
letter*
lettuce*
level
level crossing
lever
liable
liar
liberty
librarian
library
lice
license
lichen
lick*
lie
life
lifeboat
lift
light*
lighthouse
lightning
like*
likely
limb
limerick
limit
limp
line
linen
liner
lining
link
lion
lioness
lioness
lip*
lipstick
liquid
lisp
list
listen*
lit*
liter
litter
little*
live
lively*
liver
livestock
living
lizard
load
loaf*
loan
loaves*
lobster
local
loch
lock
locker
locket
locomotive
lodge
loft
log
lonely
long*
longitude
look*
looking glass
loom
loop
loose*
lord
lose*
lost*
loud*
loudspeaker
lounge
louse
love*
lovely*
low*
lower
loyal
lubricate
luck*
lucky*
luggage
lullaby
lumber
lump
lunar
lung
lurk
luxury

**M**

macaroni
machine
machine gun
machinery
mackintosh
mad*
made*
magazine
magician
magnet
magnetic
magnify
maid
mail
main
majority
make*
make up
male
mammal
mammoth
man

manage
manager
mane
manger
man hole★
mankind
man-made
manner
manners★
manor
mansion
manufacture
many★
map
marble
March★
march
mare
margarine
margin
marine
marionette
mark
market★
marmalade
marriage
marry
marsh
marsupial
mascot
mask
mass
massive
mast
master
mat
match★
mate
material
mathematics
maths
matter
mattress★
mauve
maximum
May★
may★
mayonnaise
mayor
maze
meadow★
meal★
mean
meaning
meant
meantime
meanwhile
measles
measure
meat★
mechanic
mechanical
medal
medicine
medium
meet★
meeting
melt
member
memory
men
mend★
menu
merchant
mercury
mermaid
merry
mess
message
messenger
met★
metal
meteor
meteorite
meter
method
metric
microbe
microphone
microscope
middle★
midget
midnight
might★
mighty
migrate
mild
mile
military
milk★
milkman★
mill
miller★
million
millionaire
milligram
millimeter
mime
mimic
minaret
mince
mincemeat
mind
mine
miner
mineral
minimum
minister
mint
minus
minute
miracle
mirage★
mirror
mischief
miser
miserable
Miss
miss
missile
mission
missionary
mist
mistake★
mister
mitten
mix★
mixer
mixture
moat
model
modern
moist
mold
mole
mollusk
molt
moment★
monarch
monastery
Monday★
money★
mongrel
monk
monkey
monorail
monster
month
mood
moon★
moonlight
moor
moped
more★
morning★
Morse code
mortar
mosaic
Moslem
mosque
mosquito
moss
most★
motel
moth
motor
motorway
mount
mountain
mountaineer
mourning
mouse
moustache
mouth
mouth organ
move★
movement
mow
Mr.
Mrs.
Ms
much★
mud★
muddle
mule
multiply
mummy
mumps
mural
murder
muscle
museum
mushroom
music
musician
Muslim
mutter★
mystery
myth

**N**

nail
naked
name★
nap
napkin
nappy
narrow
nasty★

nation
national
nationality
native
natural
nature
naughty*
navigate
navy
nearby*
nearly*
neat
necessary
neck*
necklace
nectar
need*
needle
neglect
neighbor
neighborhood
neither
neon
nephew
nerve
nervous
nest*
nestling
net
netball*
never*
new*
news*
newspaper*
newt
next*
nickname
niece
night*
nightmare
nip
nit
noble
nobleman
nobody*
nod
noise*
noisy
nomad
none*
nonsense
noon
no one*
noose
nor*
normal
north
nose*
nostril
note
nothing*
notice
nought
noun
novel
November*
now*
nowadays
nowhere
nuclear
nucleus
nude
nuisance
numb
number
nun
nurse
nut
nylon

**O**

oak
oar
oasis
oat
obedient
obey
object
oblong
oboe
observe
obstinate
obvious
occupation
occupy
ocean
o'clock*
octagon
October*
octopus
odd
offer
office
officer
often*
offspring
ogre
oil
ointment
old*
old-fashioned
once*
onion*
only*
open*
opening
opera
operate
operation
opinion
opportunity
opposite
optician
orange
orbit
orchard
orchestra
order
ordinary*
ore
organ
organization
organize
original
ornament
orphan
ostrich
other*
otherwise
ought*
ounce
out*
outdoors*
outgrew
outgrow
outing
outlaw
outline
outside*
outskirts
outward*
oval
oven
over*
overalls
overcoat
overflow
overhang
overhaul
overhead
overhear
overlap
overtake
overtime
owe
owl
own
owner
ox
oxen
oxygen

**P**

pack
package
packet
pad
paddle
page*
paid*
pain*
paint*
painting
pair
palace
pale
palm
pan*
pancake
panda
pane
pant
pantomime
pants
paper*
papier-maché
papyrus
parable
parachute
parade
paraffin
paragraph
parallel
paralysed
parasite
parcel*
pardon
parent
park*
parliament
parrot
part*
particle
particular
particularly
partly*
partner
party
pass
passage

passenger
Passover
passport
password
past
paste
pasteurize
pastime
pastry
pat*
patch
patchwork
path*
patience
patient
patrol
pattern
pause
pavement
pay*
pea*
peace
peach*
peacock
peak
peanut
pear
pearl
peasant
pebble
peck
peculiar
pedal
pedestrian
pedigree
peek*
peel*
peer
pen
pence*
pencil*
pendant
pendulum
pen pal
penguin
peninsula
penknife
penny*
pension
pentagon
people
pepper
percent
perch
percussion
perennial
perfect
perform
performance
perfume
perhaps*
perimeter
period
periscope
permanent
permission*
permit
perpetual
person
persuade
pest
pet*
petal
petrol*
pew
pharaoh
phase
philosophy
phone
photograph
photostat
phrase
physical
physics
piano*
piccolo
pick*
picnic*
picture*
pie*
pier
piece*
pig*
pigeon
piglet
pigsty
pile
pilgrim
pill
pillar*
pillow*
pilot
pimple
pinch
pine
pineapple
ping-pong*
pink*
pint*
pioneer
pip
pipe*
pirate
pistil
pistol
pit
pitch
pitchfork
pity
pizza*
place*
plague
plain
plait
plan
plane
planet
plank
plankton
plant*
plastic
plate*
plateau
platform
play
player*
playground*
please*
pleasant*
pleasure
plenty*
plot
plow
plug
plum*
plumber
plunge
plural
plus
p.m.
pneumatic
pneumonia
pocket*
pod
poem
poet
poetry
point*
poison
polar
pole
police
policeman*
policewoman*
polish
polite
pollen
pollute
polythene
pond*
pony
pool
poor*
pope
popular
population
porcelain
porch
porcupine
pore
pork
porpoise
porridge
port
porter
porthole
portrait
position
possess
possible*
post*
post office*
poster
postman*
pot*
potato*
potter
pottery
poultry
pound
pour*
poverty
powder
power
powerful
practical
practice
practise
prairie
praise
pray
prayer
precious
predator
predict
preface
prefer
pregnant
prehistoric

prepare
prescription
present
presently*
preserve
president
press
pressure
pretend*
pretty*
prevent
prey
price*
priceless
prick
prickle
pride
priest
primary
prince
princess
principal
principle
print
prison
prisoner
private
prize
probably
problem
process
procession
produce
producer
product
profit
program
progress
project
promise
pronoun
pronounce
proof
propel
propeller
proper
property
prophet
protect
protein
protest
Protestant
proud
prove
proverb
provide
province
prowl
prune
psychology
pterodactyl
public
publish
pudding*
puddle*
pull*
pulley
pulpit
pulse
pump
pumpkin
punch
punctual
punctuation
puncture
punish
pupa
pupae
pupil
puppet
puppy*
purchase
pure
purple
purr*
purse*
pursue
push

**Q**

quack*
quadruped
quadruplet
quality
quantity
quarantine
quarrel
quarry
quart
quarter
quartet
quay
queen
queer
question
question mark
queue
quick*
quiet*
quilt
quintuplet
quite*
quiz
quote

**R**

rabbi
rabbit*
race
racket
radar
radiate
radiator
radio
radius
raft
rafter
rag*
rage
raid
rail
railroad
rain*
rainbow
rainfall
raise
raisin
rake
ram
ran*
ranch
rang*
rank
ransom
rap
rapid
rare
rash
raspberry*
rat*
rather*
rattle*
raw*
ray
razor
reach*
read*
ready*
real*
realize
really*
rear
reason
rebel
recall
receive
recent
recipe
recite
recognize
record
recorder
record player
recover
rectangle
red*
reduce
reed
reef
referee
reference
reflect
reflection
refresh
refrigerator
refuse
region
regret
regular
rehearse
rehearsal
reign
reindeer
reins
reject
relative
relax
relay race
relief map
religion
remain
remainder
remember*
remind
remote
remove
rent
repair
repeat
replace
reply*
report
represent
reproduce
reptile
republic
require
rescue
resemble
reserve
reservoir

resident
resign
resources
responsible
rest*
restaurant
restore
result
retail
retire
retreat
return*
revenge
reverse
revolution
revolver
reward
rhinoceros
rhyme
rhythm
rib
rice
rid
rich*
riddle
ride*
rider*
ridge
ridiculous
rifle
right*
rim
rind
ring*
rink
rinse
rip
ripe*
ripple
risk
river
road*
roar
roast
rob
robber
robe
robot
rock
rocket
rod
rode*
rodent
rodeo
roll
roller skates
rolling pin
roof*
room*
roost
root*
rope*
rose*
rot*
rotate
rotten
rough
round*
roundabout*
route
row
royal
rubber
rubbish
ruby
rucksack
rudder
rude*
rug*
rugby
ruin
rule
ruler
rumor
run*
rung
runway
rural
rush
rust

**S**

sabbath
sabotage
sack
sacred
sacrifice
sad*
saddle
safe
safety
safety pin
saga
said*
sail
sailor*
saint
salad
salary
sale*
saliva
salt*
salute
same*
sample
sanctuary
sand*
sandal*
sandwich*
sang*
sank
sap
sari
sash*
sat*
Satan
satchel
satellite
satisfactory
satisfied*
satisfy
Saturday*
sauce
saucepan
saucer
sauna
sausage
savage
savanna
save*
savings
saw*
saxophone
saying
scab
scaffolding
scald
scale
scales
scalp
scar
scarce
scare
scarf*
scarlet
scatter
scene
scenery
scent
scholarship
school
science
science fiction
scientist
scissors
scold
scooter
scorch
score
scorpion
scout
scowl
scramble
scrap*
scrapbook
scrape*
scratch*
scream*
screen
screw
screwdriver
scribble
scroll
scrub*
sculptor
sculpture
scythe
sea
seagull
sea horse
seal
sea level
seaweed
seam
search
season
seashell
seat*
second*
second hand
secret*
secretary
section
sector
secure
see*
seed*
seek
seem*
seesaw
segment
seize
seldom
select
self
self-defense
self-service
selfish
sell*
semaphore

semi circle
send*
senior
sense
sensible*
sent*
sentence
sentry
sepal*
separate
September*
serf
sergeant
serial
series
serious
serpent
servant
serve*
serviette
set
settee
settle
settlement
sever
several
severe
sew
sewer
sex
shade
shadow
shaft
shake*
shall*
shallow
shame
shampoo
shape
share
shark
sharp
shatter
shave

shawl
sheaf
shear
shears
sheath
sheaves*
shed
sheep*
sheep dog
sheer
sheet*
shelf*
shell
shellfish
shelter
shepherd
shield
shift
shilling
shin
shine*
ship
shipwreck
shipyard
shirt*
shiver
shoal
shock
shoe*
shone*
shook*
shoot
shop*
shore
short*
shorts
shortsighted
shot
should*
shoulder
shout*
shove
shovel
shower

shrank*
shriek
shrill
shrimp
shrink
shrub
shudder
shut*
shutter
shy
sick
side*
sideways
siege
sieve
sigh
sight
sign
signal
signature
silence
silent
silhouette
silk
sill
silly*
silver
similar
simple*
sin
since
sincere
sing*
single
singular
sinister
sink
sip*
sister*
siren
site
size
skate
skeleton

sketch
ski
skid
skill
skin*
skip*
skirt*
skull
skunk
sky*
skylight
skyline
skyscraper
slain*
slang
slant
slap
slash
slaughter
slave
slay
sled
sledge
sleep*
sleeping bag
sleepy*
sleet
sleeve*
sleigh
slender
slept*
slew*
slice*
slide
slight
slim
slime
sling
slipper
slippery*
slit
slope
sloppy
slot

slow*
slum
sly
smack
small*
smart
smash*
smell*
smile*
smith
smoke*
smooth*
smoulder
smuggle
snack
snail
snake
snap
snare
snarl
snatch
sneeze*
sniff
snob
snore
snorkel
snout
snow
snug
soak
soap*
soar
sob
soccer
social
society
sock*
socket
sofa
soft*
soil
solar
sold*
soldier

sole
solemn
solid
solitary
solo
solve
some★
somersault
something★
sometime★
sometimes★
somewhere★
son★
song★
soon★
soothe
sorcerer★
sore
sorrow
sorry★
sort
sought★
soul
sound
sound barrier
soup
sour
source
south
souvenir
sovereign
sow
space
spacecraft
spade★
span
spank
spare
spark
sparkle
sparrow
spat★
spawn
speak★
spear
special
species
specimen
speck
spectacles
spectator
spectrum
speech
speed
speedometer
spell
spend★
sphere
spice
spider
spied★
spies★
spill
spilled★
spin
spine
spiral
spire
spirit
spit
splash
splendid
splinter
split
sponge
spoon★
spore
sport
spot★
spotlight
spout
sprain
sprang★
spread★
spring
sprout
spun★
spy
square
squash
squat
squeal
squeeze
squint
squirrel
St.
stab
stable
stack
stadium
staff
stag
stage
stagger
stagnant
stain
stair★
staircase★
stale
stalk
stall
stallion
stamen
stammer
stamp
stand
standard
stank★
star
starboard
stare
start★
startle
starve
state
station★
stationary
stationery
stay★
steady★
steak
steal★
steam
steamer
steel
steep
steeple
stem
step
stepfather
stepmother
stereo
stereophonic
sterilize
stern
stethoscope
stew
steward
stewardess
stick★
stiff
still★
stilts
sting
stink
stir
stirrup
stitch
stock
stole★
stomach
stone
stood
stop★
store
stork
storm
story★
stove★
stowaway
straight★
straighten
strain
strait
strange★
stranger
strap
straw
stray
stream★
street★
strength
stretch
stretcher
strict
stride★
strike
string★
strip
stripe★
strode
stroke
stroll
strong★
struck★
structure
struggle
stubborn
stuck★
student
study
stuff
stuffy
stung★
stump★
stupid★
stutter
style
subject
submarine
substance
substitute
subtract
subway
successful
such★
suck
sudden★

suffer
sufficient
suffocate
sugar*
suggest
suicide
suit
suitable
suitcase*
sum
sun*
Sunday*
sundial
sung*
sunrise
sunset
sunshine*
superior
supermarket
supernatural
supersonic
superstitious
supper*
supplied*
supply
support
suppose
sure*
surf
surface
surgeon
surgery
surname
surprise
surrender
surround
survive
suspect
suspend*
swallow
swam*
swap
sway
swear
sweat
sweater
sweep
sweet*
swell
swept*
swift
swim*
swing*
switch
swop*
sword
swore*
swung*
syllable
symbol
symmetrical
synagogue
synonym
syringe
syrup

**T**

table
table tennis*
tack
tackle
tadpole
tag
tail*
tailor
take*
tale
talent
talk*
tall*
talon
tambourine
tame
tan
tangled
tank
tanker
tap*
tape
tape recorder
tapestry
tar
tart
task
taste*
taught*
taut*
tavern
tax
taxi
tea
teach*
teacher*
team*
teapot*
tear*
tease
technical
technology
teeth*
teethe
telegram
telegraph
telephone
telescope
television
tell*
temper*
temperate
temperature
temple
temporary
tempt
tend
tender
tennis
tent
tentacle
term
terminal
termite
terrible
terrify
territory
terror
test
text
textbook
textile
texture
thank*
thatch
theatre
their*
then*
theory
there*
therefore
thermometer
thermos
thermostat
thick*
thief
thigh
thimble*
thin*
think*
third
thirsty*
thorough
though*
thought
thousand*
thread
threaten
thresh
threw*
thrill
throat
throne
through*
throw*
thumb*
thunder
Thursday*
tick
ticket*
tide
tidy
tie
tight*
tights
tile
till
timber
time*
timetable
timid
tin
tiny
tire
tired*
tissue
title
toad
toadstool
toast*
tobacco
toboggan
today*
toe*
together*
toilet
told*
tomato
tomb
tomorrow*
ton
tongue*
tonight
tonne
too*
took*
tooth*
toothbrush*
top
torch
tore*
tornado

tortoise
torture
toss
total
touch
touching*
tough
tour
towards*
towel*
tower
town*
toy*
trace
track
tractor
trade
trademark
trade union
traffic
tragedy
trail
trailer
train
traitor
tram*
tramp
trample
transfer
transistor
translate
transparent
transplant
transport
trap
trapeze
trapezoid
travel*
trawler
tray*
tread
treason
treasure
treat
treaty
tree*
tremble
trendy
trial
triangle
tribe
tributary
trick*
tricycle
tried*
trifle
trigger
trim
trio
trip*
triple
trod*
troll*
trolley
trombone
tropics
trot
trouble*
trousers*
truant
truck
true*
trumpet
trunk
trust
truth*
try*
tub*
tuba
tube
tuber
Tuesday*
tug
tumble
tundra
tunic
tunnel
turbine
turkey
turn*
turtle
tusk
twilight
twin
twinkle
twist
type
typewriter
typical
tyrant

**U**

udder
ugly*
umbrella*
umpire
unanimous
uncle*
unconscious
uncover
under*
underline
underneath*
underpass
understand*
understood*
undid*
undo*
unearth
unemployed
unfortunate
unicorn
uniform
union
unique
unit
unite
universal
universe
university
unknown*
unless*
unpack*
unsightly*
unskilled*
until*
upholstery
upon*
upper
upright
uproar
upset
upside down*
upstairs*
urban
urgent
use*
used
useful
useless
usual
usually
utensil
utter

**V**

vacant
vaccinate
vacuum
vague
vain
valley
valuable
value
valve
vampire
van
vandal
vane*
vanish
vapor*
variety*
various*
varnish
vase
vast
vat
vault
vegetable*
vegetarian
vegetation
vehicle
veil*
vein
venom
verb
verse
versus
vertebra
vertebrae
vertebrate
vertical
vessel
vest*
vet
veterinarian
viaduct
vibrate
vice
vicious
victim
victory
videotape
villa
village*
villain
vine
vinegar*
viola
violet
violin
viper
virus
visible*
visit*
visitor*
vital
vitamin
vixen

vocabulary
voice*
volcano
volt*
volume
vomit
vote
vow
vowel
voyage*

## W

wade*
wag*
wage
waggle*
wagon
wail
waist*
waistcoat
wait
waiter
waitress
wake
walk*
wallet
walrus
waltz*
wand
wander
wangle*
war
ward
wardrobe
warehouse
warm*
warn
warning
warp
warren
warrior
wart*
wash*
washer
wasp
waste
watch*
watchman*
water*
waterfall
water logged*
waterproof
watertight*
watt
wave*
wax
weak
wealth
wealthy
wean
weapon*
wear
weary
weather*
weave
web
webfoot
Wednesday*
wee*
weed
weep
weft
weigh*
weird
welcome
welfare
well
west
western*
whale
wharf
what*
whatever*
wheat
wheel*
wheelbarrow*
when*
whenever*
where*
wherever*
whether*
which*
while*
whine*
whip
whirl
whirlpool
whirlwind
whisker
whisper*
whistle
white*
who*
whoever*
whole
wholesale
whose*
why*
wick
wicked
wide*
widow
widower
width
wife*
wig
wigwam
wild
will*
willing
wilt
win*
wind
windmill*
window*
windshield
wine
wing
wink*
winter*
wipe*
wire
wisdom
wise
wish*
wishbone*
witch
witchcraft
with*
withdraw
without*
witness
wizard
woke*
wolf
wolves
woman
won*
wonder
wonderful
wood
wooden
woodwork
wool
woolen
word*
wore*
work*
worker
workshop
world
worm
worn
worry
worse
worship
worst
worth
worthless
would*
wound
wrap
wreath
wreck
wrestle
wretched
wriggle
wrist
write*
writing*
written
wrong*
wrote*
wrung*

## X

X ray
xylophone

## Y

yacht
yak
yap
yard
yarn
yawn
year*
yearly
yeast
yell
yellow*
yesterday*
yet*
Yiddish
yield
yoga
yogurt
yoke
yolk
young*
youth

## Z

zebra
zero
zigzag
zipper
zone
zoo
zoology